Conflicting Commitments

CONFLICTING COMMITMENTS

The Politics of Enforcing Immigrant Worker Rights in San Jose and Houston

SHANNON GLEESON

ILR PRESS

AN IMPRINT OF

CORNELL UNIVERSITY PRESS

ITHACA AND LONDON

First published 2012 by Cornell University Press
First printing, Cornell Paperbacks, 2012
Printed in the United States of America

Library of Congress Cataloging-in-Publication Data

Gleeson, Shannon, 1980–
    Conflicting commitments : the politics of enforcing immigrant worker rights in San Jose and Houston / Shannon Gleeson.
        p. cm.
    Includes bibliographical references and index.
    ISBN 978-0-8014-5121-8 (cloth : alk. paper)
    ISBN 978-0-8014-7814-7 (pbk. : alk. paper)
    1. Foreign workers—California—San Jose.   2. Foreign workers—Texas—Houston.   3. Foreign workers—Legal status, laws, etc.—California—San Jose.   4. Foreign workers—Legal status, laws, etc.—Texas—Houston.   5. Employee rights—California—San Jose.   6. Employee rights—Texas—Houston.   7. Illegal aliens—California—San Jose.   8. Illegal aliens—Texas—Houston.   I. Title.
    HD8081.A5G54   2013
    331.6'2097641411—dc23   2012024641

Cornell University Press strives to use environmentally responsible suppliers and materials to the fullest extent possible in the publishing of its books. Such materials include vegetable-based, low-VOC inks and acid-free papers that are recycled, totally chlorine-free, or partly composed of nonwood fibers. For further information, visit our website at www. cornellpress.cornell.edu.

Cloth printing   10   9   8   7   6   5   4   3   2   1
Paperback printing   10   9   8   7   6   5   4   3   2   1

Para mi mamá y abuelita, Maristela Robinson y Marta Aldana Cruz
Debo todo mi éxito a sus sacrificios
To my mom and grandma, Maristela Robinson and Marta Aldana Cruz
I owe all my success to your sacrifices

Contents

ACKNOWLEDGMENTS

After years of researching and writing this book, the process of accounting for all the people who have helped me reach this point seems the most daunting. I will do my best.

The seeds of this book were planted over a decade ago in O'Connor Hall at Santa Clara University. My mentors at SCU, especially Marilyn Fernandez, Chuck Powers, and Laura Nichols, sparked my sociological imagination and have supported me every step of the way since. My committee members in the Departments of Sociology and Demography at UC Berkeley helped lay the foundation for this research. I offer thanks especially to Irene Bloemraad, Sam Lucas, Mike Hout, Kim Voss, Michael Burawoy, Ron Lee, and Margaret Weir. Each fueled my intellectual curiosity in ways that weren't always immediately apparent, but which always came full circle. Special thanks to the Interdisciplinary Immigration Workshop, the Migration Working Group at the Center for Latino Policy Research, Gene Hammel, Lauren Edelman's law and society workshop, and Claude Fischer's sociology writing workshop. Countless colloquia at the Center for Law and Society, the Survey Research Center, the Center for Latin American Studies, the Institute for Research on Labor and Employment, and the Institute of Governmental Studies created fertile ground for the development of this book as well. I owe a debt of gratitude to all the Berkeley staff who worked behind the scenes to make these events a success. Thanks go especially to Carl Mason and Carl Boe in the Department of Demography, Jon Stiles at the SRC, and Terry Huwe at IRLE for all the technical assistance you provided over the years.

So many other colleagues and friends at Berkeley read early drafts, tore them apart, and helped me build them back up. Thanks in particular to Ming Hsu Chen, Roberto G. Gonzales, Rebecca Hamlin, Damon Mayrl, Helen Marrow, Ben Moodie, Osagie Obasogie, Marcel Paret, Karthick Ramakrishnan, Aliya Saperstein, Rachel Sullivan, Laurel Westbrook, and Phil Wolgin for offering your candid thoughts and never-ending encouragement. This book could not have been possible without two amazing scholars: Els de Graauw and Amada Armenta read more versions than any writing partner should ever be forced to, had the patience to walk me through difficult paragraphs, and always stepped up to the plate for my last-minute requests.

My colleagues at UC Santa Cruz have been beyond supportive. Jill Esterás and Alessandra Álvares welcomed me and instantly made me feel at home. The faculty in the Latin American and Latino Studies Department, the Chicano/Latino Research Center, and the Center for Labor Studies created an intellectual community where I could thrive. Gabriela Arredondo, John Borrego, Jonathan Fox, Susanne Jonas, Steve McKay, Hector Perla, Cecilia Rivas, and Pat Zavella in particular offered constructive feedback and thought-provoking discussion. Sandra Alvarez, Eric Arce, Jimmy Chiu, Susana Duro, Joe Garcia, Brian Jimenez, Claudia Medina, Anel Morales, Catherine Lagayan, Mariela Rodriguez, and Angelica Rodriguez all provided awesome research assistance. Ruth Homrighaus provided impeccable editing skills, and Paula Durbin-Westby masterfully created this book's index.

In the brave new world of research and publishing, I was privileged to be supported by several funders, including the National Science Foundation, the Ford Foundation, the UC Labor Employment and Research Fund, the UC Center for New Racial Studies, UC MEXUS, the UCSC Chicano/Latino Research Center, and the UCSC Committee on Research. My year as a Ford Postdoctoral Fellow at Santa Clara University and the

Katharine and George Alexander Community Law Center was invaluable for bringing this book to fruition. The generosity of the Hellman Family Fund also supported publication expenses. I am grateful also for the patience of Fran Benson, Kitty Liu, Susan Specter, and the rest of the editorial staff at Cornell University Press, and to the anonymous reviewers who provided me with their vital suggestions.

Parts of this book, in revised form, were previously published in "Organizing for Latino Immigrant Rights in Two U.S. Cities: The Case of San Jose and Houston," in *Civic Hopes and Political Realities: Immigrants, Community Organizations and Political Engagement*, ed. S. Karthick Ramakrishnan and Irene Bloemraad (New York: Russell Sage Foundation Press, 2008), 107–33, and in "Labor Rights for All? The Role of Undocumented Immigrant Status for Worker Claims-Making," *Law and Social Inquiry* 35, no. 3 (2010): 561–602.

My dear friends have been an immense source of support. Heartfelt thanks go to Angelina Bouchard, Rhonda Campbell, Shelly Grabe, Darren Noy, Cheryl Holzmeyer, Milton Magaña, Cristina Mora Torres, Chris Sullivan, and Leslie Wang for the many hours on the phone, on the couch, and on the trails. My family has seen me through this process, and been there every step of the way. Above all, my mother's love and support have always been unfailing, and it is she who taught me the dignity of work, and the importance of justice and equality for everyone. It is her example that I have strived to follow my entire life. My little brother Danny has kept me out of the dark ages of pop culture, given me unconditional love, and made me so proud. To Grandma, Abuelita, Tia, Dad, Arthur, Aunt Steph, Uncle Michael, Tom, Carol, Poppy, Bud, Erin, Estela, Ms. Turner, and all my other aunts, uncles, and cousins—thank you for all your support and for always keeping a smile on my face. Chahta and Hya have kept me company for hours on end of writing, and snapped me back to reality when there was nothing more important than dinner and playing ball. Catch-A-Bear, I miss you. And most important, Gabriel Carraher has stood by me through it all, somehow knowing exactly when to let me work, when to feed me, and when to force me to go to bed. Thank you for all your love, support, and patience. I can't wait to get back to the beach with you.

I am forever indebted to the dozens of government bureaucrats, non-profit staff, and consular representatives who agreed to speak with me, despite clearly more pressing matters. Thank you all for telling me your story and helping me understand the importance of the work you do. Final and deepest thanks go to the workers who motivate this book. For all the immigrants who continue to cross the border every day to make a better life for themselves and their families, and whose struggle for justice continues, this book is for you.

Abbreviations

ABA	American Bar Association
ACORN	Association of Community Organizations for Reform Now
AFL-CIO	American Federation of Labor and Congress of Industrial Organizations
AIR	Americans for Immigration Reform
AJC	American Jewish Committee
BLS	Bureau of Labor Statistics
BPUSA	Building Partnerships USA
Cal/OSHA	California Occupational Safety and Health Administration
CDLE	Colorado Department of Labor and Employment
CIPC	California Immigrant Policy Center
CJD	Casa Juan Diego
CRA	Civil Rights Act
CTW	Change to Win

DFEH	Department of Fair Employment and Housing
DHS	Department of Homeland Security
DLSE	Division of Labor Standards Enforcement
DOL	Department of Labor
DOL-WHD	Department of Labor—Wage and Hour Division
DOS	Department of State
DWU	Domestic Workers United
EBASE	East Bay Alliance for a Sustainable Economy
EEOC	Equal Employment Opportunity Commission
FLSA	Fair Labor Standards Act
GAO	Government Accountability Office
HCIR	Houston Coalition for Immigration Reform
HERE	Hotel Employees and Restaurant Employees International Union
HIWJ	Houston Interfaith Worker Justice
HIWS	Houston Initiative on Worker Safety
HPD	Houston Police Department
HRW	Human Rights Watch
ICE	Immigration and Customs Enforcement
IME	Instituto de los Mexicanos en el Exterior
INA	Immigration and Nationality Act of 1952 (McCarran-Walter Act)
INCITE!	INCITE! Women of Color against Violence
IOM	International Organization for Migration
IRIS	Immigrant Relations and Integration Services
IWFRC	Immigrant Workers Freedom Ride Coalition
IWJ	Interfaith Worker Justice
JEWP	Justice and Equality in the Workplace Program
KGACLC	Katharine and George Alexander Community Law Center
LCCR	The Lawyers' Committee for Civil Rights Under Law
LIUNA	Laborers' International Union of North America
LSEA	labor standards enforcement agency
LSLA	Lone Star Legal Aid
MACIRA	Mayor's Advisory Committee on Immigrant and Refugee Affairs

MOIRA	City of Houston Mayor's Office of Immigrant and Refugee Affairs
MPI	Migration Policy Institute
MTA-ABAG	Metropolitan Transportation Commission and Association of Bay Area Governments
NCOSH	National Council for Occupational Safety and Health
NELP	National Employment Law Project
NILC	National Immigration Law Center
NLRB	National Labor Relations Board
NRA	National Restaurant Association
NRTWO	National Right to Work Organization
OECD	Organisation for Economic Co-operation and Development
OEHHA	Office of Environmental Health Hazard Assessment
OMB	Office of Management and Budget
OSHA	Occupational Safety and Health Administration/Agency
PACT	People Acting in Community Together
PHC	Pew Hispanic Center
ROC-NY	Restaurant Opportunities Center of New York
SBLC	South Bay AFL-CIO Labor Council
SCC	Santa Clara County
SCC-OHR	Santa Clara County Office of Human Relations
SCOPE	Strategic Concepts in Organizing and Policy Education
SEIU	Service Employees International Union
SIREN	Services, Immigrant Rights and Education Network
SRE	Secretaría de Relaciones Exteriores
SVAIR	Silicon Valley Alliance for Immigration Reform
SVTC	Silicon Valley Toxics Coalition
TMO	The Metropolitan Organization
TWC	Texas Workforce Commission
TX-SIP	Texans for Sensible Immigration Policy
UFCW	United Food and Commercial Workers

UNITE HERE!	Union of Needletrades, Industrial, and Textile Employees and the Hotel Employees and Restaurant Employees International Union
WCRI	Workers Compensation Research Institute
WHISARD	Wage and Hour Investigative Support and Reporting Database
WPUSA	Working Partnerships USA
YWU	Young Workers United

Introduction

Immigrant Labor in the United States

A hundred years ago, 146 young immigrant women died in one of the largest industrial accidents in U.S. history. Unable to escape the fire at the Triangle Shirtwaist Factory in Manhattan because locked doors sealed them in the building, the young women fell victim to an employer who offered them the "low wages, excessively long hours, and unsanitary and dangerous working conditions" that had become endemic to the industry as a whole (Kheel Center 2011). The exploitation of the mostly Jewish garment workers at the Triangle Shirtwaist Factory has become a touchstone in U.S. labor history. This incident kicked off an extensive labor organizing campaign that fought to institutionalize protections for all low-wage workers, including collective bargaining rights (won in the 1935 National Labor Relations Act), the minimum wage and overtime provisions (the 1938 Fair Labor Standards Act), protections against racial discrimination (the 1964 Civil Rights Act), and industrial health and safety standards (the 1970 Occupational Safety and Health Act), among others.

In today's de-unionized, postindustrial economy, these protections remain vital for workers. In this book, I examine how these rights are enforced for the growing population of low-wage immigrant—and particularly undocumented—workers. Immigrant workers—not unlike those who perished at Triangle—labor in nearly every low-wage industry across the United States. We interact daily with industries built on cheap immigrant labor. Each morning many of us don designer clothing likely made by an immigrant garment worker who recoups only a fraction of the profit (DOL 2004a), pass construction sites teeming with injured and underpaid immigrant laborers (Valenzuela et al. 2006), and eat food picked or prepared by immigrant women subjected to rampant sexual harassment (Castañeda and Zavella 2003). An estimated 8 million of the 35-million-strong immigrant workforce are undocumented and considered among the most vulnerable and underpaid (Passel and Cohn 2009; BLS 2010). Their ongoing exploitation has been the focus of much scholarly research and journalistic reporting, such as Stephen Greenhouse's 2005 exposé of work conditions in the immigrant-dense Brooklyn neighborhood of Bushwick, a short train ride away from the old Triangle Factory (Greenhouse 2005). Recent one-hundred-year-anniversary commemorations of the tragedy at Triangle remind us that the unpaid wages, dangerous workplaces, and outright discrimination experienced by workers in 1911 are alive and well for workers today. Hourly wages that are almost $4 less than the federal minimum, language discrimination, and the indiscriminate firing of pregnant women are all par for the course in Bushwick and nearly every city in the nation.

Unlike the laborers of one hundred years ago, immigrant workers today have access to a range of formal protections. In theory even undocumented workers enjoy a modicum of labor rights, despite ongoing legal challenges to these rights. Though employers are prohibited from hiring undocumented workers, when they do so they are compelled to pay those workers at least the minimum wage and compensate them for any overtime they accrue. They must adhere to antidiscrimination standards and are expected to implement appropriate health and safety protections for all their employees. These rights reflect no arbitrary benevolence, but rather the acknowledgment by labor standards enforcement agents and other worker advocates that the protection of "even [undocumented] workers, is important to prevent the exploitation of any employees, legal or not, and to discourage employers from hiring illegal immigrants for cut-rate wages" (Greenhouse 2005).

Even as formal protections have proliferated over the years, their implementation is not a given, particularly for vulnerable populations like undocumented workers. As union membership has declined, workplace rights have become even more important. Nonetheless, ensuring that worker rights exist is only half the battle: getting workers to make claims on those rights, and getting responsible agencies to follow up on those claims, is the other half. Many of the immigrant workers in Bushwick interviewed by Greenhouse knew little of their rights under the law, while others were surprisingly familiar with them but terrified to speak out due to fear of deportation or job loss. A few had actually complained but were ultimately distrustful of the New York Labor Department. For all these workers, the formal existence of rights had little effect on the constant violations they experienced. Thus, immigrants' labor rights must be activated in order to be useful; and while some individual workers can muster the resources and legal consciousness to activate them on their own, most require the assistance of a trusted—and creative—advocate to make these rights real. For those who can afford it, a private lawyer can be an important advocate. Those who can't often turn to a network of community organizations for help. This book examines the strategies deployed by a wide variety of stakeholders who intervene in the enforcement of immigrant workers' rights.

One approach such intermediaries take is simply to help aggrieved workers file claims. Lawyers reach out to workers in order to funnel them to the appropriate bureaucratic apparatus, which might help the workers recoup their lost wages, issue discrimination penalties, or provide other compensation in the wake of injury. In addition to this direct "lawyering" approach, as Gordon (2007) dubs it, labor advocates engage in long-term worker organizing, sometimes with the aim of formal unionization (Fine 2006). Advocates may also focus on advancing policy reform, such as living wage ordinances, or promoting the implementation of existing policies, such as wage theft prevention policies, which have proliferated (Luce 2004; Huq et al. 2006; Bernhardt 2010).

This book examines how immigrant workers' rights are enforced in practice, how claims are channeled, and why and how advocates take on particular battles. In the chapters that follow, I draw on an in-depth comparative case study of two immigrant-receiving destinations—San Jose, California, and Houston, Texas—to examine the dynamics of enforcing immigrant worker rights. I consider how certain solutions become commonly understood as appropriate responses to a given issue that affects immigrant laborers, and which actors take on responsibility for the advancement of particular worker problems. For example, why does a construction worker who has been cheated of a week's pay in San Jose get funneled to a local legal aid clinic and eventually a state agency to file a formal claim, while his counterpart working in one of Houston's sprawling track developments will struggle to find any lawyer willing to serve him and will perhaps never set foot in a government office to file a claim? Why do the San Jose police have little to offer this worker, while in Houston any police officer is required to make a theft-of-service report when asked? How is it that if this nonunionized worker were to call the South Bay AFL-CIO Labor Council in San Jose, he would be advised to call the California Department of Labor Standards Enforcement or seek out a local legal aid clinic, while in Houston the Harris County AFL-CIO Council would be more likely to encourage him to pay a visit to city hall, the federal building, or perhaps even a worker center to help organize a direct action, depending on his situation? And how do we understand the vastly different support immigrant workers will find from their consulates in these two cities?

The goal of this book is to help answer these questions and expand our understanding of how immigrant worker rights are enforced and advanced. I situate the rights of immigrant workers in the space between both labor standards enforcement and immigration control, two conflicting jurisdictions whose implementation can vary widely, depending on their local political context. I then look beyond government bureaucrats to understand how enforcement strategies are influenced by local intermediaries who may have diverse interests in the advancement of immigrant worker rights. These include local elected officials, who can either intensify or mitigate the surveillance of undocumented immigrants and promote or stymie the interests of workers; civil society actors, who have direct knowledge of and access to immigrant workers, and who work in diverse ways to advance their rights; and consular institutions, whose unique combination of political legitimacy, institutionalized resources, and unfettered support for their emigrant population creates a unique pathway for rights enforcement.

Making Rights Real

This book examines how actors on the ground promote the rights of immigrant workers and do the work Epp (2010) refers to as "making rights real." Rather than view rights as self-propelled imperatives rooted solely in the law, this analysis highlights the complexity of the enforcement process and the variety of actors implicated in struggles for immigrant workers' rights. Legal scholars have focused at length on the role of the courts (Rosenberg 1991; McCann 1994; Epp 1998), how social movements advocate for particular policy interests (Minkoff 1995; Andersen 2006), the ways individuals develop legal consciousness (Merry 1988, 1990), and the individual and institutional barriers they face to claims-making (Felstiner, Abel, and Sarat 1980; Albiston 2005). In most conceptions of "rights in action," laws are created by political actors influenced by competing interest groups, such as parties and social movements. These policies then often face a series of judicial challenges in which they are subject to various interpretations of the Constitution and legal precedent. The resulting statutes are filtered through the internal regulations of the bureaucracies charged with enforcing them, and those organizational cultures shape the individual behavior of front-line bureaucrats (Lipsky 1980; Mashaw 1985; Brehm and Gates 1999).

Three elements are often missing from this analysis. First, while the discretionary role of bureaucrats has been well documented, the strategies bureaucracies adopt for carrying out their mandates are often not uniform across different contexts. Federal agencies can have dozens of field offices spread across the country, each with distinct challenges and resources at its disposal. In the arena of workplace rights, for example, the federal Equal Employment Opportunity Commission has over fifty offices. The Department of Labor's Wage and Hour Division alone has nearly ninety. In each of these places, federal law must coexist with state and local policies. Even in a context of federalism, where federal law trumps state legislation, the efforts of states and cities can be neutral, helpful, or can pose a significant hindrance to the implementation of federal policy. Popular examples of policy arenas in which federalism creates conflict include drug policy, gay marriage, and, increasingly, immigrant rights. The significance of overlapping jurisdictions is not simply bureaucratic: overlapping jurisdictions can also influence how policy goals are implemented. If resources and political will are uneven, the more powerful agency may take the lead. Where there are few resources in place to reach out to claimants, bureaucracies have to get creative with their resource allocation and outreach strategies.

A second piece often missing from the puzzle of rights enforcement is the constellation of organizations outside the bureaucracy that can affect the process. While jurisdictional boundaries are often tightly drawn to define the scope of agencies' activities, the actual process of enforcement frequently lures in additional interested groups. Elected officials can influence how resources are allocated to enforcement bureaucracies and can then pressure them to be used in particular ways. The mayor of a city, for example, may rally for state and federal resources to assist his community, as Ray Nagin famously did for New Orleans in the wake of Hurricane Katrina. City councils and boards of supervisors, often compelled by their constituents, may also decide to invest in certain initiatives that seem insufficiently covered by the responsible bureaucracies at the state and federal level. Social movements not only advocate for particular laws but can also be just as vigilant regarding their implementation. Other civil society groups also make demands on how enforcement resources should be deployed, and some even function as intermediaries in the effort to reach out to potential claimants.

Last, rights do not exist in a vacuum, and policies often clash. These conflicts can become manifest between different levels of government, but the federal government is certainly not itself a unitary actor (Evans, Rueschemeyer, and Skocpol 1985). This is a result not only of a complicated electorate that yields inconsistent popular support but also of the competing demands of nationhood. Laws are formulated to maintain order and protect those who lack power in the social structure. The goals of law enforcement agencies frequently clash with the goals of agencies designed to protect civil rights. The nature of this struggle may vary substantially across contexts, with public support for one agency's goals potentially dwarfing support for that of the other. One of the clearest examples of this contradiction, and the focus of this book, is the simultaneous efforts to deter and deport the estimated 5 percent of workers who are unauthorized on the one hand and to protect them from workplace abuse on the other. To this end, the following pages will focus on the institutional dynamics of enforcing the rights of immigrant workers.

Protecting Those Who Work in the Shadows

As the total undocumented population has grown from a mere 3–6 million in the period prior to the 1986 Immigration Reform and Control Act (Bean, Telles, and Lowell 1987) to close to 12 million by 2009, the fate of the 8 million workers among them has become an increasing topic of concern (Passel and Cohn 2009). Though undocumented workers constitute only 5 percent of all civilian laborers, it is estimated that approximately a quarter of drywall workers, dishwashers, maids and housekeepers, meat and poultry workers, and roofers are undocumented, as are nearly 70 percent of farmworkers (Greenhouse 2008, 226; Passel and Cohn 2009). Many of the industries where undocumented workers are concentrated are almost completely nonunionized. A mere 1.6 percent of all restaurant and food service workers, 2.2 percent of crop production workers, and 1.1 percent of car washers were union members in 2008 (Hirsch and Macpherson). Union protections are also virtually nonexistent in informal sectors such as day labor and domestic work, where undocumented workers are also common. For these and other nonunionized workers, federal, state, and local labor laws are the sole protection against employer abuse. Immigration status has been deemed irrelevant to a worker's ability to file a grievance against his or her abusive employer.[1] Failure to provide these protections, most argue, accelerates the race to the bottom for workplace standards.[2]

Yet those attempting to protect the rights of undocumented workers face a legal conundrum. Though these rights exist, undocumented immigrants are barred from legally working by employer sanction provisions instituted through the 1986 Immigration Reform and Control Act, which for the first time interpreted hiring undocumented workers as illegal and punishable by fines.[3] Employer sanctions were designed to deter employers from hiring unauthorized workers, and proponents assumed they would reduce the demand for migrants seeking work. The net effect of the law as a deterrent to migration flows is negligible, but its chilling effect on undocumented workers has been well documented (Wishnie 2007; Golash-Boza 2009). Rather than keep undocumented migrants out, employer sanctions make them more vulnerable to employer abuse by creating a perverse set of incentives for employers to exploit them and by deterring undocumented workers from speaking out against this abuse (Wishnie 2007; Bacon and Hing 2010).

One of the most far-reaching responses to the conflict between immigration enforcement and noncitizen rights was the 2002 U.S. Supreme Court Case *Hoffman Plastic Compounds, Inc. v. National Labor Relations Board*. In a 5–4 decision, *Hoffman* ultimately banned the provision of back pay to undocumented workers who have been unjustly fired for organizing a union and effectively removed the National Labor Relations Board's ability to require reinstatement in such cases (Berman 2004). This decision has had ripple effects for efforts to protect undocumented workers from exploitation. The majority opinion, penned by then chief justice Rehnquist, argued that providing full rights to undocumented workers would ultimately serve as a magnet for future flows and encourage their employment. The minority opinion, written by Justice Breyer, on the other hand, argued that to deny rights to undocumented workers "lowers the cost to the employer of an initial labor law violation [and] increases the employer's incentive to find and to hire illegal-alien employees."[4]

Since *Hoffman*, the protections of back pay and reinstatement have not been available to undocumented workers, but other formal protections remain in place. These include the ability for labor standards enforcement agencies to collect unpaid wages for a claimant's hours worked and to protect workers against arbitrary discrimination and harassment prohibited under civil rights legislation, to enforce basic health and safety standards, and in some cases even to require compensation and medical treatment in the wake of an injury. In fact, one of the first things many labor standards enforcement agencies did following *Hoffman* was to issue public statements that reiterated their stance toward undocumented workers. The Department of Labor, for example, emphasized that the Court's decision in *Hoffman* "does not mean that undocumented workers do not have rights under other U.S. labor laws" and reassured the public that the agency would "continue to provide core labor protections for vulnerable workers . . . without regard to whether an employee is documented or undocumented" (DOL 2008). Similarly, the Equal Employment Opportunity

Commission issued a press release avowing that the *Hoffman* decision "does not affect the government's ability to root out discrimination against undocumented workers," and it reiterated that "enforcing the law to protect vulnerable workers, particularly low income and immigrant workers, remains a priority for EEOC" (EEOC 2002b). Despite these assurances, a wide gulf persists between the rights afforded to undocumented workers on the books and those that ultimately materialize in practice.

One could argue that the existence of workplace rights for the undocumented defies classic understandings of citizenship that presuppose political membership as a prerequisite for access to social citizenship (Marshall 1950). Yet the simultaneous efforts to identify and deport undocumented immigrants while also attempting to protect them from exploitation reflect what Bosniak (2006) refers to as the "two faces of citizenship" in modern liberal democracies. That is, despite the impulse to police the physical and political borders of membership, the United States is also compelled to offer some modicum of rights and equality even to noncitizens. The need to enforce immigration laws and the need to enforce labor standards are dual aspects of maintaining law and order. Ultimately, however, the paradoxical existence of undocumented workers affects not only individual claims-making behavior but also how bureaucracies collaborate (or stay out of each other's way) and how advocates strategize in the complicated dance of enforcement.

On the bureaucratic end, labor standards enforcement agencies have deployed resources to reach out to undocumented workers and reaffirm their interest in protecting undocumented workers' rights. This challenge is closely tied to the dismal state of labor standards enforcement more generally. Despite a 900 percent increase in the size of the American workforce since 1941, the Department of Labor's Wage and Hour Division relies on 50 percent fewer investigators today than it did then (Bobo 2008, 116). The Occupational Safety and Health Administration has also been criticized for being ineffective at reducing injury rates and for failing to adequately regulate several hazardous chemicals that pose risks to workers (Michaels 2007). These inadequacies are intensified by the fact that private-sector union coverage today is at its lowest level since 1973, the first year for which reliable data is available (Hirsch and Macpherson).

President Obama has promised to reverse this trend, pledging to stop globalization's race to the bottom for U.S. workers by strengthening collective bargaining provisions, promoting health and safety laws, and ensuring that "dollars earned are dollars paid" (Talbott 2008; OMB 2010). The 2009 confirmation of Hilda Solis to head the Department of Labor was seen as a hopeful sign of positive changes to come in the enforcement of worker rights. Solis, the daughter of Latino immigrant parents and someone with deep connections to organized labor, declared she would confront those employers who intend to "cut corners and disregard safety in the workplace" or seek to "to deny workers a voice" (Solis 2010). Within her first year in office, Solis launched a campaign to tackle the long-ignored issue of wage theft and deployed the "We Can Help" / "Podemos Ayudar" campaign, which ran public service announcements explaining how workers could seek out help and emphasizing that all workers would be treated equally, regardless of immigration status (DOL 2010c). Solis has coupled her commitment to immigrant labor with outspoken calls for comprehensive immigration reform (DOL 2010a). In the interim, the Department of Labor has pushed for clear commitments from Immigration Customs Enforcement not to interfere in DOL investigations.[5]

The devastating effect of immigration enforcement on labor standards enforcement has been demonstrated by several high-profile incidents over the years, such as the May 2008 raid in the small northeastern Iowa town of Postville. Following a daylong Department of Homeland Security operation at the nation's largest kosher slaughterhouse, a major organizing campaign and workplace violation investigation was disrupted, and nearly four hundred mostly Mexican and Guatemalan workers were deported.[6] These workers' access to formal workplace rights diminished nearly to the vanishing point in the face of their impending incarceration and eventual deportation. For months, the United Food and Commercial Workers had been waging an organizing campaign while the Iowa labor commissioner investigated alleged workplace violations at the plant. Violations ranged from run-of-the-mill wage and hour infractions to egregious abuses of power, such as the beating of a worker whose eyes were first duct-taped by a supervisor wielding a meat hook (Hsu 2008; Landon 2008). What Postville reveals is that despite the well-intended efforts of labor standards enforcement, such as those launched under the leadership of Obama and Solis, the overarching threat of detention and removal permeates all aspects of the undocumented work experience. The accessibility of workers' formal rights on the books must be understood within this context.

The power of immigration enforcement reaches further than just the workers who are unfortunate enough to be caught in a raid. The majority of undocumented immigrants working in the United States are never detained or deported. For example, compared with the estimated 11.2 million total unauthorized immigrants living in the United States in 2010—a number that reflects the decline that followed the recent recession (Passel and Cohn 2011)—only 580,107 "aliens" were deported by Immigration Customs Enforcement in 2009 (DHS 2010). While immigration enforcement is certainly devastating to those deported individuals and the families they left behind, perhaps the larger power of the enforcement apparatus is not the particular raids or deportations that take place but rather the ever-present potential for a raid that hangs over workers' heads.

The challenge that labor standards enforcement agencies face, therefore, is how to distinguish their mission from that of immigration enforcement agencies in order to reach out to a vulnerable population that is likely to be skeptical of their efforts. Though President Obama has infused resources into the Department of Labor, his employer audits, or "silent raids," have also garnered support among anti-immigrant lobbyists who argue that the president is not doing enough to curb undocumented migration (Krikorian 2011). While seemingly less controversial than the Bush-era policies of border militarization and mass deportations, these raids have in fact reached many more companies and are considered a "far more effective enforcement tool" (J. Preston 2010). They also send a chilling reminder to all workers who labor in the shadows that their place in U.S. society is precarious.[7] Undocumented workers' vulnerability is further complicated by their usually low levels of education, by language barriers, and by their general lack of familiarity with U.S. legal systems. The availability of formal protections is therefore insufficient to truly protect the rights of all immigrant workers, and the role of institutional intermediaries is particularly important for the undocumented population.

Beyond the Bureaucracy

Within this context, a complex bureaucratic system has emerged to enforce workplace rights. At the federal level it includes the Department of Labor's Wage and Hour Division and Occupational Safety and Health

Administration, the Equal Employment Opportunity Commission, and the National Labor Relations Board. Many state enforcement agencies work in tandem with these federal offices. To focus only on the bureaucrats is to miss the many other actors involved in the process of policy implementation and rights enforcement, however. Though significant attention has been paid to how individual workers engage in claims-making (Merry 1990; Bumiller 1992), as well as to the policy advocacy and legal mobilization that social movements promote (Rosenberg 1991; McCann 1994; Minkoff 1995; Gould 2009), I contend that in order to understand *how* rights are enforced we must also account for the broad set of actors necessary for claims to even materialize. Furthermore, while social movements can engage people in "active citizenship" (Miraftab and Wills 2005), to focus solely on movement organizations assumes that the only way for individuals to activate their rights claims is through organizing collectively. Figure 0.1 provides an overview of these institutional actors, which include enforcement agency bureaucrats as well as elected officials, civil society organizations, and foreign consulates. Each of these intermediaries must navigate the overlapping policy realms of immigration and worker rights in order to address the abuses facing undocumented workers in particular.

Labor standards enforcement agencies are naturally front-and-center in the process of enforcing worker rights, yet even they have developed outreach strategies that rely on a wide array of organizational linkages to gain

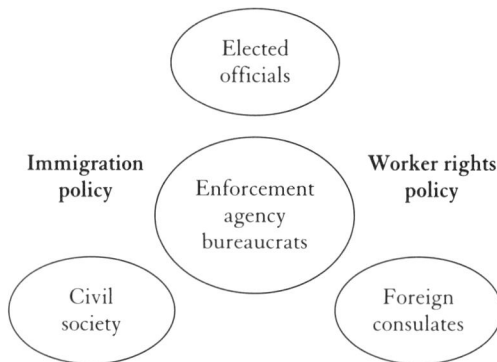

Figure 0.1. Institutional actors in the process of enforcing immigrant worker rights.

access to immigrant communities and other vulnerable populations. Tactics include partnering with local media organizations and collaborating with trusted local elected officials, community organizations, and consular institutions. Some efforts to promote immigrant worker rights are tied to formal collaborations with labor standards enforcement bureaucracies, while others are quite independent. Oftentimes community organizations are critical to pressuring government agencies to be accountable to their core missions. This book evaluates the broader system of enforcement by examining how these intermediaries relate to each other and together form distinct local systems of rights enforcement.

Efforts to address the needs of undocumented workers in Postville, Iowa, are emblematic of the myriad organizations involved in protecting immigrant workers. After the historic raid bled Agriprocessors of half its workforce, the company hired replacements under unchanged conditions, and the UFCW remained diligent, fighting to keep the spotlight on the company and pressing for accountability (Leys 2010). Spurred by their constituents, congressional representatives also pressed ICE to back off and urged the Department of Labor to pursue investigations aggressively (Braley 2008; Treviño 2008). Reacting to Agriprocessors' status as the largest kosher poultry processing plant in the United States, Jewish faith leaders and their allies in other traditions rallied alongside immigrant rights advocates to bring attention to the immoral conditions consumers had been supporting in their patronage of the Agriprocessors label. Several rabbis even met with the remaining workers to hear their concerns (Harris 2008a, 2008b). In addition, the Mexican consulate, whose presence in Iowa was relatively recent and whose general policy is to not interfere in U.S. domestic policy, also joined the legions of representatives of community-based organizations and legal advocates who descended on Iowa to assist workers (Chaudry et al. 2010). While every organization shared a central desire to enforce the rights of the undocumented workers in Postville, each also had a particular set of motivations for doing so and faced a distinct set of institutional constraints. At every turn, each of these efforts to address immigrant-worker abuse also confronted counterefforts intent on maintaining the status quo.

As exhibited by the ambivalent response of Postville leaders, only some of whom spoke out against the raid (Drash 2008), local elected officials and departments can also act as intermediaries in the process of immigrant worker advocacy. For the most part, municipal governments do not regulate workplaces.[8] Yet even governments without local jurisdiction may create local enforcement mechanisms. Several cities have developed "wage theft" provisions, for example, that allow police to go after offending employers to pave the way for the district attorney to press charges (Smith, Sugimori, and Yasui 2004; Verga 2005; IWJ 2009). Although immigration enforcement is a federal responsibility that involves only limited state intervention, a number of cities and counties have become involved in either collaborating with or resisting immigration enforcement efforts. Dozens have instituted policies that target a wide area of immigrant life, including education, housing, and work (Rodriguez, Chishti, and Nortman 2007). As of January 2011, seventy-two local law enforcement agencies in the United States had signed memorandums of understanding to participate in the controversial 287(g) program, which gives local officers the power to aid in enforcing federal immigration laws (Capps et al. 2011; ICE 2011a). City and county officials are therefore crucial to channeling enforcement efforts in particular ways. While immigrants, and especially those who are undocumented, often lack direct political influence, their rights are a touchstone for broader interest groups—including organized labor and the growing Latino community—whose support local politicians rely on for reelection. Conversely, those opposed to advancing immigrant worker rights can wield significant political power as well.

Civil society organizations also have a stake in promoting the rights of immigrant workers and were among the primary actors to draw attention to the workplace violations at Agriprocessors. Increasingly, worker rights have become a key platform for the broader immigrant rights movement (Baker-Cristales 2009), which has rallied for comprehensive immigration reform while also pressuring for piecemeal solutions to support the well-being of immigrant workers and their families (Milkman 2006b). Perhaps one of the strongest allies of the immigrant rights movement is organized labor, though its involvement has been relatively recent. After years of supporting employer sanctions, in the last decade the AFL-CIO leadership has conceded that unions are made stronger by standing with immigrants (AFL-CIO 2001). In an era of declining union membership, worker centers have also become key advocates (Fine 2006). Beyond organized labor, other aspects of civil society too have taken on the banner of immigrant worker rights. Viewed from the lens of civil rights, standing with immigrants is a way to build a unified front toward the goal of achieving racial justice and structural change (Cottman 2006; Morris 2010). Human rights advocates see the enforcement of immigrant worker rights as a crucial tool for holding the United States accountable for universal protections handed down by the international community (HRW 2005a, 2005b). Driven by their faith and conviction, religious leaders have raised the alarm about immigrant worker abuse as a moral issue, which has turned out to be a common tool used to publicly shame offending employers into compliance (Bobo 2008; IWJ 2009). For all these groups, immigrant worker rights are a social movement goal for the members and communities on whose behalf they advocate (Chacón 2008).

Lacking conventional avenues for political voice in the United States, many immigrant workers have also found an ally in their consulate, which often serves as the first point of contact for immigrants detained in raids such as Postville (Ramos 2008). As the largest sending country of immigrants overall, and undocumented immigrants in particular, Mexico has been present at every turn of the debate over immigration reform and the treatment of its immigrant expatriates, providing support through *matrículas consulares* (identity cards) (IME 2005) and referrals to health care resources through its *ventanillas de salud* (a program that provides on-site assistance and health outreach) (IME 2012g; Ventanilla de Salud 2010). As the key "diasporic bureaucracy" of the Mexican government in the United States, boasting over fifty-two offices, the Mexican consulate has become more than simply a place to process passports and visas (Délano 2009; Laglagaron 2010). Many offices double as cultural centers, information and assistance hubs, and, increasingly, spaces to find ways to navigate the bureaucracy of the host society. Though traditionally viewed with skepticism by their countrymen—who have good reason to be wary of the corruption, inefficiency, and nepotism their government is famous for—the Mexican consulates wield significant resources and authority, making them an important ally. And considering that Mexico receives over $20 billion a year in remittances from workers in the United States (even during recessionary times), the Mexican government's ability to protect the rights of its migrant workforce is economically essential and crucial to the government's maintaining legitimacy with Mexican nationals. To this end, many offices collaborate with unions to educate workers about their rights, and some have gone so far as to create a *ventanilla laboral* (labor window) to address queries on site. In 2004, a collaboration between the U.S. Department of Labor and the Mexican government was institutionalized (DOL2004b), and many more formal agreements have been struck with state agencies.

In this book, I will examine the role each of these sets of actors—labor standards enforcement agencies, local governments, civil society groups, and Mexican consulates—has played in advancing the rights of immigrant workers, and especially those who are undocumented. I also consider how the approach of each of these types of organizations differs from that of the others and across time and place.

The Political Field of Immigrant Worker Rights

The immigrant workforce is not a monolith, and neither is the system that exists to protect immigrant worker rights. It varies not only from actor to actor but also from place to place. Political cultures vary, and elected officials have a different set of constituents to please in each city. Unions and immigrant rights groups often take on particular priorities from place to place, developing distinct movement strategies and collaborations with their allies. Further, even consular institutions are not uniform in how they protect their nation's interests, and diplomats are trained to learn the specific needs of diasporas in which they operate. The policy regime for worker rights and immigrant enforcement is also variable and can be best understood as an overlay of federal, state, and local policies that sometimes complement but often compete with each other. States not only vary in their engagement with the immigration enforcement process, they also differ in their approaches to protecting workers. As of January 2011, employers were required to pay workers above the federal minimum wage in sixteen states (DOL 2011a), and enhanced state-run OSHA plans regulated workplace safety in twenty-two states and jurisdictions (OSHA 2011).[9] Many states also offer additional protections against discrimination (EEOC 2001),[10] and state workers' compensation provisions vary widely (WCRI 2010). Unions, too, wage an uneven battle across the country, facing business-friendly "right-to-work" legislation in twenty-two states (NRTWO 2007).

How then should we understand the varying approaches to advocating for immigrant workers? In this book I draw on the concept of a *political field*, which Ray (1999) defines as "a structured, unequal, and socially constructed environment *within which* organizations are embedded and *to* which organizations and activists constantly respond." Often employed by social theorists as an alternative to reductive models that focus on exogenous variation, field theory is most often attributed to Bourdieu's critique of the "dry empiricism" of sociology, which offers a "mesolevel concept denoting the local social world in which actors are embedded and toward which they orient their actions" (Sallaz and Zavisca 2007, 24). Criticized as a tautological approach by some, this perspective argues that to explain the actions of individuals and their representatives, one must examine their relations to other actors and the context in which they exist (J. Martin 2003). Fields do not exist in isolation, and the very act of attempting to define the boundary of a field requires that we also identify what type of capital and resources are active therein and how they are distributed among relevant actors. Yet the actors within a political field do not operate autonomously, but do so "in response to" and "within" the political field they inhabit (Bourdieu and Wacquant 1992).

Political sociologists have adopted the term to help explain why social movements, for instance, adopt particular strategies in one place but not another. In her examination of the women's rights movements in Calcutta and Bombay, for example, Ray (1999) highlights two key elements of a political field: the political culture of a place and the distribution of power among various movement actors. More recently, Fligstein and McAdam (2011) also use the field approach to develop a theory of strategic action in order to understand how social movements orient themselves to states and markets. They provide an alternative to rational-choice models for understanding why actors behave how they do, and they offer that "rules" institutionalize social relations within a strategic action field, and new fields are likely to pop up as stakeholders develop new interests and strategies. The authors provide the example of the civil rights movement, in which movement groups, various levels of state actors, and other civil society organizations were each drawn to the cause for distinct reasons and with varying resources, and often in reaction to pressure from one another.

In this book I use the concept of a political field to analyze the dynamics of enforcing immigrant worker rights. To do so, it is necessary to first examine the factors that make the political field of immigrant worker rights cohere. Perhaps more so than other areas of rights—such as women's, disability, or LGBT rights—the political field of immigrant worker rights is a patchwork of institutions with varying organizational missions. Labor standards enforcement agencies talk about undocumented workers as potential *clients* whose immigration status is irrelevant to the validity of their claim (Gleeson 2011b). Local elected officials in sanctuary cities have promoted their policies under the umbrella of public safety for their *residents* and the community as a whole, and their opponents rely on the same understanding of the issue (Ridgley 2008). Civil society actors rally on behalf of their *members*, which often includes a broader community of low-wage workers or the shared interests of Latino or Mexican communities (often to the exclusion of smaller groups of undocumented immigrants) (Jones-Correa 2007). Acutely aware of their noninterventionist norms, consular officials will almost always frame their relationship to the issue as a commitment to their *diaspora*, or to their nationals living abroad (Délano 2009). Consulates are able to influence the enforcement of their co-national workers through "social skill," which Fligstein and McAdam (2003) define as "a given actor's ability to motivate cooperation in other actors by providing those actors with common meanings and identities in which actions can be undertaken and justified" (3).

Aside from organizational missions, the calculus of what is politically feasible in a particular time and place also drives the language and frames that advocates use. Because undocumented immigration in particular is a politically charged topic in many circles, immigrant worker advocates often choose to not explicitly engage the issue. They make this choice in order to avoid backlash from opponents or to bring together as broad a coalition as possible toward a common policy goal. Consequently, the issue of immigration status often becomes the unspoken elephant in the room. For example, in order to deter abusive employers from claiming they have no responsibility to their undocumented workers and to encourage undocumented workers to come forward, labor standards enforcement agents have created outreach programs that reiterate their agencies' accessibility to all and promote language that elides the importance of immigration status, as in the national Podemos Ayudar campaign described above. As a result, a worker's immigration status can remain ambiguous throughout the life of a claim unless a specific remedy mandates that an investigator dig further.

Similarly, the policies of local governments and the posture local elected officials adopt toward immigrant communities often elide the direct issue of immigration status. Many city programs, such as the initiative in support of municipal IDs, tend to determine eligibility in terms of an individual's presence in the city rather than his or her federal immigration status.[11] Even punitive programs such as 287(g) are publicly rationalized as targeting only a very narrow group of residents for their inquiries into immigration status (though their effect can be widespread and chilling in practice). During election season, it is also rare that elected officials can safely flaunt their advocacy for immigrant communities without making a simultaneous statement in support of enforcing existing immigration laws. For example, many sanctuary city policies have been scrutinized during election seasons, as was the case during Mayor Chuck Reed's reelection campaign in San Jose (Normand 2007). Similarly, in Houston, the Mayor's Office of Immigrant and Refugee Affairs quickly became a liability to Mayor Bill White's bid for reelection and his subsequent run for governor. Eventually the office was forced to tone down its mission statement, removing a clause in which the office promised to advocate for all immigrants regardless of immigration status.

This delicate dance is also evident in civil society, where actions are theoretically governed by organizational membership and not the government. Even the member base of unions that represent immigrant-dense sectors can be diverse, and framing the issue of worker rights strategically has the potential to draw in a broader base of coalition members. As a result, union organizers rarely focus on the undocumented status of workers, preferring instead to rally workers around the common cause of shared labor conditions.[12] Even recent challenges to the notorious Social Security "no-match letters" have adopted a broad frame. Advocates contended that notices sent by the Social Security Administration that alerted employers when information provided in hiring documents did not match SSA records would impact native-born and legal immigrants alike. A lawsuit, supported principally by Bay Area central labor councils and their legal counsel, focused not only on the large numbers of undocumented workers who could be terminated if they were unable to resolve a discrepancy within 90 days but also on the inherent errors in the Social Security Administration's database that would inevitably affect documented workers who have changed their name through marriage or naturalization (Weinberg, Roger, and Rosenfeld 2009). Though immigration reform is perhaps most central to the issues taken up by immigrant rights groups, even in this context the issue is often subsumed to broader concerns of language acqui-sition, cultural preservation, and the struggle to challenge xenophobia and discrimination—all of which are more likely to attract philanthropic sup-port than are politicized cries for amnesty (INCITE! 2007).

Consular offices, too, are uncomfortable discussing immigration status in public forums and routinely declare it an issue that is irrelevant to their relationship to their co-nationals. Every outreach program promoted by the Mexican consulate that I have examined emphasizes the range of rights immigrants have regardless of their legal status. Further, whether or not a Mexican immigrant is documented is completely irrelevant to his or her status as a Mexican national eligible for consular protection. Viewed from this perspective, the consulate's widely popular and widely criticized pro-gram to issue *matrículas consulares* (consular IDs) is carefully framed as a tool to help Mexican nationals "open bank accounts, rent apartments and function in a security-conscious United States" (P. Martin 2005, 456). Ul-timately, as evidenced even by pointed exchanges between heads of state like the 2010 exchange between President Felipe Calderón of Mexico and President Obama in the wake of the controversial Arizona SB 1070 bill (LaFranchi 2010), consular diplomats must pursue noninterventionist, muted advocacy.

Each of the actors at the center of my analysis—labor standards en-forcement bureaucrats, local elected officials, civil society, and foreign consulates—acknowledges and understands the particular challenges im-migrant workers face, yet each is nonetheless bound by particular norms and conventions when advocating on their behalf. I therefore structure my argument in the pages that follow around the process of enforcing immi-grant worker rights, rather than any one actor or policy arena. I also use the phrase *immigrant worker rights* to refer specifically to the formal protec-tions afforded to the mostly low-wage immigrant workforce, a substantial proportion of whom are undocumented and Latino. While I do not mean to ignore other significant components of this population and the issues they face—including, for example, the precarious position of both high- and low-skilled guest workers—in this manuscript I focus specifically on the issue of undocumented status, the vulnerability it foments, and the cen-tral role it plays in the labor and immigrant rights movements. Further, while union organizing and collective bargaining are central functions of worker advocacy, my focus here reflects the reality that the vast majority of workers in the United States, and especially immigrant workers, do not enjoy union representation. When I speak of *immigrant worker rights*, therefore, my aim is to evaluate the basic protections afforded to foreign-born workers and the mechanisms that have been established to enforce them under federal, state, and local law.

To this end, I assess the relevant actors in the process of advocating for immigrant worker rights and the division of labor that has emerged across this political field. A *specialized* division of labor, I posit, occurs when various actors hone specific organizational skills and defer to experts within the field for advancing a particular goal. This approach assumes that the enforcement objective (in this case, protecting immigrant workers) enjoys sufficient resources and political support to build confidence in the viability of the formal bureaucracy. In this scenario, while advocates may continue to pressure the system for improvements, institutional intermediaries focus on promoting existing logics and procedures. Conversely, a *diversified* division of labor emerges from a contentious political field and a weak formal bureaucracy. In this scenario, no one group has sufficient resources to advance its objectives alone, and collaboration and coordination between institutional intermediaries becomes essential.

In order to examine the system of immigrant worker rights enforcement, I compare two cities that share common histories of immigrant labor but which have also developed distinct policy regimes for protecting them: San Jose, California, and Houston, Texas. I focus specifically on how and why local governments channel claims-making, how civil society organizations frame the issue of immigrant workers' rights and strategize to broker claims-making, and finally how consular institutions leverage their political weight and credibility with the Mexican immigrant community in the United States.

This book reaffirms that the gap between legal protections and actual claims is wide, as is the field of actors involved. I analyze what accounts for the types of bridges that are constructed to balance the dual systems of labor standards enforcement and immigration enforcement, offer thoughts about the efficacy of different models that have emerged, and analyze the dynamics of conflicting institutional imperatives facing multilayered enforcement bureaucracies.

Throughout this book I examine why and how, for example, state agencies predominate in one place, while federal bureaucrats take the lead in another. In San Jose, one of twenty-two California Division of Labor Standards Enforcement offices across the state is the go-to agency for filing a wage and hour claim. Operating from a nondescript downtown office, the DLSE actively enforces a provision written into the California Labor Code following *Hoffman* that "[a]ll California workers—whether or not they are legally authorized to work in the United States—are protected by state laws regulating wages and working conditions." Its counterpart at the Department of Fair Employment and Housing takes a similar stance. State actors in Houston, on the other hand, have not made as strong a declaration in this matter and are practically absent from labor standards enforcement.[13] As a result, the federal Department of Labor has a much more active role in claims outreach and processing. The Houston Mayor's Office of Immigrant and Refugee Affairs (MOIRA) is also a major local partner, as is the Houston Police Department, which enforces a wage theft provision that was initially aimed at protecting day laborers in the city. While the California Labor Code offers protections against wage theft, and the San Jose City Council has shown enormous support for immigrant rights, analogous city programs in San Jose have invested relatively little in directly enforcing the *workplace* rights of immigrants.

Beyond local government, civil society in San Jose and Houston has also taken up the flag of immigrant worker rights in distinct ways. While organized labor and immigrant rights advocates have garnered significant political strength and face few opponents in San Jose, the tables are turned in Houston. The South Bay Labor Council in San Jose has leveraged its power to advance several high-profile organizing campaigns in immigrant-heavy industries such as hotels and ethnic markets, as well as to promote progressive policy change in the health care, transportation, and housing sectors. The work of individual claims-making has been left to nonprofit legal clinics and state agencies. On the other hand, the dynamic yet under-resourced Harris County AFL-CIO in Houston faces an exponentially more hostile environment for organizing and policymaking and possesses few legal advocates who can help process individual cases for immigrant, and especially undocumented, workers. As a result, this dedicated labor council finds itself wearing many hats while engaging in a widespread collaboration with federal agencies, MOIRA, and other community actors to address the individual claims of immigrant workers. Similarly, while the Mexican consulate is a major presence in both San Jose and Houston, its authority to directly address complaints over workplace rights diverges; the consulate takes a relatively passive role in San Jose and a more hands-on approach in Houston.

In sum, I argue that specialization in San Jose emerges from a political field that allows various actors to advocate for immigrant workers from different perspectives in resource-intense ways while also ultimately encouraging a single logic of formal claims-making via the state enforcement apparatus. Conversely, a strategy of diversification and collaboration in Houston reflects a risky political field characterized by a weak state enforcement apparatus and contentious labor and immigration politics. This environment, in turn, requires advocates to multitask and collaborate not only to make the formal claims-making route tenable for undocumented workers especially but also to encourage the creation of alternative avenues of seeking recourse outside the system.

Research Design

This book is based on nearly five years of research in San Jose and Houston, two traditional immigrant destinations (Singer, Hardwick, and Brettell 2008) with widely varying political fields of immigrant worker rights. A third of San Jose residents, versus a quarter of those in Houston, are foreign born, and both cities are home to large Latino immigrant populations (see table 0.1).[14] The economies of both San Jose and Houston provide classic cases of the postindustrial labor market: workers are concentrated in the service sector, while agricultural and manufacturing employment represents less than a quarter of jobs in each place. Yet the policies, administrative structures, and political cultures for dealing with immigration and labor enforcement vary widely between the two cities. I argue that while the situation facing immigrant workers in each city is remarkably similar, the avenues for claims-making are strewn with distinct challenges in each place. To this end, I compare how public institutions and civil society shapes the cities' distinct approaches to rights enforcement.

The first glaring difference between San Jose and Houston is rooted in the very standards California and Texas have evolved for workplace protection. Apart from providing more stringent wage and hour provisions,[15]

TABLE 0.1. Demographic profiles of San Jose and Houston

	San Jose, CA	Houston, TX
Race (%)		
White	49.0	56.0
Asian	31.0	6.0
Some other race	13.0	13.0
Two or more races	3.0	1.0
Black or African American	3.0	23.0
American Indian and Alaska Native	1.0	0
Native Hawaiian and other Pacific Islander	0	0
Hispanic or Latino (of any race) (%)	32.0	41.0
Unemployed (%)	8.0	8.0
Median household income ($)	78,660	42,797
Language other than English (5+) (%)	54.5	44.6
Foreign born (%)	37.8	27.9
Naturalized U.S. citizen	51.1	27.2
Entered 2000 or later	23.4	33.6
Asia	58.0	17.1
Latin America	33.2	73.7
Europe	5.9	4.2
Africa	1.4	3.9
Northern America	1.1	0.8
Oceania	0.4	0.3
Economic characteristics		
Unemployed (%)	7.6	7.7
Median household income ($)	78,660	42,797
Major industries (%)		
Manufacturing	20.2	9.1
Education, health care, social assistance	16.6	17.9
Professional, scientific, management	14.7	13.6
Retail trade	10.4	10.2
Arts/entertainment, recreation, accommodations, food services	7.9	9.0
Construction	7.3	11.1
Finance/insurance, real estate, rental/leasing	5.5	6.6
Other services, except public administration	4.7	6.0
Transportation, warehousing, utilities	3.5	6.2
Information	3.5	1.6
Wholesale trade	2.8	3.8
Public administration	2.7	2.4
Agriculture, forestry, fishing and hunting, mining	0.3	2.4

Source: American Community Survey, 2005–9.

California offers some of the most expansive discrimination protections of any state,[16] has some of the more strenuous workplace health and safety standards on the books, and is home to one of the most comprehensive state workers' compensation policies in the country. Locally, the San Jose metropolitan area is also home to one of the strongest union movements, boasting private-sector union membership of 7.5 percent, compared to only 3.6 percent in Houston (Hirsch and Macpherson). Conversely, Texas policies are designed to enforce the basic federal minimums for wage and hour, discrimination, and worker safety protections, and Texas is also the only state in the nation where employers are not required to carry worker's compensation insurance.[17] Lastly, right-to-work legislation has severely hampered Texas unions.[18] As a result of these distinct policy contexts, the state apparatus in California is much more developed than it is in Texas. Indeed, these are two very different places to be a low-wage worker.

Furthermore, the political debate surrounding undocumented immigration in San Jose and Houston is also very different. While both cities have some of the most active and dedicated immigrant rights movements, it is fair to say that advocates in Houston face a fiercer set of opponents who command a greater share of political power. While the last several mayoral administrations in Houston have been relatively supportive of immigrant communities, significant opposition has emerged on the city council, such as pressure to shut down the Mayor's Office of Immigrant and Refugee Affairs and to rescind the city's informal "sanctuary" policy and to establish a 287(g) agreement with the Department of Homeland Security. Conversely, while the political leadership in San Jose is by no means unanimous in its support for undocumented immigrants, at every turn in recent debates an overwhelming majority of council members has affirmed their rights. Both cities are also couched in the broader context of state politics, with several of the stalwarts against comprehensive immigration reform representing Houston districts. By comparing the enforcement of immigrant worker rights in the context of these two political cultures, I am able to identify not only differences in how actors relate to each other but also how similar organizations deploy resources differently across the two.

The bulk of the data for this book comes from ninety interviews across the political field of immigrant worker rights in San Jose and Houston conducted from October 2005 to June 2009. Interviewees included labor standards enforcement agents, representatives of civil society groups, and consular staff.[19] Within this scope, I focused on institutions directed at Mexican immigrants (who constitute 87 percent of the Latinos in San Jose and 76 percent of those in Houston) and to a lesser extent Central Americans (particularly in Houston) (U.S. Census Bureau 2009a). In each city, I concentrated on those organizations that have direct jurisdiction over or are otherwise involved with shaping the focus and direction of addressing labor standards enforcement and immigrant advocacy, and I interviewed personnel at sister organizations whenever relevant. To identify these various organizations, I relied on directories of nonprofits,[20] as well as referrals provided by government agencies.[21] I requested interviews via e-mail or phone and conducted all but a few in person. Though not the key focus of this analysis, the arguments I advance in the book are also partly informed by fifty interviews I conducted during the study period with Latino immigrant restaurant workers and by an ongoing study of workers who have filed a claim at one of six San Francisco Bay Area workers' rights clinics.[22] All individual and institutional interviews ranged from one to two and a half hours in length and were conducted between October 2005 and June 2009. All references to workers use a pseudonym, and wherever I was requested to do so I also preserve the anonymity of my bureaucratic and organization contacts.

Looking Forward

In the pages that follow I explore the factors driving the divergent strategies that emerge in the process of advocating for immigrant worker rights in an expanded context of immigration enforcement. Chapter 1 launches my account with an overview of the evolution of the postindustrial United States and the path San Jose and Houston have taken. I sketch the evolution of the Valley of Heart's Delight into what we know today as Silicon Valley and how the Bayou City has grown into the third-largest city in the nation, known for being the home of the space program, a pioneer in medical research, and the epicenter of the oil industry. Low-wage immigrants, I show, have been central to the unequal story of progress for both cities, and I identify the particular barriers immigrant workers must confront. I describe the economic events that have given rise to the modern U.S. economy, characterized by steadily decreasing rates of union representation and the particularly precarious condition of undocumented workers. Within this context, I introduce the ever more essential, though increasingly underfunded, labor standards enforcement bureaucracy, and the many factors that divide rights in theory and rights in practice. These challenges, as subsequent chapters show, are paramount for undocumented workers.

Chapter 2 shifts away from a discussion of rights on the books to an assessment of how bureaucrats incorporate immigrant workers into their mission, drawing on interviews with the staff at the helm of labor standards enforcement agencies (LSEAs) in San Jose and Houston. I begin with a close examination of the aftershocks of the 2002 *Hoffman Plastic Compounds, Inc. v. National Labor Relations Board* Supreme Court decision and the legislative and regulatory responses handed down in California and Texas. Next, I examine the ways that agency bureaucrats interpret their relationship to undocumented workers. I find that while agents in both places remain committed to the goal of serving all claimants without regard to their immigration status, they still face significant barriers to doing so. I present findings from a sample of Latino immigrant restaurant workers that provide insight into the effects of undocumented status, legal consciousness, and eventual claims-making. The chapter ends by describing the ways institutional intermediaries can act as brokers between LSEA bureaucrats and immigrant workers.

Chapter 3 turns to the role of local government in channeling enforcement efforts. After comparing the struggle between business and labor in San Jose and Houston, I recount the debate over undocumented immigrants in the two cities and compare the policy responses that have emerged in each place. In the face of creeping federal interior enforcement efforts, elected officials in San Jose have offered repeated symbolic reaffirmations of their support of their cities' immigrant residents. Meanwhile, though antilabor and nativist groups have amassed significant influence in Houston, noncitizens are still able to demand substantive representation. Yet the balance of political power in each city has shaped the behavior of public institutions. I argue that a political culture in San Jose that has been generally supportive of immigrants and workers, coupled with strong state institutions for labor standards enforcement, has spurred a minimalist approach to enforcement that generates little demand for city and county to invest resources in the arena of workplace rights. Conversely, an inaccessible Texas labor standards enforcement bureaucracy, a caustic environment for union organizing, and a hostile context for immigrant mobilization has yielded significant pressure on Houston officials to actively create alternative pathways for immigrants who have experienced a workplace violation.

In chapter 4, I venture beyond the state apparatus to evaluate the role civil society organizations have played in implementing the rights of immigrant workers. I evaluate both the framing of the issue in each place and the strategies that have emerged. Specifically, I draw on Fine (2006) to specify three ways civil society organizations are advancing immigrant worker rights: (1) direct service *to* individuals, (2) collective organizing *with* workers, and (3) policy advocacy *on behalf of* workers. Rather than focus on any one actor, I examine a range of civil society organizations involved in promoting immigrant workers' rights, including but not limited to central labor councils, worker centers, immigrant rights groups, faith-based agencies, legal advocates, and even business groups. In San Jose, I uncover a specialized division of labor whereby accessible state agencies and legal advocates work to provide direct services for even undocumented workers, leaving unions to focus on innovative campaigns buttressed by faith leaders and immigrant rights advocates to organize workers and advocate for policy change. In Houston, by contrast, a hostile climate for labor and immigrants has led to a much more diversified advocacy approach, whereby labor standards enforcement agencies, the Mexican consulate, city officials, the central labor council, immigrant rights groups, and a new worker center all collaborate in a coalition to provide outreach and direct service to the Hispanic community. Meanwhile, unconventional alliances have also emerged in Houston between moderate business leaders interested in immigration reform and labor and immigration leaders who lack comparable levels of access to and influence over local and state politics.

Chapter 5 evaluates how the Mexican consulate leverages its diplomatic power to advance the rights of its nationals in the United States. Though emigrant advocacy has an established tradition in Mexican consular history, I argue that current efforts to engage in labor standards enforcement represent a new manifestation of the activist state. I contrast consular efforts in San Jose and Houston to engage in transnational advocacy. Facing a strong bureaucratic apparatus and well-developed legal advocacy community, the Mexican consulate in San Jose has deployed its influence primarily through "sideline" advocacy that focuses on worker education, referral, and specialized assistance with cases that require legal counsel. Conversely, the Mexican consulate in Houston has adopted a more "frontline approach" that has generated an integrated bureaucracy and collaborations with federal agencies, the City of Houston, the Harris County AFL-CIO, and several community-based organizations. Put together, the Mexican consulates in San Jose and Houston reflect the consulate as a hybrid institution that possesses the institutional resources of the state but also has the ability to deploy a unique set of cultural, linguistic, and institutional resources in particular ways. I explore the specific organizational dynamics that shape each office's path to advocacy and suggest several benefits and liabilities to this involvement, as well as promises for the long-term viability of the consulates' continued participation.

The conclusion offers several lessons learned from assessing the political field of immigrant worker rights in San Jose and Houston. I begin by addressing the question of whether workers are better served by a strong formal bureaucracy in San Jose or a diffuse set of alternatives in Houston. While I provide some preliminary evidence gleaned from administrative records, I emphasize the many challenges that make interpretation of these data problematic. I then move beyond policy efficacy to consider the theoretical implications of the increased institutionalization of rights and opportunities for immigrant civic engagement. I reflect on the significance of the San Jose and Houston enforcement models in light of stagnant workplace rights and the increasing surveillance of undocumented immigrants. I consider the limits of piecemeal local solutions on the one hand and the need for a comprehensive overhaul of our systems of both immigration and labor standards enforcement on the other. I end by suggesting that in the interim, each of the actors discussed in this book will remain relevant to the project of making rights real for immigrant workers.

1

WORK IN POSTINDUSTRIAL AMERICA

Since the end of World War II, the average median family income in the United States has grown by 50 percent.[1] However, lurking beneath that apparent progress is growing inequality that is now more extreme than at any other point since the three-decade era of "Great Prosperity" that began in 1947 (Reich 2011). Unionization rates are today at their lowest points, and the modern U.S. economy has slipped into a serious "time of troubles" (Lichtenstein 2002). Although workers enjoy more formal rights today than ever before, effective enforcement mechanisms do not exist (Bernhardt et al. 2008a), and the segmented labor market that Piore (1979) identified at the end of this era has become further polarized. High-paid blue-collar jobs can seldom be found outside the public sector, and contingent workers have replaced once well-paid workers who enjoyed a range of benefits including health insurance and generous pensions.

In an era of efficiency and flexibility, immigrant labor has played a key role in the transition into what Massey (1996) describes as an "Age of Extremes." Though often invisible, low-wage immigrant labor and the poor working conditions they often face are ubiquitous to our everyday lives. Migrant field workers who pick the food we eat often live in poverty (Martin, Fix, and Taylor 2006), day laborers looking for work on our street corners are frequently the victims of wage theft (Valenzuela 2003), and the car washers we patronize often survive on tips alone (Nazario and Smith 2008). When we dine out, it is highly likely that our food is prepared by an immigrant kitchen crew that commonly works long and dangerous shifts (ROC-NY 2005), and the clinics, banks, and schools we pass through are cleaned nightly by legions of subcontracted immigrant janitors who earn a meager wage and rarely receive benefits (Zlolniski 2006). The crowded factories and dangerous mines of yesteryear have been replaced by what Gordon (2007) refers to as the "suburban sweatshops" of our modern economy.

In this new postindustrial era, workers change jobs often, employers frequently evade workplace laws, and few unions are interested in and able to organize on a mass scale. Many low-wage jobs offer only part-time schedules that pay far below the living wage and almost never have access to health insurance.[2] Within this context, significant economic disparities have emerged, sharply dividing the haves and the have-nots and leading to rising levels of income inequality and poverty in the United States (OECD 2008). A borderless global market allows companies to trade goods and capital freely in most regions, driving a race to the bottom at home and abroad (Singh and Zammit 2004). Migrant workers are a key element of this process, and those who are undocumented are most likely to work low-wage jobs, least likely to be unionized, and discouraged by a number of challenges from coming forward when abuse occurs (Bernhardt et al. 2009; Gleeson 2010).

While many consider the predicament of migrant workers who lack legal status to be proof that the system is "broken," critical legal theorists argue that in fact the structural location of undocumented workers perfectly serves and reproduces the dominant economic system (De Genova 2002). That is, what makes these workers vulnerable to abuse—their illegal status in a cheap and flexible labor force that lacks effective government oversight for worker rights—is often also precisely what allows many employers to be viable and profitable. Therefore, while workplace standards like the Fair Labor Standards Act of 1938, the Civil Rights Act of 1964, and the Occupational Safety and Health Act of 1970 have been in place for decades, they are perhaps more significant today than ever before for the changing workforce.

The Hourglass Economy and Low-Wage Immigrant Labor

As its name implies, the hourglass economy is characterized by a bifur-cated structure, with a concentration of high-paying professional jobs at the top and an army of low-wage blue-collar and service workers at the bottom. Though not a perfect metaphor for the modern economy, it high-lights the contradictory structural positions of immigrant workers, who are key components of both these strata in the United States. High-skilled immigrant workers continue to fill jobs in health care and technology (Saxenian 2007), while low-wage immigrant workers have filled the ranks of the poorly regulated lower tiers of construction crews, service jobs, and what remains of the de-unionized manufacturing industry (Bernhardt et al. 2009). The presence of "low-skilled" undocumented Mexican work-ers is also nearly ubiquitous in agriculture.[3] Missing, however, is the mid-dle of the income distribution, once filled by skilled manufacturing and production positions, which have since been discontinued or outsourced, as well as by other middle-class jobs that allow for crossover between the primary and secondary labor markets.[4] The economic restructuring of the 1970s eviscerated these well-paying sectors that were once accessible even to high school graduates. This is evident in figure 1.1, which reflects the sharp increase in average income for the top 5 percent of earners, who have diverged dramatically from their counterparts in the lowest quintiles over the last several decades.

What is striking is that the two seemingly disparate worlds of high-paid work at the top and struggling low-wage workers at the bottom tightly depend on each other. The disposable income of high earners fuels the demand for the services of those at the bottom. When that demand contracts, as it did following the tech bust at the end of the 1990s and the plummet in the housing market that started in 2008, manual labor and service-industry jobs become vulnerable as well. Over the next decade, the number of jobs in goods-producing industries is predicted to stay the same, while service-providing industries will create 14 million new jobs (BLS 2009a). Some of those new service jobs will certainly be filled

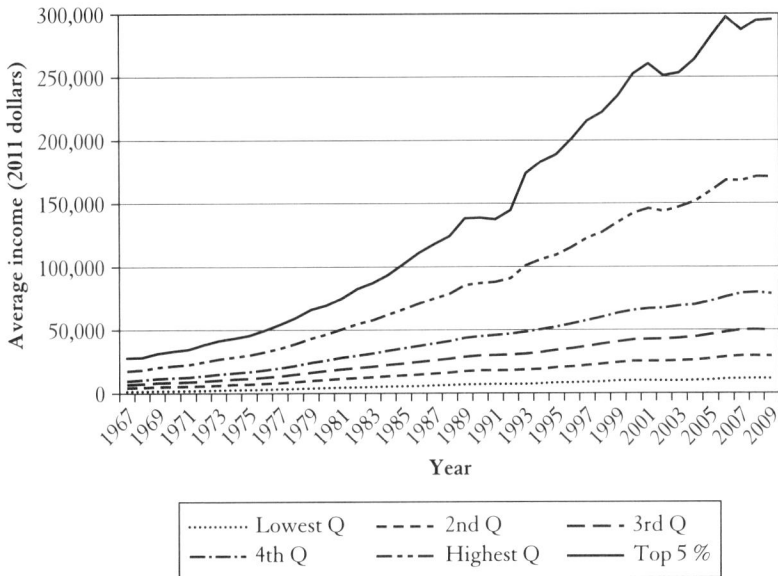

Figure 1.1. Average income by quintile and the top 5 percent, 1967–2009. Data from U.S. Census Bureau. 2011. "Income Inequality"—"Historical Income Tables." Washington, DC. http://www.census.gov/hhes/www/income/data/historical/inequality/index.html.

by white-collar and professional workers, but a substantial number will be in low-wage industries that cannot be exported, such as construction, food service / hospitality, retail, health care, and janitorial services (BLS 2009b).

In 2005, when I started this study, three-quarters of all workers earning below the minimum wage were employed in service occupations, mostly in food preparation (BLS 2006). Recent results of a study on wage theft cases processed by the Houston Interfaith Worker Justice also cites "construction workers, day laborers, domestic workers, and tipped workers" as particularly vulnerable to wage theft. These cases constitute a full quarter of the organization's caseload and are jobs heavily filled by immigrant workers (HIWJ 2010). Similarly, a nascent survey of five San Francisco workers' rights clinics finds that the top five industries for clients include restaurants, retail, construction, and janitorial services (Gleeson 2011a). Fewer than half of all claimants surveyed reported receiving health insurance, safety training, or sick pay. While conditions are precarious for all workers in these sectors, some of the most vulnerable are those who are undocumented.

Undocumented Labor in the United States

The deluge of communications we receive daily from all over the world and the cosmopolitan lives many of us lead make it seem plausible at times that we are moving toward a borderless world. Some scholars have suggested that we have entered a new era marked by the "decline of citizenship" (Jacobson 1997) and the "decline of sovereignty" (Freeman 1998). The disintegration of global trade barriers has led to the creation of multilateral institutions such as the European Commission, the Association of Southeast Asian Nations, and the North American Free Trade Association (NAFTA) commission. The resulting free-trade agreements have spurred investment across borders, as well as mass movements of labor migrants.

For undocumented workers, however, national borders have become more salient, not less. Just as economic restrictions have been lifted, massive resources have been poured into patrolling national borders, and identification papers remain the "currency of the modern state administration," to borrow a phrase from Torpey (2000). In the United States, earlier calls for open borders have been replaced by arguments for earned amnesty and a recognition that national borders are here to stay (Carens 1987; 2009). As walls have gone up, the flow of undocumented migrants has continued, swelling from an estimated 3–6 million in the period prior to the landmark 1986 Immigration Reform and Control Act (Bean, Telles, and Lowell 1987) to close to 12 million by 2009 (Passel and Cohn 2009).

While noneconomic factors such as family and cultural connections certainly contribute to undocumented migration (Adler Hellman 2008), most migrants leave in search of better economic opportunities (Massey, Durand, and Malone 2003; Durand and Massey 2006). The effect of neoliberal economic policy in spurring or stemming these flows has been debated. Early on, one popular argument posited that free trade would create a "rising tide" that would "raise all boats" (Weintraub 1992). Proponents argued that free trade policies such as the North American Free Trade Agreement would help developing countries grow their economies, create jobs, and reduce the need for workers to migrate. In campaigning for

NAFTA, proponents of the legislation, including President Carlos Salinas de Gortari of Mexico, petitioned the U.S. Congress on the premise that the deal would help Mexico "export goods and not people" (Durand, Massey, and Parrado 1999, 531). Conversely, critics charge that free trade policies have decimated economic opportunities in rural communities and created new cohorts of emigrants (Stalker 2000). Research supporting this view has shown that while free trade development may have created new job opportunities for some, the lure of American wage rates continues to draw migrants north (Massey and Espinosa 1997; Massey, Durand, and Malone 2003).[5]

Today, options for legal entry are very limited for low-wage workers in the United States. Since 1965, they have included employment-based and family-based visas. The H2-A and H2-B visa program provides temporary visas to seasonal agricultural and nonagricultural workers.[6] Those who do not manage to obtain visas and who do not qualify for asylum or temporary protected status have no viable route to legal migration. In consequence, 40 percent of the immigrant flow to the United States (IOM 2008a, 2008b) is estimated to be undocumented.[7] In response, the United States has developed an aggressive border control policy to try to mitigate this flow.

Race and class have always played a central role in the way the United States regulates whom it allows in and who is kept out (Ngai 2004). The Immigration and Nationality Act (INA) of 1952 (also known as the McCarran-Walter Act) emerged during the Cold War era and built on an existing national origins quota system. The act allotted visas for "one-sixth of one percent" of each nationality's population in the United States in 1920. This meant that 85 percent of the 154,277 visas awarded in the act's first year of operation went to individuals of northern and western European descent. The act also notably removed bars to Asian immigration and naturalization and introduced a system of preferences based on skill sets and family reunification (DOS 2009).

Thirteen years later, the 1965 Hart-Celler Act amended the INA. The act came on the heels of the more than two-decades-long Bracero Program, under whose aegis the United States sponsored 4.5 million Mexican workers to fill wartime labor shortages in the railroad industry and then later in agriculture (Calavita 1992). The 1965 changes eliminated the long-standing national origin quota system and instituted hemispheric caps in lieu of national origin quotas: 170,000 for the Eastern Hemisphere and 120,000 for the Western, with a limit of 20,000 annually from any nation. These caps seemingly set an annual limit of 290,000 visas, but many more were doled out outside these limits, mostly to eligible family members of legal permanent residents and citizens. The 1965 act also allotted 6 percent of the global immigration cap to refugees, while leaving in place the "presidential parole power" that would later facilitate the movement of refugees from politically charged countries such as Hungary, Cuba, Vietnam, and Tibet (Daniels 2008). Taken together, these changes would eventually revolutionize the migrant flow to the United States and open up legal migration channels for immigrants from Asia and Latin America.

The most sweeping reform of the last three decades was the 1986 Immigration Reform and Control Act (IRCA), which is best known for the broad amnesty program it instituted.[8] IRCA also introduced the "I-9" hiring process, which required employers to verify the eligibility of prospective employees, mandated monitoring of employers, and provided resources to expand border enforcement.[9] Increasingly, employers have been handed the power to screen the work authorization of potential employees through Social Security "no-match letters" and the growing "E-Verify" program (NILC 2009a; Wolgin 2011).[10]

In addition to these ongoing interior enforcement efforts, several more recent border enforcement operations continue to have ripple effects.[11] A decade after IRCA, the Illegal Immigration Reform and Immigrant Responsibility Act (IIRIRA) of 1996 doubled the size of the U.S. Border Patrol to ten thousand agents over five years and funded the construction of fences in heavily trafficked areas along the U.S.-Mexico border.[12] These operations significantly increased border arrests during the late 1990s (Rytina and Simanksi 2009). Rather than reducing undocumented migration, the ultimate effect of these militarization efforts was to shift popular crossing points to more dangerous sections of the border, leading to an increase in deaths. In 2006, the Government Accountability Office reported a doubling of border deaths since 1995 (GAO 2006), and recent estimates place the number of deaths from October 2009 to September 2010 at 253 (No More Deaths 2011). A secondary effect of the border buildup was to shift traditionally temporary and circular migration flows toward more permanent settlement patterns (Reyes, Johnson, and Van Swearingen 2002; Massey, Durand, and Malone 2003). Today, one in twenty workers is estimated to be undocumented (Passel and Cohn 2009), and most of these workers have no imminent way to legalize their status.

In many low-wage sectors, such as agriculture, immigrants fill many of the jobs. There are many disagreements over the impact of these new immigrants on other categories of low-wage workers, such as older waves of immigrants, the native born, and African Americans in particular (Borjas 2001; Card 2005; Peri 2007; Chiswick 2009). These debates notwithstanding, Cornelius (1998) and others highlight how immigrant labor has become "structurally embedded" in the low-wage labor market and ultimately resistant to both economic downturns and changes in political leadership. Therefore, as long as there is some demand for immigrant labor, as long as family and cultural connections persevere, and as long as the conditions in countries of origin propel migrants out, undocumented migration will persist, despite the lack of legal sanction and despite the current recessionary climate (see also: Adler Hellman 2008; P. Martin 2009; Papademetriou and Terrazas 2009).

Declining Unionization

As foreign-born and undocumented labor has boomed, union density has declined. Scholars debate which came first, and there is evidence that while demographic change impacted organizing efforts in some industries, plummeting unionization first led to the degradation of working conditions in others (Ness 2005; Milkman 2006a). Whatever the lasting impact of the current recession will be, any economic rebound is unlikely to reverse one of the clearest trends of the American economy: the steady and drastic decline in union participation over the last several decades (see figure 1.2). Over the last thirty years, core industries that were once strongholds for organized labor have lost much of their union membership. From 1983 to 2008, union membership in the construction industry dropped from 28.0 percent to 16.5 percent, nondurable manufacturing unionization is down from 29.2 percent to 11.8 percent, and even union membership in coal mining plummeted from a high of 61.5 percent to 14.5 percent (Hirsch and Macpherson).

According to Lichtenstein (2002), this drop is the result of a dialectical relationship between economic restructuring and a shift in the political

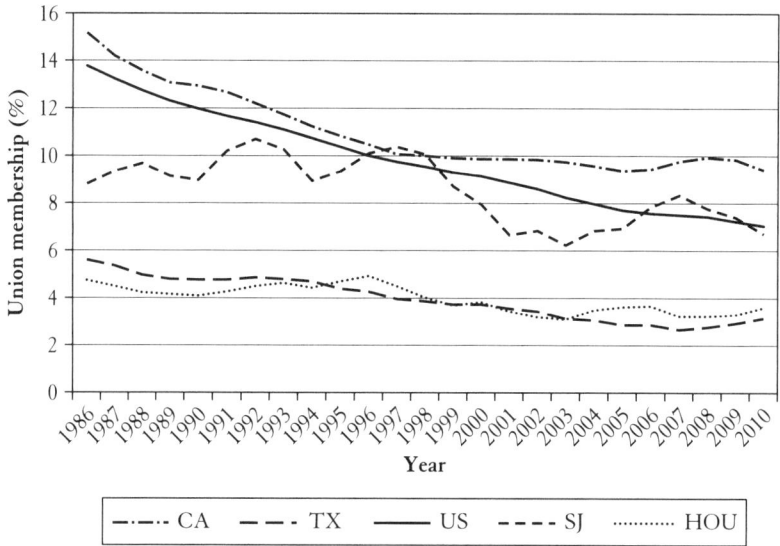

Figure 1.2. Union membership, private-sector workers, 1986–2010. These figures represent three-year moving averages, in order to account for small sample size. Data from Hirsch, Barry T., and David A. Macpherson. 2011. "Union Membership and Coverage Database from the CPS." Georgia State University and Trinity University. http://www.unionstats.com/.

culture of work: "The law, the managerial ethos, the opinion-forming pundits, indeed many workers themselves, have marginalized and ridiculed the idea that democratic norms should govern the workplace," he explains. "Little in American culture, politics or business encourages the institutionalization of a collective employee voice" (3). As a result, with no collective bargaining contract in place, most employers have been given significant latitude to cut payrolls and benefits, and quite often even to defy existing laws. Within this context, American unions have been criticized for moving away from organizing and focusing inordinately on politicking. The changing occupational structure of the U.S. economy, as well as the changing demography of the U.S. workforce, has posed particular challenges. However, this drop in union organizing has accentuated the vulnerability of undocumented workers.

Even though unionization levels have gone down as immigration rates increased, the importance of immigrants for organized labor has surged.

Not so long ago, undocumented immigrants in particular were assumed to lack any real potential as union recruits. Fantasia and Voss explain: "They were thought to view their situation in relation to their home countries, where conditions were even worse, and they were vulnerable to deportation and thus fearful of any confrontation with authority" (Fantasia and Voss 2004, 138). As the demography of the American workforce shifted toward more immigrant workers, whom union leaders had long perceived as a direct threat, the American Federation of Labor and Congress of Industrial Organizations (AFL-CIO), which represents most U.S. unions, finally decided under the leadership of John Sweeney to "stand in solidarity with immigrant workers," reject its earlier support of employer sanctions, and call for an amnesty for all undocumented workers and their families (AFL-CIO 2001; Hamlin 2008).

A 2005 split between the AFL-CIO and the newly configured Change to Win (CTW) coalition stemmed in part from differing priorities for allocating union resources (Estreicher 2006), and particularly over the question of whether and how to unionize the growing service sectors where immigrants commonly work. Despite the split, both organizations made strides to support immigrant workers, especially the seven CTW-affiliated unions that broke away, which included the International Brotherhood of Teamsters, the Laborers' International Union of North America, Service Employees International Union, the United Brotherhood of Carpenters and Joiners, the United Farm Workers of America, the United Food and Commercial Workers, and the hotel and restaurant union UNITE HERE. Some of these unions, SEIU and UNITE HERE in particular, had waged very public organizing campaigns in which immigrant workers played important roles. The now twenty-five-year-old Justice for Janitors campaign, for example, has organized 225,000 janitors—many of them Latino immigrants—in more than thirty cities (SEIU 2009). By 2009, UNITE HERE's Hotel Workers Rising campaign had launched strikes in Boston, Chicago, New York, San Francisco, and other cities in support of a largely female immigrant workforce (UNITE HERE! 2009). Change to Win leaders saw immigration as a central issue, though by no means the only one at hand, and according to Cornfield (2006) mobilized this new workforce to resurrect "the strategic organizational legacy of the Jewish labor movement to revitalize the labor movement by organizing the most marginalized workers of the emerging corporate service economy" (222).[13]

Immigrants are today seen as the "future" of the labor movement (Milkman 2006a) and their organization "imperative" for its survival (Milkman 2000). Despite the division between the AFL-CIO and the CTW, the organizations made a joint announcement on April 14, 2009, to insist that comprehensive immigration reform must remain a priority for Congress and the Obama administration. Their proposal urged: "1) an independent commission to assess and manage future flows, based on labor market shortages that are determined on the basis of actual need; 2) a secure and effective worker authorization mechanism; 3) rational operational control of the border; 4) adjustment of status for the current undocumented population; and 5) improvement, not expansion, of temporary worker programs, limited to temporary or seasonal, not permanent, jobs" (CTW 2009; Parks 2010).

The demographic shift that necessitated these campaigns, and which some argue revitalized the union movement, has been decades in the making. Yet the actual political shift among national union leadership came much later, and even unions that are known as being "pro-immigrant" continue to struggle at the local level to bring their native-born members on board (Jacobson and Geron 2008). In 2006, I sat in a Laborers' International Union of North America union hall in San Jose and witnessed a tense debate unfold about the use of translation for the majority of workers present that night, who were Spanish-speaking immigrants. Tired and impatient to head home after a long day, the native-born workers argued that translation would prolong the meeting, while their frustrated immigrant counterparts commented that without the translation their presence would be essentially ignored. An even tenser situation was recounted to me by a Sheet Metal Workers leader in Houston, who explained that while his union formally accepted the right of all workers to organize, many of his members nonetheless were very resentful of "all the illegals that take our jobs."[14]

Reflecting this lay anxiety, the share of American workers in the private sector who are foreign born rose from 10 percent in 1994 to 17.8 percent in 2010. Simultaneously, the same share of union members who are foreign-born increased from 10.4 percent to 16.8 percent over the same period (see figure 1.3). Foreign-born workers, therefore, certainly represent a significant component of union membership (Fan and Batalova 2007; Parks

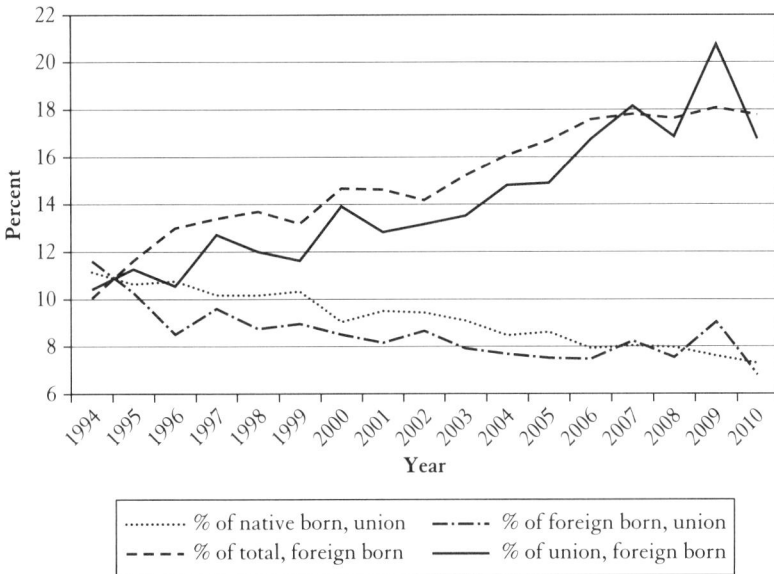

Figure 1.3. Nativity by union affiliation and union affiliation by nativity, 1994 to 2010. Author's calculations using the Integrated Public Use Microdata Series (IPUMS), March Current Population Survey (CPS), Survey Documentation and Analysis (SDA), http://cps.ipums.org/cps/sda. Universe: private sector wage and salary sector population sixteen and older, using weight "earnwt."

2007). This growth in the share of immigrant workers, however, and the narrowing of the gap between unionization levels for the two groups, cannot mask the reality that union membership rates over the same period fell precipitously for *both* native and foreign-born workers, from 11.2 percent to 7.3 percent of private sector native-born workers and from 11.6 to 6.8 percent of the foreign-born from 1994 to 2010. For all workers, therefore, the provision of formal workplace rights remains crucial now more than ever.

Employment and Labor Law in the United States

Workers' jobs are governed by a complex web of laws, policies, and industry norms, some of which are more strictly followed than others

(Bernhardt et al. 2008b). Employers often use a range of strategies to evade formal law, such as hiring only subcontracted temporary workers to avoid taking direct responsibility for the conditions of their work. They may engage in practices that directly violate the law, such as not paying overtime or failing to carry workers' compensation insurance. These actions and evasions are all governed by federal, state, and sometimes local law. On the other hand, employers may also cultivate an organizational culture that erodes the strength of workplace protections, such as implementing entirely legal policies that deter worker organizing (Kaplan 2007), or they may simply refuse to provide benefits not mandated under the law, such as health insurance, paid sick leave, and regular raises.

Both these laws and norms shape how worker rights are translated from policy to practice and can differ substantially over time and place. The political culture of a place has a direct impact on how laws are created and norms cultivated. Despite their equal right to minimum wage protections in all states, for example, undocumented workers in a relatively immigrant-friendly climate may have an easier time accessing these protections through formal means than those in cities where anti-immigrant sentiment runs high.

In the following sections, I lay out the constellation of employment laws that regulate work in the United States and consider how they apply to undocumented workers. These laws have been instituted over years of negotiation and compromise and have spawned vast bureaucracies charged with enforcing them. In the United States, basic worker protections are established by the federal government, but states and localities have substantial room to innovate beyond these basic minimums. I divide the following discussion into four main areas of workplace policy: wage and hour rules, health and safety, discrimination protections, and the right to organize. I then discuss the pervasive nature of workplace violations in the United States and the practices that have eroded the power these laws have to protect workers at the bottom of the hourglass economy, particularly those who are undocumented.

Wage and Hour Rules

If we consider workers' needs as a hierarchy of concerns, it is likely that getting paid is at the top of the list. For nonsalaried workers, the bedrock of wage and hour protection is the Fair Labor Standards Act (FLSA), enacted in 1938 in the midst of Depression-era politics. The act set a maximum of forty-four hours a week before overtime—one and a half times the normal wage—kicks in, and it also eliminated child labor. The forty-hour work week was introduced two years later by amendment. Wage and hour provisions of the Fair Labor Standards Act are enforced by the Wage and Hour Division of the Department of Labor's Employment Standards Administration, which has seventy-six district and area offices throughout the country (DOL 2009b). Approximately 750 Department of Labor (DOL) investigators are responsible for enforcing wage laws that cover 130 million workers at approximately 7 million workplaces. Following the election of President Obama, many offices received a much-needed injection of resources, and new outreach programs were launched. The Houston office, for example, got thirteen new investigators in 2009. It will take two full years to train and implement these new staff, however, before they can begin to efficiently tackle the massive backlog the agency confronts.[15] The accumulation of wage and hour claims is so severe, meanwhile, that it prompted a 2009 congressional proposal to freeze the standard two-year statute of limitations (three for willful violations) in order to give workers reasonable time to pursue their grievances (GAO 2009a, 2009b).[16]

By the time the FLSA had passed Congress, many states had already created standards of their own. The first to do so was Massachusetts in 1912, and by 1923 fifteen states, the District of Columbia, and Puerto Rico had implemented their own laws (Neumark and Wascher 2008). Yet not all states have kept up with the federal standard, which is periodically amended. By 2009, five states had no standard at all, five others lagged behind the federal minimum (with Kansas trailing the pack at $2.65), twenty-six remained in lockstep, and fourteen surpassed it (with Washington State leading at $8.55) (DOL 2009a). States also differ significantly in their overtime provisions: fourteen states have none, some states' laws apply only to certain employers and employee categories, and one state, California, has provisions for double time (Workplace Fairness 2009). In places where the state standard is absent or inferior to the federal minimum, the federal standard takes precedence. Where the state standard is more generous, it becomes the law of the land.

Even in this most basic element of the employer-worker relationship (that is, wages for labor performed), there is substantial variation in worker rights. These differences extend beyond the basic levels of protection to also encompass actual employer practices and the enforcement mechanisms that predominate in each place. Given the complicated variation in legal standards and administrative bureaucracies, it is difficult to compare violations across contexts. We do know, however, that the state with the highest percentage of workers earning below the federal minimum wage of $5.15 in 2005 was Texas, at 8.6 percent, and that California, which has one of the highest minimum wages, ranks better than all but seven other states, at 4.4 percent (BLS 2006).

States also differ significantly in their capacity to enforce wage theft violations. Texas and California have two vastly different bureaucracies. In Texas, the process for filing a wage claim requires that a worker mail in a form to the Texas Workforce Commission (TWC) in the state capital of Austin. In 2005, 2,309 claims were filed with the TWC, which ultimately collected $219,677 in overtime and minimum wage awards. In California, by contrast, the Department of Labor Standards Enforcement accepts claims at all its twenty-one field offices. In that same year, 40,277 cases were docketed with the California Labor Commissioner, ultimately yielding $43,635,207 in back pay.[17] While the federal Department of Labor plays a much more prominent role in Texas, even accounting for claims filed at the federal and state level, these claims levels reflect uneven enforcement approaches (Gleeson 2007).[18]

Apart from the federal and state apparatuses, local contexts also matter for enforcing wage and hour standards. Leading up to the landmark 2007 shift in the federal minimum wage, which had remained at $5.15 for over a decade, worker advocates across the country rallied to expose the inadequacy of the federal standard.[19] Local governments grew tired of Congress's (and state legislatures') inaction, and several cities decided to restore a meaningful wage floor. In over 122 cities across the country, worker advocates have successfully established a living wage for workers employed by establishments receiving government contracts (ACORN 2009), and the four cities of San Francisco, Albuquerque, Santa Fe, and Washington, DC, have been able to establish a minimum wage for all workers employed within city limits.[20]

Even cities that have not passed their own wage policies can be proactive in investing resources to encourage the enforcement of existing wage policies (Smith, Sugimori, and Yasui 2004; Verga 2005; IWJ 2009). In some places, this entails passing actual ordinances (see Evans 2009; Maestrelli 2010); other cities simply encourage police to enforce existing "theft of service" provisions, as is the case in Austin (Apple 2002), Denver (Riccardi 2006), and Phoenix (González 2006). In the overwhelming majority of these places, it is the plight of contingent workers (most often Latino immigrant day laborers) that has largely propelled advocates to find alternatives to the existing bureaucracies. Central to each of these efforts has been a robust network of civil society groups that not only rally to get local governments more involved but in some cases are major players themselves in combating "wage theft" (Bobo 2008).

In San Jose, city and county offices are not proactively involved in this process. However, a coalition of union leaders in conjunction with the Mexican consulate conducts regular outreach to workers through weekly workshops and targeted campaigns. A local university law clinic has also played an important role in shepherding workers through the California Labor Commissioner process (Dickey 1994). In Houston, the Mayor's Office of Immigrant and Refugee Affairs, in conjunction with the Mexican consulate, has reached out to day laborers robbed of their wages, the city and county police enforce theft-of-service provisions, and cases are routinely routed to small claims court (Pinkerton 2007b). Simultaneously, the Harris County Central Labor Council and the newly formed Interfaith Worker Justice Houston have taken their direct action "Justice Bus" to the streets demanding recourse for workers (Thompson 2009). These examples from San Jose and Houston suggest the diversity of responses to wage and hour violations at the local level.

Health and Safety

Getting paid is a tangible priority that propels workers to action fairly quickly. Conversely, workers often withstand years of unhealthy or dangerous working conditions before coming forward. An outreach officer for the Occupational Safety and Health Administration in Houston explained the difference as follows:

> You know, it's a hierarchy. . . . You'll find that Wage and Hour probably gets a hundred or more phone calls . . . versus only a few calls we get, and the big reason is, What's more important to you? That you're not being given a pair

of gloves to clean out a basin that you're working in? Or [that] you're not being paid your $250 for working this week? You know, which one are you going to complain about more?[21]

Not only are wage and hour rights more concrete than are health and safety protections, but they also encompass an entirely separate bureaucratic space. Employers in the United States have been subject to federal wage and hour laws for over seven decades. Health and safety protections have been codified for over forty years, since Congress passed the Occupational Safety and Health Act (OSHA) in 1970. The landmark legislation "heralded a new era in the history of public efforts to protect workers from harm on the job . . . and established for the first time a nationwide, federal program to protect almost the entire work force from job-related death, injury and illness" (MacLaury 2009). OSHA protections include regulations for things like scaffolding, trench construction, asbestos protection, the availability of water and shade for farmworkers, and limits on exposure to toxic chemicals.

To enforce the act's provisions, Congress created the Occupational Safety and Health Administration within the Department of Labor, which today has offices spread across ten regions. Though both OSHA and the Wage and Hour Division are subsumed under the DOL, the two agencies operate quite differently. Rather than processing and adjudicating individual claims, OSHA screens the complaints it receives, launches investigations into those its agents deem credible, and levies fines and other penalties on noncompliant employers. The agency does not, however, provide direct recourse to workers. Those who have become injured or ill must instead pursue relief through state workers' compensation systems, or via tort litigation when insurance benefits are not available.

Though the Occupational Safety and Health Act is a federal mandate, workers in twenty-seven states are covered under alternative state-run programs. States that have opted to create their own programs receive 50 percent of their enforcement funds and 90 percent of funds for consultation services from the federal government.[22] State OSHA standards must be "at least as effective as" federal standards but can include additional regulations as well. Since its passage in 1986, for example, California's Proposition 65 has required employers to provide a warning whenever workers are exposed to chemicals known to cause cancer or reproductive toxicity (OEHHA 2007). Acceptable exposure limits to hazards such as carbon monoxide in California are stricter than those set by federal standards (Cal/OSHA 2005), and the state even has provisions for ergonomic safety. Conversely, nearly half of all states, including Texas, have chosen to rely solely on the federal bureaucracy.

Federal enforcement efforts have been subject to scrutiny. A damning 2008 report prepared by the Senate Health, Education, Labor and Pensions Committee, chaired by Edward Kennedy, characterized OSHA's criminal and civil enforcement tools as "weak and ineffective." It also slammed the agency's willingness to assess and collect fines, noting that "$27.5 million in penalties involving the death of more than 600 workers since 2004 remain unpaid." The report charges the agency to investigate following most fatalities. It pays particular attention to enforcement efforts in Texas, where between 2003 and 2008 thirteen workers were killed at job sites for Patterson-UTI Drilling Company; the agency responded to these fatalities with a mere "slap-on-the-wrist approach" (Majority Staff 2008). In his testimony before Congress, President Obama's new appointment to head OSHA, David Michaels, similarly criticized the agency for being ineffective at reducing injury rates and for failing to adequately regulate several hazardous chemicals that pose risks to workers (Michaels 2007). OSHA's poor record-keeping has prompted congressional investigations (GAO 2009c), and before his death Senator Kennedy helped introduce a reform bill (Senate Bill 1580, Protecting America's Workers Act) that would revamp OSHA's record-keeping procedures, increase employer penalties, and expand the act's coverage to include public-sector workers.

While state-run health and safety programs are generally considered to be more resource-rich than their federal counterparts, they too have been criticized for being understaffed and overstretched. A 2009 probe of Nevada's program, for example, came on the heels of twenty-five worksite fatalities, most of them in construction near the booming Las Vegas strip. The final report found an array of problems, including an absence of large fines, reduction of fines following negotiations, poor communication with the families of deceased workers, and cases of state investigators who were discouraged by their superiors from placing company violations in the more damning and expensive "willful" category (Mascaro and Mishak 2009). Despite providing for some of the most stringent protections in the country, California's Cal/OSHA has been faulted for its treatment of the heat-related deaths of farmworkers each year. Worker advocates argue that these deaths are due in no small part to the agency's unwillingness to compel growers to provide the requisite shade, water, and training to prevent them (R. Rodriguez 2010).[23]

All OSHA programs, both state and federal, have been critiqued for adapting too slowly to the modern workforce, and worker advocates continue to push OSHA to move more rapidly to protect workers from modern hazards (AFL-CIO 2009b). The director of the California occupational safety watchdog group WorkSafe! comments on OSHA's limitations: "If it's a trench that isn't shored up properly, then OSHA can be very effective. They walk down the street, they take out their little orange card, they hang it up, and they say, 'Nobody gets in this trench until it's shored up.' That's very effective, that's right away. . . . But no one thinks about the toxics. You can't see them . . . and OSHA isn't as effective with these tougher issues."[24] In newer industries, worker safety is less tangible and the science less clear: the effects of toxic exposure, for instance, can take years to manifest themselves. In Silicon Valley, the infamous "clean rooms" that were central to electronic assembly were mocked by worker advocates, who charged that companies were more focused on the integrity of the chip than the health of their workers—often low-wage Latina and Asian immigrant women with limited English proficiency (Stranahan 2002).

At all levels of the health and safety bureaucracy, OSHA is sorely underfunded and spread very thin. While mean appropriations for OSHA remained relatively stable over the first three decades of the agency's life despite major swings in partisan power, the public and political consensus has been that the agency is still not doing enough (Weil 2003). A Houston OSHA representative blamed the lack of resources. When asked about the scope of his enforcement efforts, he had a hard time even remembering the names of all the counties his jurisdiction covered, and he lamented that his staff of thirteen compliance officers could not handle a mission on this scale: "People and money are probably our two greatest needs. We are sorely understaffed and sorely underfunded. . . . For each business to be visited by a Compliance Officer, if that's all that we did . . . would take us fifty years."[25]

Furthermore, the political culture of the agency changes under new administrations and across contexts. The former head of a worker safety collective in San Jose recalls moments of progress under the Carter administration that helped fund the development of material for educating employers and workers in the electronics industry. "But," she lamented, "once the Reagan administration took over, that was the end of that."[26] She contrasted the assistant secretary of labor for OSHA under Carter, a "visionary" chemist named Eula Bingham who became known for instituting worker "right to know" standards for workplace hazards, with her Reagan-appointed successor, who removed all funding. This shift, she argued, devastated the ability of community allies to develop materials, do training, and advance locally tailored initiatives that were effective at preventing injuries.

The bureaucratic barriers facing OSHA are colossal but not unique. Some might argue, however, that the consequences of these challenges can prove particularly damaging in terms of the everyday lives of workers. In 2008, the Bureau of Labor Statistics recorded 3,696,100 cases of nonfatal workplace injuries and illnesses. Though this was down from the 4,356,420 cases recorded five years prior, critics charge that the drop is in part due to changes in the structure of the economy (Azaroff et al. 2004) and the poor record-keeping of the agency (GAO 2009c). Even more consequential, 5,071 workers died on the job in 2008. Immigrant workers in particular are vulnerable to occupational fatalities. A 2004 report based on five years of surveillance data found that while the share of foreign-born workers in the U.S. workforce increased by 22 percent from 1996 to 2000, their share of fatal occupational injuries increased by 43 percent. This disparity occurred despite a 5 percent decrease in the overall rate of fatal occupational injuries to U.S. workers (Loh and Richardson 2004).

Not only are their workplace conditions more dangerous, but undocumented workers' ability to speak up is compromised by their vulnerable legal status (Ahonen and Benavides 2006; Holmes 2006; Cho et al. 2007; Tsai, Salazar, and Cohn-S 2007). Though OSHA has joined other agencies in reaching out to immigrant workers (as the following chapters will show), those who are undocumented face particular challenges in accessing those rights afforded them. In order to submit a complaint to OSHA, a worker must provide full disclosure to ensure the agency that the claim is legitimate. This presents obvious risks to any worker who is afraid that his or her job security will be compromised, particularly those who have reason to fear retaliation on the basis of their immigration status.

Workers face yet another set of bureaucracies once they become ill or injured. While OSHA creates standards that should in theory protect workers from possible injury or illness, workers' compensation systems are intended to provide financial relief and medical care in the event of an accident. "Workers' comp," as it frequently called, was created as an implicit compromise between employers and workers. It is an administrative insurance procedure that operates on a "no fault" assumption intended to avoid the need for litigation. Workers are insured to receive benefits regardless of whether they are at fault for their injury or illness, and in turn they waive their right to sue their employer. Unlike most other workplace standards, workers' compensation programs are entirely administered by state governments (except for the program for federal employees), and the state programs vary widely in their minimum standards.[27] As discussed in the following chapter, undocumented workers are generally eligible for workers' compensation benefits, though this eligibility has been contested in some jurisdictions.

With one exception, all states require employers to provide workers' compensation insurance. True to form, the Lone Star State is unique in allowing private employers to opt out of workers' compensation insurance. In exchange, injured Texans whose employers choose not to purchase workers' compensation—a third of all Texas employers (Betts and Geeslin 2006)—are eligible to sue their employers in court. Critics argue that realistically this prospect is almost nonexistent for low-wage workers, who lack the means to sue.

Yet even in states where workers' compensation is mandated, thousands of employers are not covered by formal provisions, and many who are may evade these requirements. Some small employers are exempt, for example, and others may simply choose not to provide coverage in order to avoid the expense (just as some drivers do not purchase car insurance). When employees find themselves injured in these contexts, their options are severely limited. Some states provide funds to support uninsured workers (for example, California's Uninsured Employers Benefits Trust Fund provides some relief), but not all workers qualify. Also, the practical process of filing a workers' compensation claim is enough to deter some workers. It is not unusual for insured employers to dissuade injured workers from filing claims in order to avoid having to pay higher premiums. Even when employers are supportive, workers' compensation insurance adjusters—like the employees of any other insurance company—often do all in their power to deter claims from proceeding (Biddle 2001).

In sum, the workers' compensation bureaucracy too can be difficult for workers to navigate, and even when the process proceeds as it should, workers' compensation provides limited resources to help workers recoup their physical, emotional, and financial losses. Temporary disability payments may carry workers through the initial months but take weeks to start and provide only a fraction of workers' full wages. The employability of injured workers is often drastically reduced, and their options for retraining are limited and costly (Duncan 2003). Many workers simply give up.

Discrimination Protections

In addition to securing worker wages and safety, policies have also emerged to protect workers against a range of bases of discrimination, including race, sex/gender, disability status, and, perhaps most relevant for immigrant workers, national origin. The Equal Employment Opportunity Commission (EEOC) is the federal agency charged with enforcing discrimination statutes and has fifty-three offices spread across fifteen districts. The EEOC also works with over ninety state and local Fair Employment Practices Agencies (FEPAs) that also enforce relevant state and local statutes (EEOC 2003). The agency was created by Title VII of the 1964 Civil Rights Act, which was shepherded in through the leadership of civil rights leaders and advocated by President John F. Kennedy. Seven months after Kennedy's assassination, President Lyndon B. Johnson signed the Civil Rights Act into law under fierce opposition from southern politicians, and the following year the EEOC was created.

The Civil Rights Act is extensive, covering equal protection under the Fourteenth Amendment and voting rights under the Fifteenth Amendment. Each of the ten sections of the law involves various arenas of accommodation. Title VII protects workers from discrimination on the basis of race, color, religion, sex, or national origin unless that trait is deemed a "bona fide occupational qualification" for a job (EEOC 2008). The courts have incorporated additional provisions into Title VII, such as sexual harassment protections, which were added in the late seventies. Today, workers are protected from "unwelcome sexual advances, requests for sexual favors, and other verbal or physical conduct of a sexual nature." Employers are also responsible for ensuring that workers are not subject to an "intimidating, hostile or offensive work environment" (EEOC 2009a). Several protections have subsequently been added to the EEOC's mission, including those afforded by the Age Discrimination in Employment Act of 1967, the Pregnancy Discrimination Act of 1978, the Americans with Disabilities Act of 1990, and most recently Title II of the Genetic Information Nondiscrimination Act of 2008.

When the EEOC receives a claim (which can arrive in person, via letter, or over the phone), it initiates a process of administrative triage to determine if it is viable. Once a charge is assigned to an investigator, the facts of the case are assessed, and the claim can either be dismissed or rated into one of three categories. Category A claims are those that are deemed probable to result in a "cause finding" and may or may not be litigated by EEOC counsel. Category B claims require additional evidence. Category C claims are simply dismissed immediately. Most viable claims are then referred to mediation. Agency staff explain that mediation presents a bureaucratically simpler and faster solution for many claims. A Houston investigator said:

> It's not our preference, but what we realized is that we deal with a lot of claims for which it [mediation] is beneficial for both parties. . . . It's a faster process, and it's free. So it's not that we want them to, but we encourage parties to try and talk about it because in a lot of claims we get we realize that there's sometimes miscommunication, and sometimes it's just really good to try and have both parties come and sit face to face to talk about the issue. . . . So, pretty much all cases go through mediation.[28]

When cases are not good candidates for mediation or their parties are unable to reach an agreement, an investigation is prompted. EEOC counsel either attempt settlement or litigate "reasonable cause" cases, while the plaintiffs of cases lacking reasonable cause are issued a "right-to-sue letter," and the cases are closed. At that point, a claimant may decide to use a private attorney to pursue his or her case. The ability of workers to do so depends on a variety of factors, however, including the strength of the evidence, access to counsel, and counsel's assessment of whether a given case is worth an investment of time and resources. Very often, class-action cases are strategically pursued by the EEOC, and individual plaintiffs whose cases the EEOC passes over find it very difficult to locate attorneys willing to take them on.

Like its sister agencies, the EEOC has been faced with declining resources and support. The San Francisco EEOC director reflected on her career with the district offices in Houston and San Francisco:

> I worked for five administrations. I was appointed by Jimmy Carter. I worked for Reagan, Bush, Clinton, and now the other Bush. And we've always been a stepchild, despite holding the entire budget nationwide enforcing all civil rights laws. We're just a blip, not even a line item like the Defense Department or some of the bigger agencies, such as Health and Human Services or Social Security. It's just not very much money. And expenses go up, rent goes up, salaries go up. Maybe six years ago or eight years ago, we had thirty-eight hundred employees nationwide; we're now down to about twenty-five hundred.[29]

The 2010 omnibus appropriations bill passed by the U.S. House of Representatives proposed funneling an additional $23 million to the agency to combat unresolved discrimination complaints, which between 2007 and 2008 jumped 35 percent, from 54,970 to 73,951 (Baldas 2009). In 2005, the EEOC processed 135,250 charges, 73 percent of which fell under Title VII. Nearly half (49 percent) of all Title VII charges involve discrimination on the basis of race or color, 38 percent on the basis of sex, and 15 percent on the basis of national origin. Ten percent of all EEOC charges in 2005 involved sexual harassment, and 27 percent involved retaliation of some sort.[30]

When the EEOC was created, the legacy of discrimination against African Americans was certainly at the forefront of the political debate. The rights of new ethnic minorities and immigrants have also been a concern for the agency, however. Over the years, the EEOC has received significant pressure to hire "co-ethnic" investigators and has instituted a variety of community outreach programs, such as the one launched in Los Angeles in July 2010 (Watanabe 2010). Title VII's national origin discrimination protections are of particular interest to ethnic minorities and immigrant workers. The act defines national-origin discrimination as "treating someone less favorably because he or she comes from a particular place, because of his or her ethnicity or accent, or because it is believed that he or she has a particular ethnic background" (EEOC 2002a). In practice, national-origin discrimination complaints frequently overlap with other kinds of discrimination, such as discrimination on the basis of race (Parker 2005; Nielsen, Nelson, and Lancaster 2008), but national-origin discrimination can also include unlawfully enacting a citizenship requirement for hiring or promoting a worker or unlawfully harassing or retaliating against a worker based on his or her ancestry (EEOC 2002a).

Language rights have also evolved as a key civil right for ethnic minorities (Chen 2010). Over the last several decades, the EEOC has filed many suits involving immigrant plaintiffs, such as a long line of language discrimination suits mostly involving Hispanic workers (Joyce 2004; Jordan 2005), sexual harassment suits involving migrant women (EEOC 2009b; Williams 2009; EEOC 2010), and a 2010 class-action suit involving a group of West African men fired from their jobs at a Wal-Mart in Colorado (Frosch 2010).

Following the imposition of employer sanctions under the Immigration Reform and Control Act of 1986, immigrant advocates feared that employers would make assumptions about workers' immigrant status in a blanket effort to avoid hiring the undocumented. In response, the federal government established the Office of Special Counsel for Immigration-Related Unfair Employment Practices (OSC) at the Department of Justice. This office works with the EEOC to ensure that employer sanctions do not unfairly affect immigrant-origin workers nor amplify the exploitation of undocumented workers.

State and local Fair Employment Practices Agencies have a work-sharing agreement with the EEOC, and FEPA claims are cross-filed with the EEOC. The California Department of Fair Employment and Housing (DFEH) was created after passage of California's Fair Employment and Housing Act in 1949. Like the EEOC, the DFEH processes workplace discrimination claims, and both offices sometimes work with the California Division of Labor Standards Enforcement (DLSE) on cases involving retaliation. Some important distinctions do exist between the two agencies, and in general the Fair Employment and Housing Act provides greater protections for workers. Unlike Title VII, the Fair Employment and Housing Act does not limit compensatory and punitive damages that can be awarded to plaintiffs, and it also has a longer statute of limitations. California offers additional bases of protection lacking in the federal statute, including physical or mental disability and sexual orientation (Gibson 2009). In Texas, the Workforce Commission Civil Rights Division enforces the Texas Commission on Human Rights Act. This legislation generally replicates the EEOC protections, though in some cases workers have broader benefits under federal law. One must file with the Texas Workforce Commission within 180 days to begin a civil rights claim, for example, as compared with the 300 days workers have if they choose to first file with the EEOC. In either case, discrimination claims can require lengthy hearings, expensive counsel, and demoralizing trial experiences that many workers would rather avoid (Bumiller 1992; Nielsen and Nelson 2005).

The Right to Organize

Each of the three areas just reviewed—wage and hour rules, health and safety, and discrimination protections—are important for all workers, but particularly for nonunionized workers. Beyond these formal rights, there exists a range of employer practices that may be unfair and burdensome to workers and from which workers have no explicit legal protection. The introduction of new technology, for example, is a cost-saving strategy for employers that tends to eliminate jobs; the United Food and Commercial Workers opposes such technology in retail outlets as part of its struggle to save cashiers' jobs (Berberich 2007). Similarly, housekeepers at some hotels face high daily room-cleaning quotas that UNITE HERE has taken on due to rising injury rates among housekeepers (UNITE HERE! 2009). In such instances, a collectively bargained agreement is the most effective way for workers to improve their working standards and increase their job security.

Though unions represent only a small and declining proportion of workers, the context for union labor is pertinent to the argument of this book, because unions have been the most successful advocates for workers historically and have also played a central role in the immigrant rights movement. Furthermore, many of the rights that workers enjoy today are directly linked to the efforts of organized labor. The short section that follows offers a brief summary of these victories.[31]

The foundation of collective bargaining was laid by the 1935 National Labor Relations Act (NLRA), also known as the Wagner Act. The act established the procedure by which employees are allowed to form a union and the conditions under which employers must recognize and bargain with unions. In 1947, the Taft-Hartley Act revolutionized the terms on which states could define the rules of the game for unions. In turn, some states adopted "right to work" policies, which state that workers do not have to formally join (that is, pay dues to) unions that are recognized by their employers in order to benefit from the protection of those unions. Those who support right-to-work laws argue that states that allow "union shops" (that is, workplaces where employees covered by a union contract must be members of that union) violate the right to free association and force unwilling individuals to join unions if they want to be employed (NRTWO 2007).[32] Opponents charge that right-to-work laws debase union security and create a free-rider problem among nonmember beneficiaries, who also benefit from the higher wages, benefits, and political power that accompany union membership (Mishel and Walters 2003). Currently, twenty-two states, mostly concentrated in the Midwest and South, have right-to-work laws on the books (NRTWO 2007). Many studies have attempted to identify the effect of right-to-work laws on workers. This is very difficult to do, because states with these provisions also tend to be those with lower general workplace standards and more pro-business policies.

San Jose and Houston are two very different contexts for organized labor. In 2010, 11.9 percent of all U.S. workers were members of a union, compared with 17.5 percent in California and 5.4 percent in Texas (Hirsch and Macpherson). A driving factor in this disparity is Texas's right-to-work legislation. Only 5.4 percent of workers in Houston, soon to be the third-largest city in the nation, are unionized. The Harris County AFL-CIO is known to be a dynamic central labor council, but it has a spartan staff, faces fierce opposition from business leaders in power, and struggles to gain support for key legislation in Houston. Conversely, 14 percent of workers in the San Jose–Sunnyvale–Santa Clara area of California are estimated to be union members, and the South Bay Labor Council (SBLC) boasts over 110,000 union members (SBLC 2010b).[33] The SBLC has a large and diversified staff, has been quite successful at "building regional power" (Byrd and Rhee 2004), and is considered a key player in Silicon Valley politics.

The central labor councils in San Jose and Houston have worked to address the conditions of undocumented labor. Yet despite the support of these key labor institutions, undocumented workers face enormous barriers to union membership. These barriers stem from these workers' concentration in industries in which unions have never been very strong (such as food service) or where union membership has been falling precipitously (such as the building trades). The participation of many undocumented workers in the informal economy and the contingent labor force (for whom union coverage is not a practical option) poses another set of barriers, as does the intimidation of participating and voting in a union campaign while lacking legal immigration status.[34] As a result, their ability to access federal and state workplace standards—the focus of this book—remains particularly crucial.

Rights in Theory, Rights in Practice

In this era of dismal union coverage, the piecemeal protections provided by federal and state agencies are the last resort for most workers. Yet three structural challenges make accessing even these protections difficult for low-wage nonunion workers: disjointed bureaucracies that by default do very little to coordinate their efforts, a system of penalties that incentivizes litigation and does not effectively address employer recidivism, and a body of laws that leaves vast numbers of workers without protection. For undocumented workers, each of these barriers is intensified many times over.

Bureaucratic Islands

While unions can provide workers with substantial support in the wake of a rights violation, nonunion workers are often left to fend for themselves. They must first identify the right agency to turn to, which is no easy feat. The bureaucratic web of agencies that exist to protect all the various workplace rights poorly reflects how workers tend to inhabit their workplace experiences. In places where state and federal agencies are both active, workers also have to choose between them, a decision that can have substantial repercussions for the outcome of their cases. Bobo (2008) articulates this dilemma poignantly with the example of Anka, a car wash employee:

If Anka had wanted to report the problems in her workplace and had known where to report them, she would have needed to contact the Department of Labor's Wage and Hour Division or the Illinois Department of Labor for the overtime issues and the stealing of tips, the Equal Employment Opportunities Commission about the discrimination against Latinos, the Occupational Safety and Health Administration about the workplace safety issues, and the state Workers Comp. Commission about workers not getting compensation. No worker, whether an immigrant, a community college student, a busy single mom, or the 99 percent of all workers who aren't lawyers, has the time and information needed for filing complaints with so many agencies. The laws have overlapping and confusing jurisdictions. The enforcement responsibilities are scattered. (2008, 56)

Despite the bureaucratic complexity of the enforcement system, most agencies lack a robust referral network. An information and assistance officer I spoke to with the California Division of Workers' Compensation explained that while many of the workers she sees come in with wage and hour issues, she does not really have direct connections to the California labor commissioner. Instead, she simply refers these workers to the office of the commissioner, which is located nearby. Similarly, when I spoke to the director for the San Francisco EEOC district office in 2006, who was three years into her tenure there, she declared that she had yet to meet her counterpart at the Department of Labor's Wage and Hour Division and knew little about its process. She and others I spoke to cited the financial and political challenges their offices face, which are compounded by their struggle to persuade workers to make a priority of getting restitution for the discrimination they have faced: "It takes effort to file a [discrimination] charge. . . . They [workers] don't know about us. They're just trying to put food on the table and find another job."[35] Bridging this gap requires collaboration, she explained, especially when it comes to reaching undocumented workers.

This is not to say that agencies are oblivious of the problem. Federal agencies certainly build interstaff relationships through outreach activities, and at times formal collaborations emerge to target specific issues or worker subpopulations. Yet at their core, these agencies remain distinct bureaucracies tied to separate legislation and mandates. The resulting disjointed nature of bureaucratic claims-making can pose significant challenges for vulnerable workers, such as those who are undocumented. These workers often face not only the practical problem of language access and bureaucratic knowledge, but also the prospect of approaching a government entity that incites anxiety and fear (Gleeson 2010).

Unaccountable Employers

Even when workers are willing and able to file claims, their complaints are not always heard. Critics argue that employers face very little chance of confronting meaningful legal or financial repercussions for their actions, and fines have simply become the cost of doing business (Bobo 2008). Overall, the risk of having to pay fines is a cheaper one than the threat collective bargaining poses (Lichtenstein 2002). And it has become increasingly unlikely that offenders will even pay fines. The number of workers covered under the FLSA has increased 55 percent in the last three decades, while the number of investigators has dropped 15 percent and the number of compliance actions completed is down 36 percent (Bernhardt and McGrath 2005). Though some DOL cases involve back wages damages in the millions, the average reward from 2000–2004 was only $746—an insignificant amount for most employers, though a sizable one for a low-wage worker.[36] Three percent of cases over this period involved employers classified as repeat violators. The director of Cal/OSHA described the problem that repeat offenders pose for his agency:

> Our basic enforcement model is: we go out, we do an inspection, we write a citation for every single violation we see, specify an abatement date, and assess a penalty. The press seems to be very focused on this, and a lot of critics of the agency are focused on the premise that if you assess high penalties, you're fixing a problem. And it's certainly true, if you set an example, you get people's attention. . . . But one of the things that often happens, is that we cite an employer and there are huge penalties. . . . Then there's a couple of years of litigation and the matter gets resolved one way or the other, and usually it's for a reduction of penalties. And then we're back there again in two years, the same thing all over again. All over again.[37]

In other arenas of protections, employers have simply learned how to work the system. Many contractors have perfected the art of liquidating their assets to avoid liability, for example, or of disappearing as a business (and sometimes later reappearing under a different name).[38]

Frustrated by the impotence of U.S. labor standards, many civil society groups have deployed alternative strategies to pressure unaccountable employers. Worker centers have become an important element of this effort, as they frequently rally the moral authority of community leaders to pressure offenders into complying with the law. Savvy media campaigns and direct actions have become mainstays for groups like Interfaith Worker Justice and the Restaurant Opportunities Center, which have given up on relying solely on bureaucrats to defend the workers they represent. Some have gone directly to the doors of offending employers, cameras in hand, to demand compensation (Jayaraman 2005; Bobo 2008).

Uncovered Workers

No matter how inadequate and frustrating they may be, formal laws and the agencies entrusted to enforce them provide the only protection for non-union workers. Even the labyrinth of protections they offer is not available to all workers, however. An important qualification that affects a vast number of workers is whether they are legally defined as an "employee." Whether a worker is an employee affects the very core of that individual's relationship to his or her workplace rights. Officially, independent contractors are defined as self-employed individuals. Employers who hire independent contractors are not required to pay taxes and benefits, such as unemployment insurance, Social Security, and Medicare, on their behalf. They are also not required to meet basic minimum standards for those contractors by, for example, complying with minimum wage and overtime provisions and health and safety guidelines, or by offering workers' compensation insurance.

Of the 154.5 million individuals in the U.S. workforce in 2008, 10.3 million were classified as independent contractors. In addition, there were 2.5 million on-call workers, 1.2 million temporary help agency workers, and 813,000 workers provided by contract firms (U.S. Census Bureau 2009b). While self-employment is a mainstay of the American economy, both worker advocates and congressional leaders have expressed concern over employers' rampant misclassification of workers as independent contractors to cut down on labor costs and strip workers of protections. This trend is cited as a primary factor in the race to the bottom in industries that engage in intense bidding wars to drum up business, including construction, landscaping, and janitorial work (Ruckelshaus 2007). In response, civil society groups have launched a multilevel campaign to address the loopholes that workers fall through under these circumstances, with a particular focus on the effects of independent contractor status on immigrant workers (NELP 2009a).

Thousands of low-wage workers employed by small businesses across the nation also lack protection. The FLSA is limited to establishments grossing $500,000 or more, and discrimination protections under Title VII of the Civil Rights Act cover only those establishments employing more than fifteen individuals. Industries that do not engage in "interstate commerce" (such as small farms and persons who employ domestic workers in their homes) are also not covered by the Occupational Safety and Health Act, and employers with fewer than ten workers are exempt from programmed inspections and reporting requirements. In many places, state law fills this gap, but not in all. Several state governments also have (or have had) limiting provisions that overlook entire categories of workers, such as taxicab drivers (Mitra 2005), day laborers (A. Gonzalez 2007), and domestic workers (DWU and Datacenter 2006).

The logistics of contingent work present yet another set of practical barriers to claims-making. Take, for instance, a typical morning scene on a street corner where young men wait for contractors to hire them on as laborers. A worker may get picked up by an unscrupulous employer who promises him $10 an hour for eight hours of work. The employer then drives the individual to the job site, where he labors without shade or water for ten hours. At the end of the day, instead of being returned to the street corner and given his day's pay, the worker is dropped miles away without being paid a dime. Clearly, this scenario involves a series of violations of the worker's rights. The verbal contract between the worker and the contractor provides tenuous proof of their arrangement, however. Furthermore, unless the worker obtained the contractor's real name or driver's license number, it is unlikely that he will ever be able to track the violator down.

Even in situations in which the law clearly covers a worker, the employer is accessible, and the worker requires legal guidance, the worker may struggle to convince a lawyer that his or her case is worth pursuing.

Labor lawyers often only take high-profile, class-action suits in which victory—and the possibility of recouping their costs—is all but certain. A waitress who is owed $500 in missed meal breaks may desperately need that money, but she will probably be left on her own to pursue the claim unless she is able to find pro bono assistance. If she lacks the educational and linguistic skills to navigate the bureaucracies involved, and particularly if she lives somewhere where bilingual agency staff are not available and community intermediaries are few and far between, she is unlikely to be able to make any headway against her employer. And for public interest lawyers who rely on federal Legal Services Corporation funds—the primary source of legal aid funding in the United States—undocumented workers are beyond their scope of service unless they can locate an alternative resource stream (ABA 2006).

Implementing Rights, Enforcing Claims

This chapter has outlined the general contours of low-wage work in the United States, the formal laws meant to protect workers, and the gaping holes in these protections, particularly for low-wage and contingent workers. To say that immigrant and undocumented workers are vulnerable simply due to inaction on the part of regulators and advocates would be a gross oversimplification. Like other low-wage workers, immigrant workers suffer from the under-resourced lethargy of the agencies designed to protect them. Yet rights do exist on the books, though they do not magically get implemented. In the next four chapters I will focus on four actors that are central to the enforcement of immigrant worker rights in the United States. I argue that any effort to understand the dynamics of this enforcement process must go beyond the federal and state level, which is where workplace rights are most often legislated, to consider the local political fields in which immigrants live and work. The local political cultures and institutional landscapes of cities and counties across the country affect which actors take up the cause of immigrant workers and what strategies they use to advocate on their behalf.

I start with chapter 2, which focuses on the principal enforcement body: the federal government, whose charge is to enforce the removal of undocumented immigrants while also promoting the implementation of their rights. I zero in on the ways that federal and state labor standards enforcement agencies navigate the conundrum posed by an increasingly devolved immigration apparatus that counters their efforts to reach out to the growing immigrant workforce.[39] Then, in chapter 3, I zoom in to the local level of immigrant labor to examine how place matters for how these rights are implemented. I assess how the local policies in place for governing the lives of immigrant workers and the climate of either support or opposition shape the role local governments choose to play in enforcing the rights of their immigrant workforce.

Finally, chapters 4 and 5 assesses how civil society organizations and the Mexican consulate are brokering the relationship between immigrant workers and the formal government apparatus. In chapter 4, I examine three common advocacy strategies—direct service, grass-roots organizing, and policy advocacy—and I compare who has taken up the charge of each, and how, in San Jose and Houston. I focus in particular on the role that central labor councils have played, both in and outside the context of union organizing, and the types of relationships they have forged with legal advocates, immigrant rights groups, faith-based organizations, and even the business community. Chapter 5 then expands the scope of advocacy to include transnational advocacy of the Mexican consulate, which has forged top-level relationships with federal and state labor standards enforcement agencies, as well as alliances on the ground through targeted outreach to promote worker rights. I argue that as such, the Mexican consulate represents a hybrid institution that combines the legitimacy and resources of a government enforcement agency with the access to and allegiance toward immigrants that a community organization has.

In each case, I argue that in order to understand how rights in theory become rights in practice, one must understand the borders and content of the political field in which they are being implemented.

2

Implementing the Legal Rights of Undocumented Workers

The preceding chapter examined the emergence of a new global economy wherein protections for low-wage workers have become increasingly important. Undocumented workers, who make up a growing portion of this low-wage workforce, are less likely to be unionized, and they face an array of barriers for mobilizing these rights. This chapter provides an overview of the legal framework for undocumented-worker rights in the United States from 1952 through the landmark 2002 Supreme Court decision in *Hoffman Plastic Compounds, Inc. v. National Labor Relations Board*, which held that undocumented workers are summarily barred from receiving back pay and effectively ineligible for reinstatement following unlawful retaliation. Drawing on a series of federal and state cases subsequent to the *Hoffman* ruling, I highlight the legal debates that continue to fester, revealing a tension between the *rights* of undocumented workers and the *remedies* they are legally afforded in practice.

Next, the chapter moves beyond the role of the courts and, through interviews with labor standards enforcement bureaucrats in San Jose and

Houston, unpacks how these bureaucracies have crafted their outreach strategies in a contradictory context of sustained rights for undocumented workers and an increasingly robust immigration enforcement apparatus. I describe how the ambivalence in these two enforcement arenas allows for the "don't ask, don't tell" policy that operates in many labor standards enforcement offices regarding a claimant's immigration status, and I then explain why these bureaucrats' ability to help undocumented workers defend their rights may ultimately be limited. I end by drawing on the voices of workers on the ground, which reveal the need for trusted community brokers who can link the government apparatus with the workers whose rights they are entrusted with enforcing.

The Evolution of Undocumented Worker Rights on the Books

Though undocumented immigrants in the United States enjoy far more rights than they do in countries with more draconian legal systems (Chammartin 2004), their rights here are still significantly curtailed. Non-citizen immigrants lack the right to vote, and undocumented immigrants are excluded from most safety-net services and benefits, are generally barred from receiving financial assistance for higher education, and are unable to acquire basic identification documents in most states. In the arena of work, however, undocumented workers occupy a strange position that submits them to increasing vulnerability for detention and deportation while also leaving in place many status-blind workplace protections. In the current Obama administration, the workplace represents both the increasingly intense focus of immigration enforcement and a target for a reinvigorated campaign to hold employers accountable to federal and state labor law.[1] These same protections are also an ongoing focus of public debate and legal challenges.

It may therefore seem surprising in this current hypervigilant era that prior to 1986 employer sanctions against hiring undocumented workers did not exist. The emergence of these restrictions stems from a compromise struck with growers during deliberations leading up to the passage of the 1952 Immigration and Nationality Act. In the midst of the Bracero Program, which supplied the agriculture industry with immigrant labor from Mexico, debate raged over the impact of undocumented workers on native workers' wages and ability to organize unions. Within this context, Texas farmers and growers, who had grown reliant on cheap immigrant labor, vehemently resisted the ban on undocumented labor. The negotiated result was what came to be known as the Texas Proviso, which banned the "harboring of unauthorized aliens" while stipulating that employment was not considered harboring (Brownell 2009).

The issue of undocumented labor rights made its way to the Supreme Court in 1984 in *Sure-Tan, Inc. v. National Labor Relations Board*.[2] The case involved the owner of a leather processing factory who had been charged with and found guilty of retaliating against two undocumented workers involved in union organizing. The Supreme Court retained the requirement that claimants mitigate their damages (i.e., make a good faith effort to avoid additional injury or loss) and be available to work in order to be eligible for compensation under the company's back pay liability. However, these five employees returned to Mexico to avoid deportation, and were therefore not available. Nonetheless, the Court simultaneously affirmed the rights of undocumented workers to be classified as employees and protected by the National Labor Relations Act, to organize for and participate in the election of a union, and to be eligible for back pay when these conditions were met. The Court's rationale was facilitated by the absence of employer sanctions at the time, as well as by the lack of conflict between extant immigration law and labor rights under the National Labor Relations Act.

But times were changing. Two years after *Sure-Tan*, the Immigration Reform and Control Act of 1986 passed, instituting both a massive legalization program and an employer sanctions provision that made it illegal to employ (or hire back) an undocumented worker. As a result, back pay and reinstatement remedies came to be framed by opponents as compelling employers to violate federal law and incentivizing undocumented workers to illegally seek employment. The passage of the Immigration Reform and Control Act meant that the issue of undocumented labor rights was destined to reappear before the Supreme Court. As expected, on March 27, 2002, in a 5-to-4 decision in the *Hoffman* case, the Court reversed its stance.[3] Like *Sure-Tan*, the case similarly involved a NLRB decision that had awarded back pay to an undocumented immigrant fired for union organizing. During a compliance hearing, the worker's undocumented status was revealed, and the administrative law judge subsequently held that the worker's illegal status precluded his right to back pay and, effectively, reinstatement. The central conflict, the Court argued, was that both remedies were now prohibited under IRCA. Fisk, Cooper, and Wishnie (2005) explain, "Rather than harmonizing the two statutory regimes, the majority [in *Hoffman*] concluded that immigration policies . . . trump labor policies" (389). Undocumented worker rights had entered a new era.

Employers and worker advocates alike predicted that *Hoffman* would overturn the commitments made by labor standards enforcement agencies to protect the rights of all workers regardless of their immigration status. The directives of immigration authorities now collided with the goals of labor standard enforcement agencies (LSEAs), including the Department of Labor, the Equal Employment Opportunity Commission, and the Occupational Safety and Health Administration. After grappling with the meaning of the decision, however, most LSEAs concluded that with the significant exception of back pay and reinstatement remedies, *Hoffman* did not generally affect statutory remedies for undocumented workers such as minimum wage requirements, health and safety standards, and discrimination protections.[4]

In the ensuing years, employers have continued to challenge the premise of undocumented worker rights in areas far removed from union organizing, and the debate around undocumented worker rights has been reinvigorated in the courts and in the public sphere.[5] Though elite opinion often diverges from public opinion, particularly on immigration (Camarota and Beck 2002),[6] court battles can also reflect tensions brewing in the broader public. In addition to revealing a widespread ambivalence toward undocumented labor in the United States, the cases that have followed *Hoffman* also highlight an important distinction between *rights* and *remedies* in the law.

A major consequence of *Hoffman* was to draw a distinction between protecting the *hours worked* that undocumented immigrants engaged in and the *job security* and *freedom from retaliation* of these same undocumented workers. In practice, this meant that those rights connected to work already performed were largely left intact. If an undocumented worker was cheated of a day's pay, subject to sexual harassment, or injured on the job, for example, the question of compensation remained fairly straightforward. Other rights, however, such as the right to be rehired in the case of unlawful termination, were no longer guaranteed.[7]

Despite the fact that the majority of cases post-*Hoffman* reiterated the existing rights of undocumented workers, in the wake of *Hoffman*, critics feared that the decision would be the slippery slope that allowed employers who hired undocumented workers to get away with abuses "scot-free." While *Hoffman* upheld the National Labor Relations Board's order that the company "cease and desist its violations of the NLRA" and "conspicuously post a notice to employees setting forth their rights under the NLRA and detailing its prior unfair practices," advocates of undocumented workers remained skeptical that this mea culpa would be meaningful in light of the broader implications of the decision.

Whether or not we are on the slippery slope to a deterioration of undocumented worker rights is yet to be seen. However, several key cases provide a window into the legal arguments to which *Hoffman* opened the door.[8] Although they may represent the exception to the general rule that the rights of undocumented workers have been sustained, and though several of these cases have been struck down by subsequent challenges, they are instructive here as a lens into the philosophical and legal arguments that undocumented worker rights pose.

The first of these questions is simply whether immigration status should be relevant to an employer's responsibility toward his or her workers. Less than a month after the Supreme Court handed down its decision, *Hoffman* was invoked in a case involving eight California janitors working under subcontractors for several supermarket chains. In *Flores et al. v. Albertson's*,[9] the plaintiffs contended that they had been misclassified as independent contractors and denied essential wages and benefits under the Fair Labor Standards Act and the California Labor Code. Attorneys for the workers also contended that the defendants had engaged in a wide range of unfair hiring and retention practices. A key defense for the employer rested on the discovery of the workers' immigration status (Calderon-Barrera 2003). After much wrangling, an appeals decision in June 2004 prohibited the introduction of these employees' pay documents, arguing that such a move would "have the potential for *in terrorem* [in order to frighten] effects that may cause many plaintiff class members to abandon their claims." The case was ultimately settled in favor of the janitors for $22.4 million (Muñiz 2010, 223).

A similar sentiment in favor of the irrelevance of immigration status to labor protections was reflected in a decision handed down by a New York judge in *Flores v. Amigon*.[10] The decision argued, "If employers know that they will not only be subject to civil penalties . . . and criminal prosecution . . . when they hire illegal aliens, . . . [but also that they are] required to pay them at the same rates as legal workers for work actually performed, [then] there are virtually no incentives left for an employer to hire an undocumented alien in the first instance" (NILC 2002a). Similarly, in *Rodriguez v. The Texan, Inc.*,[11] a federal judge reprimanded the offending employer by declaring, "[I]t surely comes with ill grace for an employer to hire alien workers and then, if the employer itself proceeds to violate the Fair Labor Standards Act (which this Court does not of course decide, but must assume for purposes of the present motion), for it to try to squirm out of its own liability on such grounds" (NILC 2002b). In both cases, the rationale for placing a firewall between immigration enforcement and labor standards enforcement was not only a reverence for the rights of individual workers but also the argument that equal rights for all workers would ultimately reduce the comparative advantage of undocumented workers as cheaper and more easily exploitable.[12]

Yet the reaction post-*Hoffman* was not universally supportive of protecting undocumented immigrants. At the heart of this opposition was the perceived criminality of undocumented migration. Indeed, many judges were indignant that those who had committed the criminal act of illegal migration should subsequently be rewarded with rights. These opinions concurred with the majority opinion in *Hoffman*, penned by Chief Justice Rehnquist, which characterized the National Labor Relations Board's decision to reinstate the undocumented plaintiffs as "discounting the misconduct of illegal alien employees" and subverting the Immigration Reform and Control Act. They argued that providing remedies to aggrieved undocumented workers, rather than reducing demand for future undocumented flows, "not only trivializes the immigration laws, [but] also condones and encourages future violations."[13] Citing the technical prerequisite that in order to receive compensation plaintiffs had to also "mitigate" their damages by seeking alternative gainful employment in the interim, attorneys for the defendant argued that workers seeking back pay would have to remain in the United States illegally and continue to work without authorization, clearly violating immigration law.

This argument prevailed in *Sanchez et al. v. Eagle Alloy*,[14] a Michigan case involving two injured foundry workers who were presented with

Social Security Administration "no-match letters" soon after filing for workers' compensation. Unable to produce the required documentation, the two were subsequently fired and their workers' compensation claims ignored. In response, the workers sued their employer for medical damages and lost wages under Michigan's workers' compensation law. While they were eventually awarded the former, the judge deemed the workers ineligible for recouping lost wages under a Michigan provision that released employers from liability for workers who were "unavailable to work" due to their commission of a crime. Even though under Michigan workers' compensation law undocumented workers are defined as eligible employees, the characterization of undocumented work as unlawful prevented these claimants from mitigating their damages and precluded their rights to wage-loss benefits (NILC 2003).[15]

Similar debates over the criminality of undocumented work, and about the difficult decisions undocumented workers must make in order to find stable work, surfaced in the 2004 workers' compensation case *Jane Doe v. Kansas Department of Human Resources*.[16] In *Jane Doe*, concerns were raised about the validity of an injured meat packer's work authorization. The case was referred to the Worker Compensation Division's Fraud and Abuse Unit, and an ensuing investigation revealed that the injured worker had used an assumed name and false Social Security number both to obtain employment and in her subsequent workers' compensation claim proceedings. Both trial and appellate judges found that the injured worker's use of an assumed name to gain employment and to file a workers' compensation claim was "abusive" and "amounted to the concealment of a material fact."[17] The petitioner, whose name was eventually revealed to be Delia Butanda, was found guilty of intentional and willful "abuse of the system" and fined $2,000 for the fraudulent act and another $5,000 for her series of misleading statements. Though the court acknowledged that the employer, National Beef Packing Company, "actively and knowingly participated" in the employee's use of false documents, the company's actions were ultimately deemed irrelevant, and National Beef Packing was not held culpable for Butanda's losses.[18] Though the doors of employment had been wide open to Butanda, she was deemed criminal and ineligible for lost wages because she had assumed a false identity—a ubiquitous practice for those in her position (see also Ebinger 2008).

Far from settling the question of undocumented workers' rights, then, *Hoffman* reified an artificial distinction between the legality of an employer's actions (that is, it is not legal for an employer to violate a workplace statute) and whether undocumented workers are eligible for recourse when these standards are nonetheless violated. That is to say, it distinguished between undocumented workers' *rights* and the *remedies* available to them when those rights are violated. In some cases, the court imposed sanctions on offending employers, but these penalties were substantially less than those levied in cases involving authorized claimants.[19] For example, the judgment in *Fermin Colindres et al. v. Quietflex Manufacturing*[20] became local legend in Houston (Greenhouse 2003). The case involved a group of Latino workers who complained that factory management was engaging in language-based discrimination against them. Unable to reach a resolution, in January 2000 the group staged a two-week walkout, for which they were ultimately fired. Workers then filed a claim with the Equal Employment Opportunity Commission under Title VII of the Civil Rights Act. The immigration status of the workers was immediately raised by Quietflex's attorneys and deemed relevant by the court. Though Quietflex was ultimately ordered to pay $3 million in damages to workers, undocumented claimants were disqualified from receiving the compensation.[21] The turn of events in *Quietflex* furthered the justification that worker rights must yield to the priorities of immigration enforcement and that undocumented workers ought to be excluded altogether from the veil of protection.

Other cases stopped short of full exclusion, providing some compensation for aggrieved undocumented workers, though at levels well below the general standard. Such was the approach in September 2003 in *Ulloa v. Al's All Tree Service*,[22] which involved the unassuming story of an undocumented landscaper who sued his employer under the Federal Labor Standards Act for failure to pay him the hundred dollars per day he was promised over a ten-day work period. Rather than order that the original agreement be enforced, the judge ruled that the employer was only liable to the extent required by the minimum wage for the State of New York at the time: $5.15 per hour.

This double standard was replicated in a 2005 New Hampshire civil suit, *Rosa v. Partners in Progress, Inc.*,[23] involving an undocumented

Brazilian construction worker injured by an aerial lift. Rosa, who had been hired to paint a Wal-Mart store, sued the contractor who employed him for lost wages. Though the court agreed that his immigration status, which he was compelled to reveal, had nothing to do with the facts of the case, nor with the injured worker's eligibility to bring a claim under tort law, it also deemed that his compensation need not subscribe to U.S. standards under the FLSA (Weissbrodt 2007). The case eventually reached the Supreme Court of New Hampshire, which ultimately cited a string of federal and state cases suggesting that federal immigration law precludes an undocumented worker from receiving lost wages,[24] as well as other cases where an award was issued.[25] In rather contradictory fashion, the court acknowledged that not providing a remedy would create an incentive for employers to hire undocumented workers and treat them as "disposable commodities who may be replaced the moment they are damaged." Yet it also concluded that immigration status has direct bearing on the level of compensation undocumented workers are eligible for, and subsequently calibrated damages to wage levels in Brazil (NILC 2005). In this case, therefore, *Hoffman* was not found to be "controlling" but still rather "instructive" and "persuasive" in establishing a two-tier system for workplace rights. (See also Fuller 2006; Cunningham-Parmeter 2008.)

While the previous section has by no means provided a comprehensive analysis of the legal precedents for the rights of undocumented workers, it does highlight the volatility of undocumented workplace rights and the occasionally arbitrary-seeming legal decisions that decide these workers' fate. The exact character and content of undocumented-worker rights in the United States are not settled. As a result, labor standards enforcement agencies still hold substantial responsibility for enforcing undocumented worker rights. Meanwhile state, local, and federal immigration enforcement efforts continue to create an ever-chillier climate for upholding whatever rights do exist for undocumented workers. In the following section, drawing on interviews with agency directors in Houston and San Jose, I examine how bureaucrats on the ground are negotiating this ongoing paradox. I find that while the courts continue to debate, labor standards enforcement agencies seem to have neither the desire nor the patience to become deputies of the immigration enforcement apparatus.

Beyond the Courts: Bureaucratic Responses to *Hoffman*

Political sociology research examines how bureaucratic agents exercise discretion with clients with the effect of either expanding or constricting the services and benefits they ultimately receive. In some cases, bureaucrats may go the distance for clients they deem worthy (Maynard-Moody and Musheno 2003), and in others they may exercise undue discrimination against a client (Lipsky 1980). Existing research into bureaucracies in education, law enforcement, welfare, health care, and libraries reveals that even though undocumented immigrants are formally barred from many civic and political arenas, they seem to be achieving rapid bureaucratic incorporation (van der Leun 2003; Lewis and Ramakrishnan 2007; Gonzales 2008; Jones-Correa 2008; Marrow 2010).

Caught between the immigration and labor standards enforcement contexts, one of the first things many LSEAs did following *Hoffman* was to issue memorandums of understanding to reiterate their incorporating stance toward undocumented workers. The first to do so was the agency directly implicated in the case, the National Labor Relations Board. The NLRB's memo reaffirmed the definition of undocumented workers as *employees* who were eligible to vote in union elections regardless of their documentation status. It also sketched out the limitations on employers' ability to raise questions regarding workers' status and affirmed provisions for "conditional reinstatement" of any employee wrongly discharged for union activity as long as that employee was able to establish his or her work eligibility within a "reasonable time frame." The document emphasizes that immigration investigations should only occur after a "genuine issue" is established in order to avoid overtly facilitating employer efforts at intimidation. It also suggests that while *Hoffman* precludes back pay for an unauthorized worker who is wrongly discharged, it need not necessarily preclude back pay for those wrongfully demoted (NLRB 2002).

When I spoke to NLRB attorneys in California and Texas, these sentiments were reiterated, with the caveat that it was not that these attorneys were *pro*-undocumented worker but rather that their protocol was to treat the immigration status of a claimant as irrelevant unless the specific facts of the case require them to investigate further. An NLRB attorney in San Jose (Region 20) reflected on his twenty-five-year career with the agency and affirmed that even during the shift from *Sure-Tan* to *Hoffman*, his office continued to do everything possible for undocumented workers as far as the law allowed. Though prior to *Hoffman* the agency had no role in verifying work authorization when issuing back pay or reinstating a worker after unlawful termination, it is now compelled to do so. In these cases, the attorney explained, "We would give them a period of time to obtain it and some limited back pay [compensation]. We would try to find a compromise between those two conflicting laws." However, he reiterated, "I don't think anyone disagrees that the immigration law and the National Labor Relations Act didn't match very well. . . . [But] our policy now is . . . we don't ask, we don't make inquiries, but if it comes up, we act in accordance with the immigration law."[26]

His counterpart in the relatively conservative district covering Houston (Region 16) expressed similar ambivalence: "Initially we treat the whole charge on a neutral basis. But if an employer says that an employee was fired because he was an illegal immigrant using a false Social Security number . . . then we *have* to investigate the claim [of illegal status]. . . . Otherwise, we don't ask." He went on to stress that the agency's investigations into claimants' immigration status nearly always came about because employers had pushed the issue as a defense. This information, however, is held in strict confidence and is not shared with ICE. Nevertheless, he says that he and his colleagues counsel workers not to independently offer information about their status unless asked, and he admits they struggle to persuade potentially undocumented witnesses to agree to testify during hearings. While this attorney felt confident that his agency is open to protecting undocumented claimants as far as the law allows, he also wonders whether the dramatic drop in petitions his agency received post-*Hoffman* was fueled by an assumption that "they probably can't win cases post-*Hoffman*."[27]

Other federal labor standards enforcement agencies in Houston and San Jose expressed similar frustration with the conflicting messages sent by federal law. Despite the new restrictions imposed by the *Hoffman* ruling, all the representatives I spoke to were eager to carve out as broad an arena of rights as the law allowed them to. For example, in the months following the decision, the Department of Labor's Wage and Hour Division issued a fact sheet emphasizing that the Court's decision in *Hoffman* "does not mean that undocumented workers do not have rights under other U.S. labor laws." It reminded workers that the new regulations "did not address laws the Department of Labor enforces . . . [and which] provide core labor protections for vulnerable workers." The agency professed it would continue to enforce the Fair Labor Standards Act "without regard to whether an employee is documented or undocumented" (DOL 2008). The agency's director in Houston, a stern and avowedly conservative character, explained his stance that undocumented workers "were employees, with the same protections under the FLSA." In his view, *Hoffman* plainly "had no effect."[28] The director of the Wage and Hour Division in San Jose professed similar indifference toward *Hoffman*. Her office is smaller, and unlike the Houston office it refers many cases to the state labor standards enforcement system, whose statutes are more robust. Nevertheless, she plainly explained that her agency does not "solicit information" about a claimant's immigration status and that immigration status has "never been an issue."

Similarly, the Equal Employment Opportunity Commission jumped in with a press release clarifying previous guidance while avowing that the *Hoffman* decision "does not affect the government's ability to root out discrimination against undocumented workers." The agency emphatically reiterated that the ruling had no bearing on "the settled principle that undocumented workers are covered by the federal employment discrimination statutes and that it is as illegal for employers to discriminate against them as it is to discriminate against individuals authorized to work." It concluded: "Enforcing the law to protect vulnerable workers, particularly low income and immigrant workers, remains a priority for EEOC" (EEOC 2002b). As with the other two agencies, Equal Employment Opportunity Commission directors in Houston and San Jose were unfazed by *Hoffman*. The acting director in Houston stated plainly, "We don't look at immigration status of an employee." He acknowledged that a claimant's status could be raised as a defense by a defendant employer, in which case the ensuing remedy could be affected. But, he went on to explain, "We don't look at that unless it comes up at that end."[29] Repeating almost verbatim her colleague's sentiment, the San Jose EEOC director replied that in terms of evaluating the facts of a case, immigration status is "really irrelevant, so we don't even inquire." The statutes her agency enforces (including the Civil Rights Act of 1964) "apply to everyone,"[30] and the agency's outreach coordinators provided a long list of efforts they have made to quell immigrant workers' fears.

On the whole, federal bureaucrats I spoke to see their work as focused exclusively on enforcing labor rights, and they understand immigration enforcement to be irrelevant to their core mission. When I probed representatives on their rationale, many explained that it was not a humanitarian reaction. Instead, these agents saw protecting the rights of undocumented workers as central to the effort to disincentivize employers' mistreatment of *all* workers. The deputy director of the Equal Employment Opportunity Commission office in Houston, for example, explained, "A person working here in the United States can file a complaint irrespective of immigration status." He emphasized, however, that the responsibility for assessing the worker's immigration status lies squarely in the hands of the employer. His agency is simply "interested in looking at employment policies and practices of companies that may be exploiting immigrants."[31] The EEOC director in the San Francisco district office provided a parallel response. Reflecting on the large agricultural workforce in California, she acknowledged, "There are millions of them in California, they're the most vulnerable, and many of them are undocumented." Their documentation, she reiterated, is "not an issue for us."[32]

Beyond the federal apparatus, state agencies in Houston and San Jose are also compelled to enforce worker rights, even for undocumented claimants. However, in California, both the standards and the institutional infrastructure erected to enforce them are more robust. Nevertheless, when asked to describe how they negotiated the post-*Hoffman* context, representatives of both California and Texas agencies not only reiterated many of the same "don't ask, don't tell" sentiments of their federal colleagues but also added a reminder that as *state* agencies they are even further removed from any mandate to carry out the functions of federal immigration policy.

California is ahead of the pack in this regard. Following *Hoffman*, the state agencies not only issued public statements in response to the federal declarations, but the state legislature went a step further and inscribed a firewall between immigration enforcement and worker rights into the California Labor Code. Today, Section 171.5 of the code makes an individual's immigration status irrelevant to the enforcement of state labor, civil rights, and employee housing laws. In addition, the California Division of Labor Standards Enforcement, the state office charged with enforcing wage and hour provisions, formally announced, "All California workers—whether or not they are legally authorized to work in the

United States—are protected by state laws regulating wages and working conditions" (CA-DIR 2009). Similarly, the Department of Fair Employment and Housing (DFEH) posted a bulletin stating: "The Department will continue to accept, investigate, and prosecute cases involving workplace discrimination without regard to the worker's immigration status. Further, the Department will not ask for information about the immigration status of any employee filing a complaint" (CA-DFEH 2002).

The official sentiment expressed by state agencies in Texas was markedly more muted than in California but not altogether different. Texas agencies did not make public declarations or offer formal guidance on how *Hoffman* affects their treatment of undocumented workers, yet when asked about their stance on this issue, representatives from the Texas Workforce Commission reiterated their commitment to protect undocumented workers in no uncertain terms. One agency representative at the central office in Austin explained the practical necessity of this posture: if he were to ask potential claimants to present their documentation status, he would in essence be contradicting his own agency's mission and inviting employers to mistreat their undocumented workers. He elaborated in even bolder terms: "We feel that states that do not protect those workers are doing the wrong thing. So for that reason, we don't ask that question."[33]

While the goals of federal immigration enforcement continue to clash with the provision of rights to undocumented workers in the courts, then, on the ground I found that bureaucrats at federal labor standards enforcement offices are uninterested in conceding any power that would compromise their own agency's missions to hold employers accountable. The changes ushered in by *Hoffman* were understood by everyone I spoke to in both Houston and San Jose to be a challenge to—but not to preclude—enforcing the rights of undocumented workers. In response, the common strategy is to adopt a "don't ask, don't tell" approach, wherein bureaucrats were absolved of responsibility for uncovering a worker's immigration status unless forced to do so. This passive approach to the issue is less an example of shirking, as Brehm and Gates (1999) might suggest, than a method of steadfast adherence to agency missions to uphold federal labor standards and evidence of a strong effort to draw a jurisdictional divide between this goal and that of immigration enforcement.

The Limits to Good Intentions: Challenges to Implementing Undocumented Worker Rights

Despite the universal support for the rights of undocumented workers among federal and state labor standards enforcement agents in Houston and San Jose, many overarching challenges complicate the protection of these rights. In this section, I chronicle two levels of barriers. First, I provide an institutional perspective on the difficulty of reaching immigrant workers, particularly those who are undocumented. Language skills, cultural competency, and the development of trusted liaisons all pose resource demands that are not always easily met by government agencies. Second, I draw on the narratives provided by fifty restaurant workers I interviewed across the two cities. Through their voices, I highlight the ways that undocumented status shapes workers' legal consciousness and their subsequent propensity to engage in claims-making following a workplace violation.

Barriers to Reaching Immigrant Workers

In every office I visited, each director recounted a long list of translated material, culturally relevant videos, and ongoing outreach calendars the office had generated in an attempt to reach out to a range of vulnerable populations. Immigrant workers are by no means the only target. The Equal Employment Opportunity Commission, for example, was in the midst of launching a "Teens at Work" campaign designed to educate young workers about their civil rights. Similarly, the Occupational Safety and Health Administration had crafted a series of personalized flyers for particularly dangerous occupations. Yet the community that agents felt most anxious about reaching was the immigrant community. Demographically, immigrants represent a growing proportion of the agencies' outreach target, and logistically immigrants are perhaps the hardest population to reach.

Despite the long history of the immigrant population in California, the availability of Spanish-speaking personnel has proliferated unevenly across different agencies. When I visited in 2006, the EEOC San Francisco district (which covers San Jose) served fourteen different language groups, while the Houston office boasted at least ten bilingual investigators covering Spanish, Chinese, and Vietnamese. Nonetheless, both directors identified several gaps in their district's language capacity. For example, at the time of my inquiry, the San Jose office's district, where one of the largest Cantonese-speaking diasporas in the world is located, had no investigators who spoke the language. Both the San Jose and Houston offices also cited a need for more investigators who spoke various other Chinese dialects, Vietnamese, and one of the many South Asian languages. This lack of language capacity not only posed an instrumental barrier to attracting individual claimants; it also deterred a deeper connection with the community through cultural understanding.

Reflecting this challenge, the director of the Department of Labor office in San Jose relayed the story of a recent failed effort to address wage and hour violations in ethnic markets in the city. One cluster of charges involved an Indian specialty-store owner who owed $500,000 in overtime back wages to his workers. The employer followed a very common practice of paying workers a set "salary" in cash rather than maintaining hourly time cards. Through agency surveillance, the Wage and Hour Division was able to confirm that workers at the store were putting in up to sixteen-hour days and being paid far below even the federal minimum wage. The shop's workers included both Indian immigrants who spoke English well and monolingual Spanish-speaking immigrants. Though language did not pose a technical barrier for these workers, they were the target of ongoing exploitation and were vulnerable to the shop owner's pleas that they keep quiet during the investigation. Ultimately, due in large part to the efforts of Spanish-speaking DOL-WHD staff, the Latino workers eventually came forward, while the Indian workers maintained their stance that they had only worked forty hours, "no problem." The agency was ultimately unsuccessful in getting them to file a formal complaint, and the office continues struggling to hire an investigator who speaks an Indian language.[34]

The relatively small populations of South Asian immigrants and the complex linguistic diversity of these populations, compared with the number of Latino immigrants in San Jose and Houston, likely make these challenges inevitable, but I found some instances where even Spanish posed a challenge for agencies. Though the vast majority of the bilingual investigators at the Houston EEOC office spoke Spanish, their sister office in New Orleans had only one Spanish-speaking investigator in the wake of Hurricane Katrina, when the city was inundated with exploitable day laborers. Similarly, the Houston Police Department, which investigates wage-theft claims, had only one Spanish-speaking officer (out of six) in its community outreach division. In San Jose also, I found that the information and assistance officer at the local office for the Division of Workers' Compensation was one of only three Spanish speakers to hold that post in the entire Northern California Region. Other bustling offices that serve substantial Latino populations, including major Latino population centers like Oakland, Sacramento, and Fresno, in fact had no Spanish-language capacity.[35] The result is that Spanish-speaking clients drive in from all over the region to see this one San Jose information and assistance officer. Though this officer is explicitly prohibited from offering legal advice, she is able to help monolingual clients familiarize themselves with the system by providing crucial technical assistance with forms and by speaking to insurance adjusters, who are not required to communicate with clients in their native language.

Language, as many of the agency representatives I spoke to explained, is only one side of a much more fundamental key to accessing vulnerable immigrant communities. Beyond technical translation, language capacity is also crucial for building rapport. The San Jose EEOC director explains: "I do not believe that investigators need to be bilingual. . . . The agency can hire translators. However, it does make a big difference in terms of trust."[36] In some cases, lack of trust was rooted in very specific histories wherein the division between labor standards enforcement and immigration enforcement had not held firm. The director of the Wage and Hours office in Houston explained, for example, that "because of the past history of dealing with immigrant workers"—a legacy of neglect, and some cases even overt intimidation, of immigrant communities—immigrant workers are reluctant to file complaints.[37] This legacy is the residual effect of the fierce anti-immigrant sentiment of a small but vocal and powerful element of civil society groups and politicians in Houston.

Other agencies have more tangibly negative legacies to confront. The director of the Occupational Safety and Health Administration, for example, told me of a July 2005 incident that shattered the agency's reputation for a while. The episode involved a putative OSHA training at Seymour Johnson Air Force Base in Goldsboro, North Carolina, which was billed as a mandatory health and safety meeting. However, unbeknownst to OSHA officials, Immigration Customs and Enforcement officials entered the facility under false pretenses and conducted a massive work-site raid. Many undocumented workers were subsequently detained on charges of unauthorized presence. In the wake of this farce, OSHA officials were furious and demanded assurance that ICE would cease all such activities. Ultimately, under tremendous pressure from OSHA officials and Congress, Department of Homeland Security secretary Michael Chertoff conceded that he was "very concerned with the incident" and ordered ICE to put a stop to such administrative ruses under OSHA's name (Office of U.S. Senator Russ Feingold 2006). In its attempt to move forward, OSHA has invested significant resources to reach out to immigrant communities.

Yet these outreach campaigns face an uphill battle. The director of Cal/OSHA concedes, "The most difficult thing for us to do is get in front of immigrant groups of workers, who tend to view the government as a monolith, and say [to them], you know, 'There's a really big difference between us and ICE.' "[38] Incidents like the North Carolina raid have lasting effects and cast doubt on the authenticity of the separation of powers between labor standards enforcement and immigration authorities. The director went on to lament the effect of this and other similar incidents: "I've never heard the crystal clear apology that should have been given. Nor have I heard an absolute ironclad statement that Homeland Security will *never ever, ever* do something like that again. . . . I haven't heard of any more incidents. But it certainly has done a lot of damage to us." He, like immigrant workers on the ground, remains skeptical of the bounds of ICE's enforcement tactics and is concerned about his agency's effort to reach out to undocumented communities in order to compel workers to come forward.

In the next section, I delve into the chasm between workers' formal rights and actual claims-making by highlighting the way that immigration status shapes not only the instrumental barriers undocumented workers face but also the constitutive effects that being undocumented has on workers' relationship to their rights (Fleury-Steiner and Nielsen 2006).

Undocumented Status, Legal Consciousness, and Claims-Making

The power of rights on the books—however straightforward—can ultimately be realized only if individuals are able and choose to come forward to mobilize them. This is particularly the case in the arena of labor standards enforcement, where opportunities to hold employers accountable hinge almost entirely on the success of individual claims. In this regard, Felstiner and colleagues' (1980) now infamous model of "naming, blaming, claiming" reminds us that even when individuals are aware of their workplace rights and know their employer is liable for ensuring them, the final step of actually *claiming* these rights can be fraught with any number of barriers, as many socio-legal scholars have documented (Merry 1990; Bumiller 1992; Ewick and Silbey 1998). Undocumented status poses one of these practical barriers, most clearly through the ubiquitous fear of deportation. To examine how undocumented status may shape claims-making behavior, I turn to the restaurant industry, which is one of the largest employers in the country (NRA 2008), a key destination for undocumented labor (Passel 2006), and a sector where workplace violations are near ubiquitous (ROC-NY 2005, 2009).

In my conversations with fifty randomly selected Latino immigrant restaurant workers, I found that undocumented status can not only create an intense aversion to risk, but also fundamentally shapes the relationship workers have to their rights. Barred from residing or working here, these workers find themselves in a paradoxical legal position that puts them in constant danger of detention and deportation at the same time that it threatens economic disaster. The decision to engage in formal claims-making is not, therefore, an inviting one. Though fear of being discovered is certainly a part of this hesitancy, I also found that workers exhibit substantial agency in engaging in a calculated process of decision-making that weighs the effects of claims-making against current work relationships and, ultimately, their long-term goals of settlement or return migration. Though undocumented workers come to the United States for a myriad of reasons, central concerns for those contemplating whether to file a claim when a workplace violation occurs include job security, uncertainly about the bureaucracy required to file a claim, and a willingness to endure current conditions in the service of a better future back home.

One of the primary considerations any worker faces when considering a workplace claim is job security. The absence of any route to legalization means that each time undocumented workers lose their jobs, they must go through the infamous I-9 verification system again. Though retaliation against workers who file a claim has repeatedly been deemed illegal, lack of formal protections for back pay and reinstatement under *Hoffman* certainly dilute, if not invalidate, these commitments. Knowledge of the details of these rights, and their limits, is certainly limited. However, I found that many workers are nonetheless wary that "rocking the boat" could put them outside their employer's good graces. For example, Alejandro, an undocumented kitchen worker I spoke with in San Jose, described the abusive behavior of his manager: "He's the type of person that screams at waiters in front of clients, tells the dishwashers that they are stupid, curses them, and tells them that they are worthless." Though this harassment is prohibited under both federal and California discrimination protections, and there are two offices in San Jose where Alejandro could go for help, he has chosen not to come forward with a formal complaint. In fact, when asked, Alejandro conceded that he knows about the Equal Employment Opportunity Commission and his rights under the law. But, he emphasized, his decision to hold back is fueled largely by fear of losing his job in what he also clearly understands to be an "at will" employment context. Married, with two young children at home, Alejandro depends on his job. He admits: "The treatment is bad; the pay is low. . . . In reality, I just really need the job, so I stayed." Fearful of enraging his employer further and anxious about his ability to find another job, he said frankly, "We all know that right now to find another job is difficult. . . . They go over everything. . . . They have to check your social and everything." He has therefore ultimately resigned himself to "avoiding problems."

Undocumented workers are also reluctant to become mired in the bureaucracy of filing a claim. Anyone who has ever had an agency lose their forms, bungle their transaction, or drag out a theoretically simple experience forever likely shares the same sentiment. Indeed, knowing *how* to proceed with a claim is insufficient. One must also feel assured that the procedure will be successful. This confidence in one's ability to navigate the system successfully is what Bandura (1994) defines as an individual's perceived self-efficacy, or "people's beliefs about their capabilities to produce effects." These beliefs determine how people "feel, think, motivate themselves and behave" (71). For the undocumented restaurant workers I spoke to in both cities, the practical cost of coming forward is further complicated by a sense that "it won't do any good," or, in the worse-case scenario, that their situation could potentially even worsen. For example, Rubén, an undocumented dishwasher in San Jose, recounted an experience his co-worker had with a bad cut to her hand. After contemplating filing a workers' compensation claim for two weeks, she was told that it was too late to file one and that she instead had to pay for her own doctor's visit and treatment. Rubén joked cynically that if she *as a legal immigrant* had problems with the process, his experience would likely be worse.

A number of factors—including language barriers, low levels of education, and an unfamiliarity with the American system of rights—combine with a general sense of the inefficiency of government functions to fuel this cynicism. Yet the undocumented experience *itself* can also ultimately disempower undocumented individuals from accessing rights that they clearly enjoy in theory. Despite the many "memorandums of understanding" and public statements that spell out the separate functions of labor standards enforcement agencies and immigration authorities, many undocumented immigrants do not trust that their information will never leave the hands of well-intentioned agencies.[39] This is a common concern that many government agencies—not only those that enforce labor standards—must face. Indeed, it is precisely this fear that, for example, deters undocumented domestic violence victims from seeking assistance from police (Wachholz and Miedema 2000; Salcido and Adelman 2004) or prevents undocumented immigrants who may be sick from seeking help in public hospitals (Berk and Schur 2001).[40]

This is not to say that undocumented workers necessarily believe they do not have rights. Indeed, Román, an undocumented dishwasher in Houston, said quite the opposite: "I think that as a person, as humans, we [undocumented immigrants] have the *same* rights." However, he also went on to explain that he was under no delusions that we exist in a world of complete equality. He conceded, "In a certain way, yes [we are treated differently]. Because [my co-worker] is a resident, he has more rights than someone, like me, who doesn't." This raw awareness of second-class citizenship exists alongside what scholars such as De Genova (2002) and Calavita (2005) describe as an active process of economic *inclusion* that produces a legally marginalized surplus of labor willing to work under conditions of extreme vulnerability. In fact, it is precisely this extreme work ethic that workers I spoke to described as their comparative advantage in the workplace, and as a source of pride. Basilio, for example, explained to me how he holds down two jobs in Houston—washing dishes during the week and landscaping on the weekends—to support his wife and children. "Yes, I'm always a little tired, but you have to work hard to get your family ahead." Similarly, I sat with Bernardo—an undocumented prep cook in San Jose—on the steps of his recently purchased home while his wife and two children played inside. In blunt terms he explained how he and other undocumented workers like him *come to work*, not to *claim*. "Even if it's not an accident, if you feel bad, or you are sick, your throat hurts or something, you simply don't want to stop working, because you have bills to pay." This perseverance, he explained, is what set him apart from his documented and especially native-born counterparts as an exceptionally good worker.[41]

Last, the uncertain long-term prospects for undocumented workers in the United States can also play a major role in their decision whether to consider filing a claim. Though the undocumented migrant flow increasingly includes family units, and substantial investments in border security dampen circular migration patterns (Reyes, Johnson, and Van Swearingen 2002; Massey, Durand, and Malone 2003), the myth of one day returning "home" remains important to many workers living "in the shadows" (Chavez 1998). In truth, most undocumented workers have very few options for future mobility and economic security in the United States. Options for moving up the career ladder are limited, and the prospect of eventual retirement without pensions or Social Security income looms large. As a result, the time undocumented workers spend here is often spent saving enough money to start their own business or to retire comfortably. Some older undocumented workers I spoke with, such as Ronaldo in San Jose, have built a life in their home country and look forward to returning to it. He explained, "I have everything in Mexico, I have my house, and even a snack store. It's just my wife and I [here]. We plan on returning to stay and no longer imposing on our kids." For this worker and others I spoke to, injury and mistreatment are bearable conditions, to be endured temporarily in exchange for delayed rewards.

Brokering Rights: The Role of Institutional Intermediaries

Taken together, these findings suggest that the core challenges facing undocumented workers make the well-intentioned "status blind" approach that many labor standards enforcement agencies take inadequate to address the needs of this population, especially given that this approach is paired with resources constraints and a general lack of credibility

(Gleeson 2011b). I therefore argue that success in enforcing workplace rights hinges not only on the strength of formal protections and the political will of the agencies entrusted with carrying them out but also on the ability of these agencies to partner with key community intermediaries to get their message out and to bring claimants in.

One pervasive tactic is to partner with ethnic media. Agencies rely on radio spots, Spanish-language television, and local newspapers to reiterate their commitment to the communities in which they are based. Every agency had some version of a public service announcement. For example, in addition to distributing Spanish-language materials, the Occupational Safety and Health Administration has solicited the help of well-known Spanish-speaking personalities in its outreach material (Nash 2003). In one announcement, El Rey Misterio, a six-time *lucha libre* world wrestling champion, speaks to his fans from behind his mask, explaining that "a safe workplace is *everyone's* right." These and other tactics were the subject of the National Action Summit for Latino Worker Health and Safety held in April 2010. Attendees included OSHA representatives from all levels of the bureaucracy, representatives of philanthropic organizations like the Dolores Huerta Foundation, and union and worker center leaders, who discussed a range of topics on worker education and successful outreach (OSHA 2010).

Beyond simply broadcasting their good intentions, agencies also collaborate with community groups to publicize successful, high-profile cases. One recent EEOC campaign, for example, centered on the case of Olivia Tamayo, who has become the face of combating sexual harassment in the fields. Tamayo, a picker for Harris Farms, a major conglomerate in the California Central Valley, had been repeatedly sexually assaulted by her supervisor. An EEOC agent I interviewed said: "It really took tremendous courage for her to come forward. . . . It [also] took a visit from one of our lawyers who's a former farmworker herself, who went to her house and spoke to her family, and spoke to her husband, and got the trust and assured her that we would go forward with this case."[42] The EEOC had to be sensitive to the fact that Tamayo feared coming forward not only due to the social stigma of sexual assault but also from fear of losing her job and potentially being deported. Fifteen years after Tamayo's first assault and three years after a federal jury in Fresno originally granted Tamayo a $1 million award, Harris Farms finally lost its appeal when the U.S. Ninth

Circuit Court of Appeals upheld the ruling. Tamayo subsequently became the centerpiece of an outreach effort called the Esperanza Project, cosponsored by various rights groups such as the Southern Poverty Law Center, Lideres Campesinas, California Rural Legal Assistance, and Human Rights Watch (HRW 2010). The campaign has launched an educational comic book and public information campaign dedicated to encouraging other immigrant women to come forward.

Practical barriers stand in the way of making agency outreach entirely effective, however. The priorities and resources of the bureaucracies do not always align with the needs of the community. For example, in 2005, when the Texas Division of Workers' Compensation was consolidated under the broader umbrella of the Texas Division of Insurance, programs that had previously been directed specifically at worker safety and education were replaced by a "multipurpose" outreach approach. Outreach under the Texas Payday Law, which pursues wage and hour violations, is no longer specifically funded, and staff have had to be creative in their approach. One commissioner explained the new environment and the creative adjustments his staff have had to make: "HUD [the federal program for Housing and Urban Development] gave us the opportunity . . . and funds to do [outreach] in the area of housing. Well, when we go out there and do housing outreach and education, well guess what? We're gonna take our employment information also."[43] Similarly, Spanish-language workshops sponsored by the California Division of Workers' Compensation have been curtailed during furlough periods and are limited by the amount of outreach information and assistance officers are able to do. Currently, these workshops only take place in San Jose once every three months, while the workshop leader travels to other cities in the region to fill the outreach void.[44]

While labor standards enforcement agencies have invested significant resources in innovative tactics to bridge the divide between their offices and the immigrant community, then, they face an array of challenges beyond rebranding their image that dovetail with the barriers undocumented workers face in coming forward to seek help. In the next three chapters I elaborate how these challenges unfold uniquely in both Houston and San Jose. I show how community partners have asserted themselves as major players, even in some cases without the sanction of government agencies. In the following chapters I highlight three such actors that shape the form and content of community collaborations: local governments, civil society groups, and foreign consulates. Through these perspectives I contrast the range of solutions that have emerged not only to educate immigrant workers about their rights but also to promote particular paths that workers should follow in the wake of a violation. In both cities, collaboration between the bureaucracy and these intermediaries is key, but the content and form of the coalitions can vary widely, depending on the broader political field in which they exist.

3

PLACE MATTERS

How Local Governments Enforce Immigrant Worker Rights

While the enforcement of workplace standards and immigration regulations has traditionally fallen outside the jurisdiction of most local governments, every year city councils and county boards pass resolutions, vote on ballot referendums, and create memorandums of understanding that influence the lives of immigrant workers. On the labor front, dramatic union victories or lockouts tend to stand out. On the immigration front, we also often focus on the hostile contexts developing in new destinations. Yet the lived reality of these issues is often more complicated and nuanced. The strategies that advocates develop are shaped directly by the political culture of a place and largely depend on the particular configuration of political allies for and against a given issue.

In this chapter, I examine the political cultures of San Jose and Houston and trace how these two politically divergent immigrant destinations have evolved on the issue of immigrant worker rights. I argue that although there is significant political and public support in both cities to incorporate undocumented workers, the power of antilabor and anti-immigrant forces varies substantially, with significant effects. This power struggle sets the backdrop for how advocates funnel resources toward implementing immigrant worker rights. I begin by contrasting the relationship between organized labor and local elected officials in San Jose and Houston. Next, I recount the national trend toward the devolution of immigration enforcement and explain how political alliances have emerged toward either immigrant sanctuary or restriction in these two cities. Together, I argue, the two policy fields of labor and immigration have dictated the path of immigrant worker rights in very locally defined ways.

Silicon Chips and Oil Fields: Politics in San Jose and Houston

A casual observer may note the many similarities between San Jose and Houston. After serving as California's first capital for only five years, San Jose went on to become a booming agricultural center, a major destination for veterans returning from World War II, and eventually the capital of Silicon Valley. Today, San Jose is the tenth-largest city in the nation, is located in the most diverse county in the state (Castellanos 2009), and is one of the "safest big cities" in the nation (City of San Jose 2009a). Houston, which was also the capital of its state at one time, drew prosperity in its early years from cotton and sugar production, but today the city is one of the most prominent centers for medical innovation and petroleum production. Once one of the largest centers of slaveholding (Torget 2011), Houston is today one of the most cosmopolitan cities, home to the third-largest concentration of consular offices in the nation (Greater Houston Partnership 2009; Houston Guide 2010). Both cities are emblematic of the modern hourglass economy and bear the mark of urban sprawl that is typical of most fast-growing American cities.[1] The lack of any zoning ordinances in Houston, the "city of big plans and no rules" (Clark 2008), is not unlike the massive expansion San Jose experienced during the Silicon Valley tech boom (Benner 2002).

Municipal politics scholar Amy Bridges (1997) argues that while southwestern cities like San Jose and Houston began as "small, ambitious, . . . and blessed with opportunity," the ambition of their founding reformers eventually replaced "parties with nonpartisanship, party politicians with a civic elite, mayors with commissioners and managers, [and] competition with political monopoly" (31). In this regard, San Jose and Houston were born of the same womb.

Yet upon closer investigation, the political cultures of these two cities diverge.[2] Partisan politics are largely a nonissue in solidly Democratic San Jose, as they are in much of the rest of the San Francisco Bay Area, and electoral wrangling usually centers on a candidate's relative position on the Democratic spectrum. Municipal leaders often voice official support for pro-immigrant policies, and organized labor wields significant power. In Houston, by contrast, partisan politics are alive and well. Though officially nonpartisan, the city council incorporates conservative perspectives. Organized labor is often seen as a threat to free enterprise, and nativist sentiments are common among a small but very influential minority. In this sense, the two big U.S. cities are political opposites.

Despite shifts in mayoral leadership, contemporary politics in San Jose can still be characterized as among the most labor and immigrant friendly in the nation. In 1998, the city council approved one of the most generous living wage ordinances in the country (Reynolds and Kern 2004), and the South Bay Labor Council continues to wield significant influence in city matters. Ethnic minorities have also fared well in local politics. In 2005, San Jose residents elected their first Vietnamese American council member, Madison Nguyen, and in 2008 their first Indian American council member, Ash Kalra. With one exception, the entire San Jose City Council in 2009 consisted of registered Democrats.[3] This is not to say that pro-business and conservative interests have no place in San Jose politics. The anti-gay-marriage Proposition 8 garnered support from 44 percent of county voters in 2008 (Santa Clara County Registrar of Voters 2009), and the power of San Jose unions is rivaled by key industry groups such as the Silicon Valley Leadership Group, Joint Venture–Silicon Valley, and the many chambers of commerce. The political profile of San Jose residents is solidly Democratic, with 70 percent of registered voters in Santa Clara County voting for Barack Obama in the 2008 presidential election (Santa Clara County Registrar of Voters 2009). According to the fall 2009 Silicon Valley Pulse Survey, only 20 percent of registered voters in Santa Clara County considered themselves "conservative." Seventy percent view immigrants favorably, and 86 percent support some sort of legalization for undocumented immigrants (Jackson 2009a, 2009b).

Like San Jose, Houston has had a long string of Democratic mayors over the last three decades. Yet Houston is couched in the conservative politics of Texas, which leads the nation in death penalty executions, is one of only a handful of states without an income tax, and sends the largest number of Republicans to Congress.[4] In 2009, five of the fourteen Houston city councilors were registered Republicans (de Graauw and Andrew, 2011). By comparison, Harris County, which encompasses most of Houston city limits, is thought of as a liberal haven compared with rural and suburban neighbors like Fort Bend and Brazoria counties. Some of the region's most strident civil rights voices have served on Houston's city council, including Sheila Jackson Lee (who has gone on to represent Texas's Eighteenth Congressional District) and noted immigration and civil rights attorney Gordon Quan.

Despite the city's significant progressive streak, city politics are still very partisan and contentious. Houston has been ranked among the top ten conservative major cities and holds the title of largest conservative city in the nation (Alderman et al. 2005). Only 50 percent of Harris County voters supported President Barak Obama in the 2008 election (Harris County Clerk's Office Elections Division 2008), and according to the long-running Houston Area Survey, fewer than half of Harris County residents (45 percent) support the Democratic Party (Urban Research Center of Houston 2009). Major flashpoints for municipal politics in Houston include gay marriage (43 percent surveyed are opposed), abortion (54 percent support restrictions), and certainly immigration (50 percent support restricting state services for undocumented Texas residents). Overall, Houston enjoys a Democratic plurality and the diversity of a big city, but the Bayou City has a strong conservative leaning that comes out in force, particularly on the issues of labor and immigration.

In sum, San Jose and Houston represent two distinct political fields for enforcing immigrant worker rights. While the demography and economies of both cities have a lot in common, their political leadership and civil society legacies differ considerably. One of the results is two different paths to justice for immigrant workers.

National Campaign, Local Battles: Municipal Support for Organized Labor in San Jose and Houston

Beyond the federal and state bureaucracy, local governments have a role to play in advancing worker rights and responding to the demands of organized labor. Cities and counties hold the fate of vast municipal workforces in their hands, and they also have the power to legislate policies for the local private sector. While only four cities have passed their own minimum wage, dozens more have enacted living wage policies that raise the bar for government contractors and send a powerful message to the private sector. Further, every city council and county supervisor has been called on at some point to mediate a labor-business dispute or to take a stand on one of the many policy issues that affect the lives of working people. In this section, I compare the strength of labor power in San Jose and Houston and suggest that, increasingly, immigration is an integral, key issue for unions and employers alike.

Building Labor Power in San Jose

San Jose is a peculiar microcosm of liberal California politics infused with the laissez-faire gusto that powered Silicon Valley's ascendance. Yet there is no question that organized labor has a reserved seat at the political table and has attained impressive victories on causes that have hardly progressed elsewhere. Today, San Jose is one of only 122 cities in the country that has passed a living wage ordinance (Luce 2004; ACORN 2009), and it has also pioneered a "labor peace" ordinance that requires contractors to negotiate and expedite the process of union recognition (Zabin and Martin 1999). Though San Jose's labor culture is certainly influenced by the progressive climate of the San Francisco Bay Area, it differs from its "left coast" neighbor San Francisco (DeLeon 1992). Though San Jose today is home to one of the strongest labor councils in the nation and has been the site of some of the strongest public worker movements (Johnston 1994), politicians in San Jose are often simultaneously reverent about the political power of organized labor and resistant to its influence.

In April 2006, in the wake of a fierce mayoral race, the political director of the South Bay Labor Council could list only two "foes" of the labor movement on the San Jose council: the current mayor, Ron Gonzales, and the incoming mayor, Chuck Reed.[5] From his perspective, Gonzales and Reed stood in the long shadow of Susan Hammer, who had served as mayor from 1991 to 1998 and reigned over a golden age for organized labor in San Jose. As one longtime Service Employees International Union (SEIU) organizer explained, "If somebody with as high profile as the mayor is on your leaflet and says, 'I know this local, they are great!' it really makes a difference."[6] Hammer was known for opening the door to the unionization of municipal workers and for supporting many of the SBLC's political initiatives. In turn, she and others who have preceded and followed her have also relied on union support during reelection season.

Hammer's term coincided with the near-legendary leadership of Amy Dean, who served as political director and then executive director of the SBLC from 1994 to 2003 and was the youngest person and first woman to lead a major labor federation. During this time, unions had "an excellent working relationship with Mayor Hammer," and it was under Hammer's leadership that the City of San Jose adopted its generous living wage policy in 1998 (Brownstein 2000, 41).[7] Dean's election as executive director in 1993 coincided with John Sweeney's ascendancy at the AFL-CIO and marked a significant break in the SBLC's political culture. Until Dean's election, for nearly four decades following the chartering of the SBLC in 1958 the council was divided into factions, with a progressive arm of former antiwar and United Farm Workers organizers on one side and the more conservative Building and Construction Trades Council leadership on the other. Dean was revered for bridging this division and was even hailed by the *New York Times* as "Christopher Columbus in the roiling and uncharted seas of the new economy" (Greenhouse 1999).[8]

Apart from growing the size of the council staff significantly, one of Dean's primary achievements was the creation of Working Partnerships USA (WPUSA), a nonprofit research organization that works closely with the SBLC on building community coalitions around policy advocacy (Brownstein 2000; Byrd and Rhee 2004). This unique addition to the SBLC gave the organization the "capacity to work on a whole variety of issues beyond just winning good contracts for members." Connected to a "real political base with real organizing abilities," today WPUSA functions as an "innovative action tank for progressive reform" that has pushed through several victories with the city and county on issues ranging from health care to transportation and housing.[9]

Dean's revolutionary tenure would also later overlap with that of Ron Gonzales, the city's first Latino mayor, who served from 1999 to 2007. In contrast to Hammer, Gonzales has had an ambivalent history with organized labor in San Jose. Equally begrudged by the business community, he was dubbed "labor friendly" by some and called a "moderate Democrat" (a slight by progressive Bay Area standards) by others (Folmar 2002). He fought against the SBLC's city living wage proposal and during his term as Santa Clara County supervisor voted down the SBLC's campaign to expand insurance coverage for the county's children. Later, in 2004, Gonzales also actively campaigned against the SBLC's Community Benefits Initiative, which would have deployed city development funds toward an "alternative economic-development policy framework" (Rhee 2004).

In 2005 Gonzales appointed District Three councilor and former SBLC political director Cindy Chavez as vice-mayor. This move gave Chavez a leg up in her campaign to succeed Gonzales, which many predicted would be successful. Every weekend leading up to the elections, her supporters—many of them members of SBLC local unions—could be seen knocking on doors throughout the city to rally support for her. In a crowded race that included eight other candidates, Chavez managed to garner the support of every city council member not in the race, as well as key state and federal figures such as San Francisco Mayor Gavin Newsom and President Bill Clinton (Rusk 2006). Yet, likely due in part to the shadow of scandal hanging over Gonzales, the result of a backroom labor deal with city sanitation workers, Chavez lost to Reed in a November 2006 runoff ballot (Walsh 2006). Six years after Amy Dean's departure, during which the SBLC was led by another dynamic young woman, Phaedra Ellis-Lampkins,[10] the SBLC welcomed Chavez to lead the organization, while her opponent Chuck Reed took the reins on council.

Since he took office in 2007, the relationship between Chuck Reed and organized labor in San Jose has been an uneasy one. Despite being a registered Democrat whose major campaign promises included a vision for "green jobs," Reed also promised to check the power of unions over city politics (Mayor Watch 2006; Office of the Mayor Chuck Reed 2009). In his 2006 bid for mayor, Reed's list of campaign endorsements included the relatively conservative *San Jose Mercury News* and the Santa Clara County Deputy Sheriffs Association. It notably did *not* include the Santa Clara County Democratic Party or any of the major Democratic organizations in the region. Yet over his four-year term, Reed seems to have built some consensus. Endorsements in his 2010 reelection campaign included most of his fellow councilors and Congresswoman Zoe Lofgren, who is considered to be a close ally of both organized labor and immigrant rights advocates in the city (Re-Elect San José Mayor Chuck Reed 2010). Nonetheless, even prior to ascending to the mayoralty, Reed had become known for falling out of step with his more liberal colleagues on issues ranging from labor to abortion rights to same-sex marriage. One SBLC staffer critically described Reed as someone who "at every turn does not support us when we [try] to get workers organized."[11] In 2009, Reed cemented his tenuous relationship with organized labor with a manifesto that proposed a list of "ethics reforms" targeting key figures in the labor movement (Seipel 2009). In 2012, organized labor challenged Reed for attempting to cut pension costs, purportedly in order to avoid city layoffs (SBLC 2012).

Though it enjoys ambivalent mayoral support, organized labor nonetheless has a wide range of political supporters further down the political hierarchy in San Jose. In 2002, Amy Dean was credited with helping to fill six of the ten council seats with SBLC allies (Hasan 2004b). Key among these was District Five councilor and State Assembly candidate Nora Campos, whose husband is a top official at the local Building Trades Council. Other supporters have included Santa Clara County supervisors Pete McHugh and Blanca Alvarado (the first Latina to be elected to San Jose City Council), Assembly member Manny Diaz, and Congressman Mike Honda.

Within this context, pioneering labor organizing campaigns have thrived in San Jose, such as the Justice for Janitors campaign, which was launched from San Jose in the early 1990s. Justice for Janitors, whose significance continues to reverberate two decades later, depended on the power created by the SBLC and strong support from local elected officials to successfully reach agreements with several major tech companies and their subcontractors (Johnston 1994; R. Preston 2004; Zlolniski 2006). Similarly, in 2001, UNITE HERE's Local 19 won a contract for two hundred workers at the city-owned Dolce Hayes Mansion, a process facilitated by the labor peace provision of the San Jose living wage ordinance. Four years later, in June 2005, labor leaders in San Jose also won a significant victory from the city with the creation of Taxi San Jose Incorporated, a partnership between taxi drivers, the companies that employ them, the San Jose Convention and Visitors Bureau, the SBLC, and UFCW Local 5. The partnership today provides "fairer and more consistent compensation to drivers, opens up the airport market to all participating cab companies, and provides faster and higher quality service to passengers at the airport" (WPUSA 2008a). At the behest of the SBLC and SEIU Local 1877, the San Jose City Council went on to approve a living wage for airport workers in

2008 (SBLC 2008). While the position of San Jose leaders vis-à-vis unions is far from a full embrace, organized labor certainly has the ear of elected officials and has been able to leverage this power to garner key victories. It is a world away from the reality facing unions in Houston.

They Can't Even Spell "Worker Rights" in Houston

Unlike San Jose, which is known as a beacon of union power, Houston is renowned among employers and scholars alike for its business-friendly climate. For example, Joe Feagin, who conducted one of the most comprehensive sociological studies of Houston in the 1980s, described the city as the "developer's free enterprise city *par excellence*" (Feagin 1988; Orum and Feagin 1991, 132) Similarly, Fisher (1990) characterizes Houston as a place where the ideological thrust in the twentieth century has been "anti-government, anti-regulation, anti-planning, anti-taxes, anti-anything that seemed to represent, in fact or fantasy, an expansion of the public sector or a limitation on the economic prerogatives and activities of the city's business community" (40). Indeed, Houston is a city where big business thrives and organized labor still struggles for political power. Despite being the fourth-largest city in the nation, the Houston metropolitan area ranks in the lowest quartile for union membership (230th out of 290) compared with the metropolitan areas of other, bigger cities such as New York (26th), Los Angeles (82nd), and Chicago (61st) (Hirsch and Macpherson). Texas's right-to-work policy, and a local political culture that is caustic to unions, are major factors contributing to Houston's hostile organizing environment. Comparing Houston to Los Angeles, another large metropolis with an established Latino population, Meyerson (2004) directly attributes the relative lack of Latino political influence to the paucity of organized labor. True to form, the home page of the Greater Houston Partnership, the largest chamber of commerce in Houston, describes Houston as a region that is "business-ready," with an excellent "business climate" and "pro-business culture" (Greater Houston Partnership 2010). Karson (2004) situates Houston as within the broader "Texas tradition where union busting has been as much a part of the scene as the cowboy boots and chili beans" (208).

Despite being the largest city in the state, Houston is not a complete microcosm of Texas. One UNITE HERE organizer who has organized workers all across the state described Houston labor politics as "slightly more progressive" than those of other big Texas cities like Fort Worth and Dallas, a difference he attributes to the more established Latino community in Houston. This union representative feels that, compared with the rest of the state and the South more generally, organizing in Houston is easier: "For the South, it's been good. I mean, . . . it could be better, but we've had good elected officials in Houston, there has been relatively decent support for working people."[12] He cited municipal support during the massive organizing campaign for the newly built Hilton Americas, which in 2005 became the sole unionized hotel in Houston (Lazarovici 2010).

Amid these relative successes, the political climate for organizing in Houston diverges radically from that of San Jose. Many of the campaigns pioneered in San Jose have failed in Houston, and political opposition to worker-friendly policies remains fierce. Perhaps the most memorable of the failed campaigns was the attempt to institute a living wage for Houston workers in 1996 and 1997. The goal was to raise the city minimum wage to $6.50 at a time when the federal minimum was $4.75. The business community spent $1.3 million to defeat the initiative (Dyer 1996). The National Restaurant Association alone donated $100,000, dwarfing the $20,000 coming from organized labor (Luce 2004, 43). Other union foes included the Greater Houston Partnership, the Houston Hispanic Chamber of Commerce, and the Greater Houston Hotel and Motel Association. Such groups capitalized on residents' fear of job losses and rising prices. One ad from a coalition of opponents of the initiative, the Save Jobs for Houston Committee, painted a picture of Houston devastated by the effects of the higher wage rate: "Cops and firefighters yanked off the streets. Higher taxes. Thousands of jobs lost. Soaring prices for such essentials as food and prescription drugs. The wholesale destruction of small businesses. Streets riddled with potholes. Swollen welfare rolls." Its scaremongering was bolstered by a controversial study conducted by University of Houston economist Barton Smith that predicted raising the minimum wage would cost the city 52,000 jobs and $18 million in lost tax revenues (Smith 1996). The director of the WorkLife Institute, a union ally in Houston, recalls hearing the common threat from key restaurateurs, "You know, if you pass this thing, we'll close our doors and move outside city limits."[13] Though the initiative, formally known as Proposition A, had significant support on the city council, many city councilors campaigned fervently against it. Among them were Republican representative Joe Roach, who referred to

Proposition A as the "Fort Bend County Job Relocation Act," referencing the more affluent and conservative suburban county adjacent to Houston. The political opposition to a living wage was led by Mayor Bob Lanier, who, though a declared Democrat, also had deep roots in the Houston business community and had made stemming rising taxes and regulation in the city into a mantra. Ultimately, supporters of the initiative were able to collect 47,000 signatures in thirty days, yet they quickly expended their paltry resources in the effort to comply with local laws that require signatures to be accompanied by voter identification numbers. The measure ultimately garnered only 23 percent of voter support (Dyer, Feldstein, and Bryant 1997).

Lee Brown succeeded "Mayor Bob," as he was affectionately called. Before taking office, Brown had been the first African American police chief under five-term mayor Kathy Whitmire, a position that he held for eight years. He had long-standing ties to labor going back to his years in California, and he counted on the support of organized labor in each of his three successful mayoral campaigns. Many labor leaders I spoke to contrasted Brown to Lanier, praising Brown's leadership in promoting worker-friendly policies. Chief among them was a huge victory in 1999, when labor leaders successfully pressured the city to increase the prevailing wage for city contracts after fifteen years of struggling. In 2006, labor advocates also succeeded in pressuring officials to investigate and prosecute prevailing wage violations for workers under major city and county contracts at the airport, the site of the new Houston Rockets stadium, and the expanded George R. Brown Convention Center and the Hilton Americas.

Five years later, labor threw its support behind Bill White, who was eventually elected to his first of three terms in 2004. This relationship, however, was more troubled than labor's partnership with Brown had been. Against the wishes of labor advocates, for example, White rescinded his support for protecting city worker benefits, instead backing city businesses in their wish to draw on worker pensions to help balance Houston's budget (Mack 2005). Despite disapproval over city layoffs and department reorganizations, the Harris County AFL-CIO endorsed White's successor, Annise Parker, in the 2009 and 2011 election seasons. In 2011, Parker also became the target of an aggressive campaign against a wage theft ordinance that would "implement effective and efficient ways to uphold the rights of Houston workers and hold unscrupulous employers accountable" (Down With Wage Theft Campaign 2012).

Beyond the mayor's office, organized labor in Houston has also counted on several steadfast community supporters over the years. These have included Sue Lovell, a key member of the Houston GLBT Political Caucus; Adrian Garcia, who went on to be mayor pro tempore under White; and Carol Alvarado, later elected to the Texas House of Representatives. Liberal millionaire Peter Brown and African American attorney Al Green also actively supported high-profile labor campaigns like Justice for Janitors. Reflecting this partisan pattern of support, the head of the local chapter of the (now reorganized) Association of Community Organizations for Reform Now said that the chapter has an "excellent relationship with a strong Democratic mayor" but complained of the "huge conservative power" on city council.[14] Skeptical of this uneven pattern of support, however, one Sheet Metal Workers union leader complained, "Local politicians in Houston can't even spell 'worker rights,' much less 'union.' "[15] For him and many others I spoke to, the moderate support of a handful of political leaders paled in comparison with the power wielded by more conservative officials and the pro-business interests they represent.

Many of the conservative congressional representatives known for supporting such policies also call the Houston area home. They include former embattled Republican Tom DeLay, who represented much of the suburbs south of Houston,[16] and fellow Republicans John Culberson, representing much of affluent West Houston, and Ted Poe, representing north Houston suburbs. Compared with San Jose congressional representatives Zoe Lofgren and Mike Honda, both of them Democrats who have been outspoken advocates for progressive issues, Texas representatives adhere to a stridently more conservative set of priorities.[17]

Rick Shaw, the legendary treasurer for the Harris County AFL-CIO, summarized the response he received from these Texas congressional representatives after requesting their support on a recent organizing drive: "Why should we? I mean, doesn't the law say if workers wanted a union they get one? All they got to do is vote for it, right? So what's there to support?" In contrast, Shaw noted "no problem with the Dems" and emphasized that while he could not cite any obvious evidence of overt hostility from Republican leadership, overt support has never been forthcoming. As a result, he has given up the uphill battle of reaching out to conservative officials, "because we know how they vote on things, and we know who our friends are."[18]

While San Jose and Houston share similar demographic and economic histories, they are on opposite ends of the political spectrum when it comes to supporting labor-friendly policies. These divergent political cultures are a telling backdrop for the battles that play out over immigration. In the next section, I further flesh out how the worker rights debate maps onto the immigration debate. I begin by describing the overall trend toward devolution in immigration enforcement and the many opportunities that cities and counties have to stake a claim on the issue. I then contrast the distinct routes California and Texas—and San Jose and Houston—have traveled regarding immigration enforcement, and I consider the effects each path has had on the resources that immigrant workers and their advocates have at their disposal in each city to combat workplace abuse.

Beyond the Feds: The Devolution of Immigration Enforcement

Though the federal government has primary authority to regulate the flow of legal migrants and to detain and deport those who are unauthorized in the country, states have increasingly jumped into the fray in recent years. In the first quarter of 2011, 1,538 bills and resolutions were introduced in the fifty states and Puerto Rico relating to immigrants and refugees, a 30 percent increase from the first quarter of 2010. The top policy arenas included employment, law enforcement, ID / driver's licenses, health, and education (NCSL 2011). Simultaneously, cities and counties are deploying similar policies (Rodriguez, Chishti, and Nortman 2007). Combined, these federal, state, and local efforts form a ubiquitous immigration enforcement apparatus, while undocumented workers continue to be welcomed by a steady stock of jobs and employers willing to hire them.

Despite the inextricable integration of undocumented labor with the U.S. economy (Cornelius 1998), detention, apprehension, and removal efforts have continued unabated, even under the Obama administration (Reese 2009). Under the leadership of Michael Chertoff, the U.S. Department of Homeland Security ramped up "interior enforcement" efforts. These high-profile immigration raids often targeted large work sites and were lauded in the media as a long overdue crackdown on undocumented migrants.[19] Administrative immigration responsibilities have also increasingly shifted to employers' hands, oftentimes with the blessing of immigrant-friendly politicians who focus their rhetoric on punishing the employer, not workers. Many of these programs can be traced directly to the 1996 Illegal Immigration Reform and Immigrant Responsibility Act, which handed substantial power to employers and resulted in what we know today as the once-suspended Social Security no-match letters program and the increasingly popular E-Verify system.[20] Critics of these initiatives argue that inaccuracies in federal databases, employer misuse of the program, and lack of oversight by other labor standards enforcement agencies only facilitate the exploitation of undocumented workers (NILC 2008a, 2009a; Wolgin 2011).[21]

In addition to increasing work site raids and delegating enforcement efforts to employers, the federal government has also worked hand in hand with cities and counties. One of the primary vehicles for this collaboration has been the 287(g) program, which involves a partnership between local police authorities and Immigration and Customs Enforcement. The stated goal of the 287(g) program is to deport unauthorized immigrants who pose a threat to national security, public safety, or both. Following the signing of memorandums of agreement between police departments and ICE, the latter provides resources to train and certify local officers in the investigation, detention, apprehension, and deportation of "aliens" (ICE 2006). The number of local 287(g) agreements has increased substantially since the Department of Justice reversed its earlier position and announced that states have the "inherent authority" to enforce civil provisions of immigration law. By 2011, there were seventy-two active memorandums of agreement, which collectively had issued over 39,000 detainers during 2010 (ICE 2008a).[22]

Other states and localities have opted to eschew local enforcement of federal immigration law and instead have expanded rights to undocumented populations. In still other cases, the expansion of undocumented immigrant rights is happening simultaneously with other restrictive changes within the same community. By 2011, there were over seventy jurisdictions (sometimes called "sanctuary cities") that expressly limited cooperation with immigration authorities (Tramonte 2011). These cities often justify their expansive approach by citing the need to garner trust among immigrant communities in order to establish effective community policing programs; moreover, in an era of limited municipal resources, many cities simply reject the added responsibility of immigration enforcement (NILC

2008b; Khashu 2009). Policies protecting undocumented immigrants are volatile, however, and subject to political shifts. Some former sanctuary cities have gone on to enact 287(g) agreements, as was attempted in Houston subsequent to several high-profile crimes involving undocumented immigrants. Other cities have convened task forces or made other agreements that allow them to work hand in hand with immigration authorities (Chadwick and Szafnicki 1999; Varsanyi 2008; Decker et al. 2009).

In addition to direct efforts to apprehend undocumented immigrants, states and local governments also regulate the day-to-day benefits and rights these individuals are afforded. A Migration Policy Institute report found that in 2007 alone, all fifty state legislatures considered legislation related to immigrants, totaling more than a thousand separate proposals. At least 156 of these became law. Over one hundred local governments have also enacted immigration-related ordinances in recent years. Examples include an ordinance prohibiting landlords from renting to undocumented tenants in Hazelton, Pennsylvania, (Ordinance No. 2006–18) and anti-loitering and anti-solicitation ordinances that affect informal industries composed of largely undocumented workers, such as day laborers, in Glendale, California (Municipal Code §9.17.030, 2004) (Rodriguez, Chishti, and Nortman 2007). One of the most sweeping state ordinances went into effect in Arizona under SB 1070, a piece of legislation that in July 2010 prompted the Obama administration to sue the state of Arizona (NILC 2010).[23] One of the most controversial of the law's provisions allowed local officers to ask individuals whose legal status they held under "reasonable suspicion" to present their relevant citizenship documents or risk arrest, substantial fines, and even jail time. SB 1070 was dubbed "racial profiling" by immigrant advocates, while supporters championed the law as a crucial tool that allows the state to implement laws the federal government had refused to enforce. Other cities have conversely made efforts to bring undocumented residents out of the shadows by expanding rights and instituting explicit protections, such as municipal identification cards (de Graauw 2009). Yet these "immigrant friendly" policies have often been couched in broader inclusive framings and have garnered much less attention than their restrictive counterparts.

What emerges, then, is a patchwork of responses to undocumented immigrants in the United States. The localized implementation of immigration enforcement, as well as the diffuse set of policies aimed at managing immigrant integration (including labor policy), come together to shape the context of reception of all immigrants. Despite moments of local inclusivity, undocumented immigrants must inevitably confront their complete lack of political membership and the overarching specter of deportation. It is within this context that labor standards enforcement agencies struggle to carry out their own mission of protecting the rights of all workers, and local governments must decide how to relate to their immigrant constituencies. In the next section I evaluate the different roads that San Jose and Houston, two traditional immigrant destinations, have taken vis-à-vis immigration enforcement.

Responding to the Needs of Immigrant Workers in San Jose and Houston

Immigrant labor has figured prominently in the economies and politics of both San Jose and Houston, two meccas for immigrant professionals and working-class immigrants alike. Like several other western cities, according to Singer (2003), San Jose is a "reemerging" destination: a prime immigrant destination during the early 1900s, the city saw its popularity decline through the 1970s before beginning to build again, topping levels from a century before in 2000. Houston, as a "post–World War II" immigrant city, experienced fast and substantial growth of immigrant flows starting in the 1970s, and these flows show no sign of letting up (Singer 2003). Today, over a third of San Jose residents and a quarter of Houston's hail from another country.[24]

San Jose and Houston have nonetheless taken very different roads toward managing and serving the needs of their immigrant communities. The following sections contrast the story of diversity colliding with a strong base for labor organizing and liberal political culture in San Jose with the context of contentious partisan politics buttressed by strong business interests in Houston.

Asserting Legitimacy and Demanding Sanctuary in Silicon Valley

Like San Jose unions, immigrant rights advocates have cultivated a long history of support among local political leaders in San Jose. By the mid-nineteenth century, the city's economy was dominated by "the seasonal fluctuations of harvesting, transporting, and canning the produce of the surrounding Santa Clara Valley" (Bridges 1997, 38). The "Valley of Heart's Delight," as the region was once known, was reinvented as Silicon Valley, with San Jose at its geographic and economic center. Its bifurcated economy has engineers and professionals at the top (many of them high-skilled immigrants from Asia) and a concentration of Latino and Southeast Asian low-wage workers at the bottom. Anthropologist Christian Zlolniski (2006) describes this latter group of workers as the "contemporary proletarians of a postindustrial economy," whose location at the opposite end of the class spectrum from the techno-elite underscores "the paradox of poverty in the midst of the affluence that has become a distinctive mark of Silicon Valley" (3–4). It is within this context that both unions and immigrant advocates, often working side by side, have rallied to gain recognition and power.

In some ways, San Jose's demography makes immigrant political power inevitable. In addition to being located in one of the most diverse counties in the state, San Jose has been classified as one of the top five most integrated cities in the United States (Robinson and Grant-Thomas 2004). No San Jose representative, therefore, has the luxury of ignoring immigrant voters and their allies. Most elected city officials have stood in solidarity with undocumented residents, as evidenced by Resolution No. 73677, which the council unanimously adopted in March 2007 in response to 2006 raids by Immigration and Customs Enforcement in neighboring cities. The resolution reaffirmed the San Jose Police Department's policy of nonengagement with immigration officials, promising that the department "will not arrest persons merely for their unlawful presence in the United States; that no otherwise law-abiding undocumented immigrants should fear arrest or deportation for coming forward to report a crime as a victim or witness; and that no otherwise law-abiding undocumented immigrants should fear arrest or deportation by contacting any employee of the City of San Jose to express concerns or to ask questions." The document deplored the "harsh unintended consequences" of ICE raids, arguing that they "undermine the ability of [San Jose] police, fire department, and other city agencies to interact with fearful immigrants, leaving all of San José's residents less safe (San Jose City Council 2007).[25]

Yet relations between the San Jose Police Department and the city's immigrant population have not been without incident. In a 2009 photo essay, investigative journalist and activist Sharat Lin documented instances of racial profiling on Cinco de Mayo that year, noting the uneasy relationship beneath the immigrant-friendly veneer of the city. Lin charged the department with "fishing for misdemeanor violations in the Hispanic community" and thereby "alienating the community and pushing many undocumented immigrants (even if unintentionally) into deportation proceedings" (Lin 2009).[26]

Despite ongoing controversy, San Jose has come to be known ambivalently as a "sanctuary city" for undocumented immigrants. When his liberal counterparts in San Francisco and Oakland embraced the title, San Jose's mayor, Chuck Reed, instead declared, "We are going to follow federal and state laws. . . . We don't need to be a sanctuary city as other cities have done" (Normand 2007). His comments prompted a sea of criticisms from immigrant advocates and fellow council members. In subsequent public declarations, Reed reverted to reiterating statements made during his initial mayoral campaign wherein he declared that making government "honest and accessible" to immigrants was one of his top priorities (McElhone 2006). In 2010, Reed and all but two council members publicly condemned SB 1070, an act signed into law by Arizona's Republican governor, Jan Brewer, that would have allowed state and local enforcement of federal immigration law and made unlawful presence or aiding undocumented immigrants a misdemeanor (J. Rodriguez 2010; Woolfok 2010).[27] Restrictionist views on immigration are generally in the minority in San Jose, and immigrants in San Jose find that most officials and businesses appreciate their economic and cultural contributions.

This support—albeit sometimes muted by the city's moderate leaders—is reflected in the backing that councilors, including Reed, have given to immigrant mobilizations over the years. In 2003, twenty-three representatives departed from Santa Clara County to join the Immigrant Workers Freedom Ride. The caravan converged with eight hundred immigrants from ten other cities to demand that Congress "legalize undocumented immigrants, re-unify families, and protect workers' rights without regard to immigration status" (Mangaliman 2003). Officials offering their support to this cause included San Jose council members Chuck Reed, Cindy Chavez, Terry Gregory, and Nora Campos. They were joined by Santa Clara County supervisors Pete McHugh and Jim Beall and representatives of the Santa Clara Office of Human Relations

(IWFRC 2003). Three years later, over three hundred thousand mostly Mexican marchers converged at the center of the city's predominantly immigrant East Side on May 1, 2006, to voice opposition to HR 4437, a federal bill that would have made undocumented status a felony. This three-mile march downtown to city hall was the largest in the Bay Area that day (Vital 2010).

Local support for immigrants is also evident in city programming. While the City of San Jose does not have a department dedicated specifically to the immigrant population, several bodies have been established to address the needs of the city's diverse populace, including the Office of Cultural Affairs, which is dedicated to advancing the artistic and cultural diversity of the city, and the Human Rights Commission, which has taken on such issues as community-police relations. One of the most extensive sources of city support for immigrant communities is the City of San Jose's Strong Neighborhood Initiative (SNI), created under Mayor Ron Gonzales in 2002. While not explicitly designed to target foreign-born residents, SNI works in conjunction with several immigrant-serving organizations to foster civic engagement and address community concerns in twenty neighborhoods throughout the city that represent approximately a third of San Jose's population (City of San Jose 2009b).[28] In order to be selected, neighborhoods must meet the redevelopment criteria of blight, underemployment, and housing challenges.

SNI neighborhoods were drawn from each council district and assigned support staff from the Department of Planning and Recreation / Neighborhood Services. SNI staff then worked with neighborhoods to compile advisory committees and begin a yearlong planning process to develop a "neighborhood improvement plan" that identified the priorities for the communities.[29] According to a city organizer assigned to a predominantly Latino neighborhood in San Jose, the program provides much-needed support to the mostly undocumented group of community leaders he works with. He said of the program, "SNI would not happen, and would not be as successful as it has been, if all of the city workers working at SNI did not have the same point of view that we are going to work with you whether or not you're here illegally. If you live in this neighborhood, you are a resident of this neighborhood, and you deserve city services. We're going to help you. Bottom line."[30] This support, he argues, was made possible by the immigrant-friendly context cultivated by city leaders.[31]

Similarly, Santa Clara County—which has its county seat in San Jose—
has also spearheaded a regional effort to address the needs of immigrant
residents in Silicon Valley. In response to sweeping welfare reforms under
the 1996 federal Personal Responsibility and Work Opportunity Recon-
ciliation Act, the county funded a Citizenship Initiative to help reestablish
eligibility for the thousands of affected immigrants. The initiative brought
together the Santa Clara County Citizenship Collaborative, a collection
of organizations receiving county funding to provide naturalization assistance and to act as a source of referral and collaboration for immigrant
advocates (SCC-OHR 2010). Each year, the collaborative sponsors Citizenship Day; in 2009 it held its twentieth event, drawing more than a thousand immigrants and providing free orientations and legal assistance in
over fourteen languages (SCC-OHR 2009).[32]

In 2000, Santa Clara County also sponsored a Summit on Immigrant
Needs and Contributions to set an agenda for addressing the needs of
county residents. The working groups that convened ultimately made
recommendations to the Board of Supervisors in the areas of immigrant
economic empowerment, education, family support, health, and legal issues. The report, titled "Knowledge on Immigrant Needs," included a section devoted to wages and working conditions in Santa Clara County. The
authors noted that while Santa Clara County is a center of innovation and
venture capital growth, "Most workers in Santa Clara County—in particular immigrant workers—possess less security than in other regions of the
U.S. and suffer from precarious working conditions" (ImmigrantInfo.org
2004). The nearly thirty-page section detailed challenges facing workers at
both ends of the hourglass economy and across the diverse national-origin
groups that make Silicon Valley home. It singled out lack of immigration
status and exploitative working conditions as top issues for Latino workers. The report identified the East San Jose Community Law Center (today
known as the Katharine and George Alexander Community Law Center)
at Santa Clara University as the principal agency providing legal services
on employment issues in Santa Clara County, but it also acknowledged
the "overwhelming demand for its assistance." In its final recommendations in this area, the report noted a need for additional legal assistance and
community resources, as well as improved outreach mechanisms to assist
immigrants seeking redress in the area of wage and hour violations, discrimination, and health and safety issues. In the decade since the summit,

these challenges remain, and they have been exacerbated by the recessionary climate.

Soon after the publication of the report, the Santa Clara County Immigrant Action Network was established, and in 2005 it was transformed into the Immigrant Relations and Integration Services (IRIS) office within the Santa Clara County Office of Human Relations. In the five years since its creation, IRIS has funded naturalization initiatives, an immigration legal services program, and an immigrant leadership institute, as well as offering support to immigrant domestic violence survivors and other community forums intended to generate dialogue on immigrant issues. The county has also provided funding through the Language Access and Community Education Services initiative for outreach specifically targeted at immigrants.[33] In conjunction with the Office of Human Relations' Network for a Hate-Free Community, IRIS works to respond to violence targeting immigrants in the community. Originally established in 1999, the Network for a Hate-Free Community was quickly spurred into action in the aftermath of September 11, 2001, to address the many hate crimes that followed targeting immigrant residents (Mangaliman 2001). Both agencies, while committed to their core missions, have faced significant cuts to staffing and services, with only one full-time staff member devoted to IRIS programming as of this writing.[34]

Over the years, Santa Clara County has also been active in promoting state and federal action in support of undocumented immigrants. In 2003, the county joined San Francisco as one of two counties in the state that offered formal support to State Senator Gil Cedillo's drive to pass legislation that would have granted driver's licenses to undocumented immigrants (Cedillo 2003). Three years later, the county board also voiced formal opposition to the so-called Sensenbrenner Bill, HR 4437 SCC 2006, which would have tightened immigration enforcement,[35] and adopted a resolution—proposed by the county Office of Human Relations—to oppose the activities of the Minutemen in the region (SCC 2005). Support for immigrants has not always been unanimous, however. More recently, while both Santa Clara County and the City of San Jose have voiced opposition to instituting a full-scale 287(g) program and have vociferously opposed the imposition of Secure Communities, Mayor Reed "welcomed" the assistance of two federal agents from the "Operation Community Shield" task force to combat gang activity in the city (Webby 2011b).

Many county leaders have also come from, and gone on to, work in immigrant advocacy groups. As de Graauw (2008) argues, this connection between civil society and political leadership is crucial to the substantive representation of immigrant communities. Following a failed bid to the board of county supervisors, for example, the former director of the Office of Human Relations went on to serve as the associate director for the Services, Immigrant Rights and Education Network (SIREN), the flagship immigrant rights organization for Northern California, before going on to head Human Agenda, another local human rights organization. His interim replacement at the Office of Human Relations had spent many years working as a labor organizer and collaborating with the immigration program at the local Catholic Charities affiliate before starting her career in public service.

The strong tradition of immigrant rights in San Jose, and in Santa Clara County more broadly, has penetrated the fabric of city and county politics. The immigrant-friendly climate combined with a long legacy of powerful organized labor has meant that advocates of immigrant workers have garnered significant political weight in the region. In contrast, the tumultuous relationship between organized labor and the business community in Houston, combined with the persistent and vocal influence of those voicing nativist sentiments, has rendered immigrant worker rights a key point of political debate rather than a point of general consensus.

Making Concessions and Striking Deals for Immigrant Rights in the Bayou City

While Houston is home to a rich collection of immigrant rights groups, pro-immigrant sentiment is countered fiercely by restrictionist and nativist forces. Though the city council and county board of supervisors are mostly supportive, anti-immigrant elected officials form a strong minority that can rally significant public support.

Despite ongoing opposition, municipal leadership in Houston has been largely pro-immigrant and has managed to erect several institutions in support of the city's diverse population. One of the strongest is the Mayor's Office of Immigrant and Refugee Affairs. Created in 2001 during Lee Brown's era of affirmative action and diversity-promoting reforms, MOIRA came to symbolize municipal support for the city's immigrants.

Benito Juárez, a longtime organizer in the Central American community in Houston, was appointed to direct the office.[36] In addition to MOIRA, Lee Brown also established the Mayor's Advisory Committee on Immigrant and Refugee Affairs (MACIRA), whose stated purpose was to "assist the mayor and MOIRA in formulating and implementing programs, services, policies, and legislation that promote nonbiased and nondiscriminatory practices in the delivery of services for immigrants and refugees."[37] A former MACIRA member describes the committee as "a place to meet and share information" and "a coming together of different community organizations that in one way or another dealt with immigrant issues."[38] MACIRA regularly meets, sometimes to focus on planning events like the first ever Houston Citizenship Week held in November 2009 and at other times to tackle pressing issues affecting the immigrant community, such as the controversy over day laborers in the city. Several MACIRA subcommittees focus on specific immigrant issue areas, including legal and government relations, community affairs, education/research, business and labor affairs, and public health and safety issues (Gambetta and Gedrimaite 2011; City of Houston 2012).

When Bill White was elected mayor in 2003, he continued support for MOIRA and MACIRA. The relationship between the mayor's office and the immigrant community shifted substantially over the years, however. A lead organizer for the Houston chapter of Centro de Recursos Centroamericanos and a member of MACIRA described the shift as a retreat on the part of the mayor's office from allowing MOIRA to take policy positions of any kind.[39] Even in their more limited scope under Brown, MOIRA and MACIRA have faced constant threat from conservative forces on the city council, which culminated in an attempt to shut them down in June 2007, when conservative talk show host and mayor pro tem Michael Berry proposed to eliminate the program. At issue was MOIRA and MACIRA's explicit mission to advocate for all immigrants regardless of immigration status, which Berry argued violated the terms of a federal grant that funded the program (City of Houston 2007a, 2007b).

Berry's proposal was opposed by many MOIRA supporters on the council, including Carol Alvarado, who represented the heavily Latino eastern district of Houston and jousted repeatedly with her conservative detractors (L. Rodriguez 2006). In a press release advocating for the program, Alvarado cited Houston as home to the fourth-largest immigrant population in the nation, a population that she said has "just as much of a right to utilize city services as native Houstonians." She argued that MOIRA offered "a one-stop shop for immigrants to practice this right" and that its elimination would be "unfair and unjust to immigrants who legally reside in our city" (Carol Alvarado Campaign, 2007). Under pressure from Alvarado and other supporters, the council eventually tabled the amendment, though Mayor White conceded to Berry's request to tone down the program's advocacy efforts.

Day labor in Houston has also been a flashpoint for the immigration debate on the divided city council. For several years, the city awarded Community Development Block Grant funds to Neighborhood Centers Inc. to run labor centers located in the city's Second Ward near downtown. When I spoke with a Neighborhood Centers representative in March 2006, the program served about ninety workers and had received approximately $90,000 to support center services and fund a center coordinator.[40] When the group applied to renew its contract the following year, tensions flared. Speaking before the council, one opposing resident charged that the country was "being invaded by illegals!" Council member Shelley Sekula-Gibbs (who would later run for and win the seat of Republican congressman Tom DeLay) also opposed the use of public funds for the project, which she contended would attract "illegals" to the city rather than serve citizen residents who need jobs. Council member Addie Wiseman offered an amendment that would require site operators to validate the legal status of workers. Center advocates, including those from MACIRA and the now-defunct City of Houston Day Labor Taskforce, countered that the primary purpose of the center was to provide day laborers a minimum wage, provide an opportunity to track contractors accused of labor violations, and provide essential health and safety training to workers (City of Houston 2006; Colley 2006). Council member Sue Lovell, a supporter of White and the center, also argued, "The responsibility is on the employers as to whether they're hiring somebody that's illegal or not. . . . I would like the city to help employers not break the law." The vote was flooded with amendments, but eventually a swing vote by Republican council member M. J. Khan, a Pakistani immigrant representing the city's immigrant-dense Southwest neighborhoods, pushed through the contract renewal (Miller 2006).[41]

Amid this debate over day labor, immigrant rights supporters also looked to the Houston Police Department to crack down on rampant abuse of the largely immigrant day labor workforce. As in many cities, it is not uncommon for workers to be picked up by unscrupulous employers, promised a set wage, and then left empty-handed at the end of the day or even after weeks. Some workers were being abandoned at work sites, and offending employers, knowing that no effective sanction would be levied on them, often feigned indignation when accused of abusing day laborers. With access to few state resources, and given the tenuous arrangements that day laborers often worked under, worker advocates had few options to assist them. At one point, the Harris County Dispute Resolution Center, which provides mediation services to the courts, had actively reached out to day laborers, providing referrals to exploited workers and their accused employers. Yet this activity eventually sparked an outcry from top leaders at the Houston Bar Association, a key sponsor of the center, who argued that in serving the day labor population the center was also using public funds to help individuals who had a "high likelihood" of being undocumented. Though never legally prohibited from continuing its work with this population, the Dispute Resolution Center was eventually pressured to cut the program.[42]

In response to the emerging dearth of resources, then–police chief Lee Brown followed the lead of several other cities and instituted a policy of enforcing "theft of service" provisions in cases where day laborers were not compensated for their work (HPD 2008).[43] The formal policy was instituted in response to a long history of calls made by the city's day laborers—both legal and illegal, I was assured—to the Houston Police Department seeking help.[44] Many officers insisted these complaints constituted a *civil* matter and refused to pursue the claims, and the Harris County district attorney also chose not to get involved. Eventually, after some persuasion, the DA agreed to file charges where there was sufficient information on a case-by-case basis. The Houston Police Department Burglary and Theft Division was mandated to investigate theft-of-service cases.[45] Thereafter, community service officers started meeting with these workers at MOIRA and at the city's various day labor sites, which at one time numbered three, though two no longer exist.

This shift in policy faced several structural challenges. Day laborers often failed to keep track of information necessary for police investigations, including the names, addresses, and license numbers of their employers, thus hindering the police department's ability to pursue complaints. The unpredictable housing and work pattern of many recently arrived day laborers also made it difficult to effectively pursue claims. Many officers refused to enforce the policy, moreover, and the anti-immigrant climate in the city and among officers made it nearly impossible to establish trust with undocumented workers.[46]

As debate mounted over day labor in the city, questions also emerged about the role the police should play in immigration enforcement. By 2008, Houston and Austin were the only two Texas cities that restricted police involvement in the process of immigration enforcement (NILC 2008b). In 1992, Houston Police Department General Order No. 500–5 had established the policy formally: "Undocumented alien status is not, in itself, a matter for local police action. Unlawful entry into the United States is not to be treated as an on-going offense. . . . Houston police officers may not stop or apprehend individuals solely on the belief that they are in this country illegally" (HPD 1992).[47] Frustrated with this position, immigration restrictionists challenged it, arguing that local governments were obliged to enforce federal immigration laws. In December 2005, Council member Mark Ellis proposed rescinding the 1992 policy.

The Ellis Resolution, as it came to be known, would have permitted police to check the citizenship status of people arrested for Class C misdemeanors, including traffic violations, and would have required police to do so for suspects involved in more serious crimes (Kennett 2005). A group called Protect Our Citizens worked with Ellis to gather enough signatures to place the proposal on the November ballot. Various immigrant rights organizations, including the Latin American Organization for Immigrant Rights and Centro de Recursos Centroamericanos, as well as the Harris County AFL-CIO, spoke before the council, bringing with them community members who provided personal testimony. In one council meeting, an organizer for Centro de Recursos Centroamericanos argued, "If we rescind this order, we are undermining public safety." Ultimately, nine of the thirteen council members agreed, and the Ellis proposal was defeated.[48]

The debate did not end there, however. As White entered his third term, his position toward undocumented immigrants hardened in the wake of two tragic police slayings involving undocumented residents with criminal records. In October 2006, following the murder of Officer Rodney Johnson, Houston Police Department officials began considering an agreement with immigration authorities modeled after the Harris County program (Crowe 2006). By March 2009, when Officer Rick Salter was shot by a Salvadoran immigrant during a drug raid, the department had referred 420 suspected illegal immigrants to federal immigration authorities (Carroll and Lee 2009). Under pressure to once again act, and with his sights originally set on a Senate seat,[49] White responded by submitting an application to the Department of Homeland Security to enter into a 287(g) agreement (Office of the Mayor 2009).[50]

White's move shocked immigrant advocates, who had for years described his support for immigrant rights as unyielding.[51] Immigrant advocates in city office offered severe criticism of White's proposal. Police Chief Harold Hurtt spoke publicly about the damage such a program could do to the trust between law enforcement and immigrant communities.[52] At a Capitol Hill press conference, he said: "Immigration enforcement by local police is counterproductive to community policing efforts. It undermines the trust and cooperation of immigrant communities, could lead to charges of racial profiling, and increases our response time to urgent calls for service" (Pinkerton 2009a).[53] Yet 287(g) supporters, including the powerful Houston Police Officers' Union, claimed that undocumented immigrants represented an "occupational hazard" for officers (Blankinship 2009; Pinkerton 2009b). The president of the union referred to the shootings as "a 'trifecta failure' of federal, state and city government to protect citizens and police officers from criminal illegal immigrants." The pro-287(g) position gained steady support in ensuing years, particularly following the shooting deaths of Houston police officers Henry Canales in June 2009 and Kevin Will in May 2011 (Langford 2011).[54] Though the city ultimately pulled out of the 287(g) program (Carroll 2009c), White's successor, Annise Parker, reiterated that Houston was indeed "no sanctuary city" (Stiles 2010).

Facing an intimidating route to accessing federal protections, an inaccessible state bureaucracy, and few channels of municipal support within a contentious local climate for immigrant rights, Latino immigrants began to turn to the Mayor's Office of Immigrant and Refugee Affairs as their unofficial local clearinghouse. After surviving many attempts to eliminate it, MOIRA was eventually moved to a city-sponsored community center in the immigrant-heavy Southwest area. A central priority for the program continues to be the city's large population of day laborers, which its director estimates is composed of three to six thousand workers spread across at least thirty corners in Houston.[55] MOIRA's services include supporting naturalization efforts, coordinating a network of immigrant rights organizations, and engaging in ongoing (though often muted) advocacy on behalf of policies that support the large immigrant population in Houston. In August 2011, MOIRA was restructured as one of several divisions of Houston's newly consolidated Department of Neighborhoods.[56]

Overall, compared with their counterparts in San Jose, undocumented workers in Houston face a decidedly more hostile environment on both the labor and immigration fronts. Workers in San Jose enjoy a relatively strong state structure for contesting workplace violations, a liberal climate toward immigration, and an active legal community. Conversely, in Houston, they can count on little support from Texas labor agencies, face a vibrant anti-immigration movement, and have limited access to legal counsel. Within this context, the City of San Jose has invested relatively few resources toward the enforcement of undocumented worker rights, opting instead to make use of existing state channels of support, while the City of Houston has played a direct and active role in coordinating a broad set of resources that serve as an alternative to the formal labor standards enforcement system.

Crafting Local Advocacy Strategies

This chapter has considered the power that organized labor and the immigrant rights communities have forged in San Jose and Houston, the policies they have been able to promote, and the opposition they have faced in each city in the context of an immigration enforcement apparatus that has increasingly granted power to local governments. I have painted a picture of strong regional labor power combined with a broad base of support for immigrant rights in San Jose. In contrast, the entrenched business lobby and strong currents of nativism in Houston pose significant challenges to the power of unions and immigrant advocates. On the labor front, San Jose is at the vanguard of many national union organizing campaigns and has one of the strongest living wage policies in the country. Pro-immigrant policies have considerable sway on city council and the county boards of supervisors. A robust network of California labor standards enforcement agencies is both largely the result of organized labor's success in San Jose and a tool that unions, legal advocates, and their allies can use to effectively advocate on behalf of workers. The central labor council in Houston, by contrast, is outspent and outstaffed by the powerful business associations in the city. Weak state protections and a centralized state bureaucracy do little to help promote the power of working people. Houston is one of the few big cities without a living wage, and local politicians have little incentive to court unions.

San Jose and Houston have also responded very differently to the needs of their immigrant populations. While politicians in San Jose have mostly dug their heels in to preserve San Jose's reputation as a sanctuary city and absolve its already stressed bureaucracies of the burden of immigration enforcement, local government in Houston is under substantial pressure to eschew any appearance of tolerating violations of immigration law. Within the relatively progressive context of San Jose, immigrants have been mostly incorporated into existing departments, and those programs that have emerged to serve the needs of immigrants do not need to replicate the labor standards enforcement resources already provided by the state. Conversely, in the embattled context of Houston, some municipal leaders have fought to provide resources for immigrant integration, *in particular* in the area of worker rights. The chapter that follows examines how the two contrasting political fields in San Jose and Houston have shaped civil society strategies for upholding the rights of immigrant workers.

4

Beyond Government

How Civil Society Serves, Organizes, and Advocates for Immigrant Workers

Civil society groups have become essential brokers between publics and government agencies of all sorts (Salamon 1987, 2002). However, the methods these groups adopt are as varied as the communities they represent. In the realm of immigrant workers' rights, some organizations have focused on educating individuals in their rights, providing technical and legal assistance to navigate government bureaucracies, or even litigating on their behalf. Gordon (2007) refers to this type of service as the "lawyering" approach. At the grassroots level, other groups take the "organizing" approach, mobilizing workers and staging direct actions to pressure employers to comply with workers' demands (Fine 2006). A third strategy focuses on lobbying political elites for policy change (Turner and Cornfield 2007).

This chapter evaluates how each of these approaches—*direct service to individuals*, *collective organizing with workers*, and *lobbying on behalf of workers*—has been advanced by civil society groups advocating for undocumented worker rights in San Jose and Houston. I argue that each approach is the result of the efforts of a constellation of organizations. The climate for workers and immigrants, the accessibility of formal bureaucracies, the viability of union representation, and the availability of alternative resources in the community shape how groups work with one another. In the following pages, I examine a range of actors who promote undocumented workers' rights, including but not limited to worker centers, central labor councils, labor unions, immigrant rights groups, faith-based agencies, legal aid centers, industry watchdogs, and even business groups. All of these actors are invested in some component of undocumented worker rights and collaborate with other groups in particular ways to advance their specific goals within their respective political field. (An inventory of the civil society groups discussed throughout is provided in table 4.1).

The pages that follow examine *who* provides direct service to, organizes with, and lobbies for immigrant workers, and how they have allocated resources toward this advocacy. Table 4.1 provides an overview of each approach in San Jose and Houston. I argue that the division of labor among organizations in each city has emerged according to the specific rules and logics of the city's respective political field. I uncover a *specialized* division of labor in San Jose, where legal advocates work with a robust and accessible state bureaucracy to provide direct services for immigrant workers who seek to file workplace rights claims. This leaves unions and their allies, buttressed by faith leaders, to focus on innovative organizing campaigns. Meanwhile, various labor and immigrant rights allies have mobilized their political capital to lobby for broad policy change. In contrast, a hostile climate for labor and immigrants in Houston has led to a much more *diversified* approach to advocating for undocumented worker rights. Here, a broader government–civil society coalition has emerged between labor standards enforcement agencies, city officials, several consulates, the Harris County central labor council, immigrant rights groups, and a new worker center, all of which collaborate to connect undocumented claimants with their rights in various ways. Meanwhile, unconventional alliances have also emerged between these advocates and influential business leaders who together are pushing for immigration reform.

Advocacy through Service: Helping Immigrants Navigate the Labor Standards Enforcement Bureaucracy

Workplace violations are nearly ubiquitous in certain low-wage industries. One of the principal ways advocates can help exploited workers is

TABLE 4.1. Mapping civil society for undocumented worker rights

Actors	San Jose, CA	Houston, TX
Primary bureaucracies	State agencies	Federal agencies
	Santa Clara County Office of Immigrant Relations and Integration Services (IRIS)	City of Houston Mayor's Office of Immigrant and Refugee Affairs (MOIRA)
Central labor council	South Bay Labor Council (SBLC)	Harris County AFL-CIO
Legal service organizations	Katharine and George Alexander Community Law Center (KGACLC)	Lone Star Legal Aid (LSLA)
Immigrant rights	Services, Immigrant Rights and Education Network (SIREN)	Centro de Recursos Centroamericanos (CRECEN)
	Voluntarios de la Comunidad Comité César Chávez	Association of Community Organizations for Reform Now (ACORN) (former)
	Silicon Valley Alliance for Immigration Reform	Casa Juan Diego (CJD)
		Houston Unido/Houston United
		Houston Coalition for Immigration Reform
Faith-based groups	Interfaith Council on Religion, Race, Economic and Social Justice	Houston Interfaith Worker Justice (HIWJ)
	People Acting in Community Together (PACT)	The Metropolitan Organization (TMO)
	Catholic Diocese of San Jose	Archdiocese of Galveston-Houston
		Houston Interfaith Coalition for Immigration Reform
Health/safety	WorkSafe!	Houston Initiative for Worker Safety (HIWS)
Research/policy	Working Partnerships USA (WPUSA)	Texans for Sensible Immigration Policy (TX-SIP)
	California Immigrant Policy Center (CIPC)	Americans for Immigration Reform (AIR)

to connect them with the rights provided to them under the law in the wake of financial and emotional distress. This approach typically has two goals. The first, practical goal is compensation for the affected individual, who often sorely needs the money to make ends meet. The second goal, often the more meaningful one, is to advance justice for the aggrieved individual who has been wronged. In either case, advocates who provide direct service rely on rights inscribed in the law and an enforcement bureaucracy that has been set up to help individuals mobilize these rights. As we have seen, low-wage undocumented workers face a particular series of challenges that creates a wide chasm between the formal rights they enjoy on the books and their actual realization in practice. What types of services advocates provide to bridge this gap depends in large part on the nature of the political field in which these actors exist.

One of the most basic aspects of the political field is the simple issue of accessibility to the enforcement bureaucracy. This includes the physical presence and proximity of agencies to workers, the strength of their protections, and how hostile the political culture is to serving these workers. As I show in this section, a robust state bureaucracy in California, combined with a strong community of legal advocates, privileges services that support formal claims-making. Conversely, facing an enforcement bureaucracy dominated by the federal government, where state agencies are largely absent and legal services for undocumented workers in particular are few and far between, advocates in Houston have had to collaborate in a more integrated fashion to provide immigrant workers with alternative routes into an intimidating and ineffective claims-making process.

Direct Routes to Claims-Making in San Jose

The California labor standards enforcement apparatus is one of the strongest in the nation, providing workers a far higher range of protections than they are entitled to under federal laws. These include a higher minimum wage, broader discrimination regulations, and additional health and safety protections. California workers also have more time to file claims, and some who are left unprotected by federal law, including domestic workers, have greater recourse through the state (Huq et al. 2006).[1] Therefore, when workers file claims in San Jose, they are likely to go to a state agency for help. These bureaucracies are imperfect, and labor advocates have a laundry list of criticisms to lodge against them. Yet most advocates also believe that compared with "the feds," California agencies are doing a better job. "Federal agencies have been gutted over the last three decades . . . [but] the state of California is a different story," explained the political director of the South Bay Labor Council. "Here we have some folks that have actually done a really good job at enforcement."[2] Some organizers I spoke to were more critical, but the overarching assumption most held was that workers should feel fairly confident about approaching a state claims agency, be it the California labor commissioner, the Department of Fair Employment and Housing, or the Division of Workers' Compensation, regardless of their immigration status.

The confidence advocates have in the formal system stems from a long legacy of social movement pressure to create stronger protections and enforcement mechanisms. Yet that confidence is also fortified by a robust network of labor lawyers in San Jose who are available to help aggrieved workers navigate this system. While California is often criticized for being an overly litigious state, the flip side of California's oversaturated market for lawyers is a strong set of pro bono resources. In addition to the many options for private legal counsel, legal aid societies and local law clinics have capitalized on the well-developed philanthropic community and legion of volunteer lawyers who lend their services.

In San Jose, one of the primary organizations that plays this role is the Katharine and George Alexander Community Law Center, which is affiliated with the Santa Clara University School of Law (ImmigrantInfo.org 2004; KGACLC 2010). The center began its work in 1993 in the city's high-immigrant Eastside community. After receiving a generous donation, it moved to its current location near downtown San Jose in 2004. With the support of a dedicated staff, dozens of law students, pro bono attorneys, and undergraduate interns, it serves about a thousand clients a year with a variety of issues and reaches approximately twelve hundred individuals each year through mobile community workshops (KGACLC 2010) and in-house clinics. One of the most well-attended clinics focuses on workers' rights through a collaboration with the San Francisco–based Employment Law Center. In addition to the KGACLC, several nearby organizations have provided similar services over the last decades, including the Instituto Laboral de la Raza, Stanford Law School, and the Legal Aid Society of San Mateo.[3] Many other organizations in the broader San Francisco Bay region do the same. Though not in San Jose proper, they remain relevant given the high proportion of Bay Area workers who live in one place but work in another.[4] Together these groups creatively access a wide array of support—a crucial intervention, given restrictions that federal funds place on serving undocumented workers.[5]

A legal advocate is by no means required to file an administrative claim with any of the state or federal enforcement bureaucracies. Yet these services remain crucial, especially for undocumented workers, for at least two reasons. First, these advocates help educate workers about their rights, provide technical assistance in preparing claims, and serve as culturally competent brokers who guide workers through the process. Second, agency staff have developed a well-honed network with these agencies, which in turn allows them to shepherd a given case through the process in a very direct way. "If we need to check on a case, or we're not sure what's going on, or something's gone wrong, we can just contact them and they'll respond," explained one staff member of the Katharine and George Alexander Community Law Center.[6] In return, the California labor commissioner in San Jose relies heavily on the law center and other legal advocates to move claimants more efficiently through the process. In some cases, agencies are able to resolve claims before they enter the agency queue.

Centers like the KGACLC serve workers from all backgrounds, including undocumented workers. When KGACLC staffers were asked about the viability of the state bureaucracies they sent workers to, their sentiments mirrored closely the bureaucratic perspectives I described in chapter 2. For example, one law clinic student declared, "Basically, if you've earned the wages, well then, they [employers] can't say, 'You're illegal,' because it doesn't matter."[7] She and others referenced segments of California's labor code that reaffirm the equal rights of undocumented workers, and they recounted positive examples of their experiences with undocumented clients. Legal advocates' central concerns in such cases involved establishing a case's merits rather than the worker's immigration status. "I haven't found that there's a big difference [between documented and undocumented claimants]," explained one clinic staff member: "The labor commissioner is very firm that somebody's immigration status is not relevant to them. . . . I've never heard of a situation where [a worker] has ever been deported for filing a wage claim. . . . I've even asked people that worked with only undocumented workers, and they have never heard of a case [like that]." After working at the clinic for close to two years, this staff member was confident that even employer threats were formally irrelevant to workers' claims. Immigration authorities in San Jose, from her perspective, were simply "not interested" in pursuing the immigration status of workers filing claims.[8]

This is not to say that raids do not happen. More than a thousand immigrants were arrested in Bay Area workplace raids in 2008, with a large Immigration and Customs Enforcement team based out of San Jose. Immigrant advocates and local media documented the impact this had on undocumented San Jose residents (Theriault 2008). Today, similar concerns loom over the emerging Secure Communities program, which San Jose officials have fought against despite an aggressive nationwide rollout. Yet the confidence that community advocates expressed to me was rooted in the strong support voiced by local officials to not further entrench the surveillance of undocumented communities.

Though the law centers in the San Jose area offer an invaluable service to workers, they also face challenges. For one, pro bono services often rely on a shoestring staff working alongside volunteer attorneys and law students. Those clinics run by law schools provide a reliable infrastructure; however, they also have to balance an inward-looking mission of teaching against an outward-looking commitment to service and social justice. The director of the Stanford Community Law Center explained, "Our mission at SCLC is actually to educate law students, so it's not really a legal aid office in that sense."[9] The supervising attorney at Santa Clara University's Katharine and George Alexander Community Law Center similarly remarked upon the duality of the clinic's mission: "We have two main aspects of what we do here: one is teach, and the other is to provide free legal services. . . . The issue for me as a teacher is [to decide] which cases seem to have the promise of a good learning experience for our students, and what can we accommodate? There are way more people who need our services than we have resources available."[10] The center's affiliation with a Jesuit university known for its social justice mission has helped facilitate community access to this clinic. The university also offers institutional support that complements often limited funding sources. Yet ultimately the mission of centers like those at Santa Clara University and Stanford is necessarily education, rather than advocacy.[11]

These community law centers are also constrained in their ability to represent workers whose cases are overly complicated. Some services are no longer offered due to a lack of resources. For example, though the KGACLC did at one point handle workers' compensation cases, following the retirement of a key supervising attorney and in an era of dwindling resources it is no longer able to assist injured workers. Staff refer these and other, more complex discrimination cases to information and assistance officers at the state Division of Workers' Compensation, or to private attorneys through either the Santa Clara County Bar Association or their well-honed network of attorneys. Though this network is vast, the incentives for any attorney to take a typical case are paltry. "Most lawyers," a clinic staff member explained, "wouldn't even look at a wage and hour case unless there's a $50,000 claim." Most low-wage workers' claims fall far below the threshold that makes advocacy worth an attorney's time and effort.[12]

Further, though clinic staff have established close relationships with state agencies, their interventions are not always sufficient to speed up the lengthy bureaucratic process. Some employers take advantage of the slow pace, preferring to drag out a case through a hearing in the hope that the system or the worker will eventually relent. The California Labor Commissioner, for example, can take several months to reach the first formal phase of discussion with a defendant employer and his or her counsel. Once an official claim is filed, the actual hearing may not occur for a year or more, and some claims can take up to two years to reach a decision. Immigrant workers in particular may be unwilling or unable to see the process through to the end. Some return to their country of origin when work prospects fall through. Others change residences so frequently that formal correspondence becomes nearly impossible.

The limitations to the direct-service model remain evident even after a judge or hearing officer has ruled in a worker's favor. Payment is by no means certain when an administrative decision has been sent to a superior court for a final judgment. Though the court has the power to invoke a lien on the offending employer, some employers refuse to pay, and there is little a clinic can do to help. One clinic worker described a case in which two employees were awarded $85,000: "The attorney who was working on the case doesn't have any property to get a lien on, [the employer] doesn't have any bank accounts and doesn't have any money. [The attorney is] really having a hard time trying to figure out how to get the money. . . . And this particular client has been in this process for now two and a half years maybe, since he first filed his claim."[13]

Despite all these challenges, advocates I spoke to at these clinics and other organizations remained confident that investing in legal services that funnel workers into the state claims-making apparatus is the best use of advocacy resources. They consider the California system, though not perfect, to be well tested and open to even the most vulnerable workers, including those who are undocumented and lack legal representation. A supervising attorney at the community law center felt confident that "a reasonably articulate person" who received an explanation of the law and his or her rights "could probably represent [him or herself] at the labor commissioner"—and in fact, he explained, most workers and employers do so.[14]

Only one little-used alternative to filing a formal claim with a state agency has emerged in San Jose: the Santa Clara County small claims court.[15] For workers put off by the long administrative process at the labor commissioner, the small claims court can be an attractive option, particularly if the compensation being sought is relatively small. The process takes less time, and legal representation is not required.[16] Yet labor and immigrant advocates in San Jose generally opt to use the state administrative bureaucracy, relying on legal advocates to help workers who come to them for advice.

Even union organizers advise their members to take this route. This division of labor allows unions to remain focused on organizing and policy advocacy while drawing on the expertise of their attorney colleagues to provide individual services. One building trades organizer explained his local's referral protocol: "We don't [handle the cases directly], but we do investigate and help them document what they need. Then we might tell them where to go [to which agency], or if they have a good case, we tell them to get a lawyer."[17] The same is true when unions are approached by nonmembers seeking assistance. A longtime organizer for home health care workers provided me with a list of law clinics she sends workers to. There was no central union-led clearinghouse for this assistance, she explained, but rather a well-oiled system of referrals between immigrant and labor advocates.[18]

Central to the legal referral approach that civil society organizations use is a strong faith in the viability of the formal bureaucracy, a trust that undocumented workers will be safe as they navigate this process, and a lack of alternative union-based solutions. Unions can do little for nonunion colleagues in San Jose who seek help with workplace violations. Unions' focus, unsurprisingly, tends to be on organizing workers. A former SEIU organizer, for example, explained, "When you have a union . . . you have the protection of the union. . . . So, for example, if you have been sexually harassed . . . it would be a whole different process [with a union].[19] So when people call us [for help] . . . if they don't have a union, it's a lot harder for us to really do anything."[20] In the interim, the best support available for nonunion workers seeking assistance, she concludes, is a referral to the relevant state agency and a list of legal providers.

The relationship between legal advocates and union leaders is not a one-way street. In San Jose, a core group of union leaders volunteers with a weekly schedule of outreach workshops at the Mexican consulate. This effort was coordinated jointly by the Building and Construction Trades Council, the South Bay Labor Council, and the Mexican consulate in order to educate Mexican immigrant workers about their rights and the resources available to them. Workers seeking help are instructed to contact state agencies such as the California Department of Industrial Relations, the California Department of Fair Employment and Housing, or the California Workers' Compensation Appeals Board. Contact information for relevant labor unions is also provided. Workers are given a calendar to track their hours and treated to a rousing pep talk about the importance of demanding one's rights.[21]

Thus, a robust set of government standards and a bureaucratic apparatus charged with enforcing them, along with an extensive network of legal advocates, supports the streamlined "lawyering approach" in San Jose. Undocumented workers represent a particularly vulnerable constituency, but they are not seen as a group that requires extraordinary resources when approaching the state bureaucracy. This perspective stands in stark contrast to the climate I confronted in Houston, where the political culture facing undocumented workers is hostile, state structures for filing for worker rights are minimal, and access to legal counsel is nearly nonexistent.

Searching for Alternative Routes to Claims-Making in Houston

Unlike the hub of state enforcement agencies centered in downtown San Jose, the entire Texas labor standards enforcement apparatus is physically centered in Austin. Thanks to a restructuring imposed by Governor Rick Perry, workers who want to file a claim with the Texas Workforce Commission must either travel to Austin, call to speak with an investigator, or mail in a claim. Those workers covered by the mere 63 percent of Texas employers who voluntarily provide workers' compensation insurance must also work with Austin for assistance (Betts and Geeslin 2006). According to the TWC spokesperson, twenty-one investigators handle a daunting eighteen thousand wage claims per year.[22] In practice, this centralized state bureaucracy leads advocates to work more directly with the federal apparatus, which is the only enforcement system with offices on the ground in Houston.[23]

Navigating federal bureaucracies is no less complicated in Houston than it is in San Jose, and the options for affordable legal counsel are considerably sparser. At the time of the research for this book, there was only one nonprofit legal advocacy organization in Houston: Lone Star Legal Aid, located in a spartan downtown office. Led by a small but committed staff of lawyers, it is one of fourteen Lone Star Legal Aid offices across Texas that help individuals with issues ranging from family law to housing to employment. Though worker advocacy is a central part of the organization's stated mission (LSLA 2007), a peculiar mix of local politics has led the Houston office to shy away from work-related cases: Several years before I visited the office, Lone Star in Houston lost a major age discrimination case against an employer whose legal counsel was the well-known Houston firm Fulbright and Jaworski. A principal with this firm also happened to be a Lone Star board member, and he eventually pressured the center to all but cease pursuing employment cases.[24]

This shift was consequential not only for Lone Star Houston but also for workers, who lost the only low-cost legal advocate they had been able to turn to. Though limited assistance is still available through the Thurgood Marshall School of Law and the immigration law program at Catholic Charities—the only other low-cost legal providers I was made aware of in Houston—employment and labor law is not practiced by either. The loss of the Lone Star service, albeit limited, was also significant given the dearth of private attorneys willing to represent workers in Houston. One attorney cited the pro-business culture in Houston as an issue, as well as changes made to the Texas labor code that disincentivize worker claims for lawyers: "Until about fifteen years ago, there actually were a significant number of attorneys who did these types of cases. However, the legislature has since made it *impossible* to get much in the way of benefits for clients, and attorney's fees are limited [to about $400 per case]. So from the attorney's point of view, it's just not worth it."[25]

Lone Star Legal Aid is also completely unable to help undocumented residents, for any reason: the Legal Services Corporation, which requires that all of a grantee's clients be documented, topped its list of donors in 2007. A Lone Star attorney reflected that in being barred from using Lone Star services, undocumented workers lack access not simply to the provision of legal expertise but, more important, to advocates who could facilitate communication between workers and bureaucracies. Negotiation is much of what she does for claimants. With other clients, she said, "We are able to pick up the phone and call individuals in places of power to get a case moved through, and even to get an order enforced." Without access to a low-cost legal service like Lone Star, undocumented workers face a "bleak option" in terms of finding direct legal assistance to navigate government bureaucracies.[26]

With both hands reluctantly tied, Lone Star attorneys in Houston actively encourage undocumented immigrants with simple claims to "buck up" and go through the process at the Texas Workforce Commission. While the TWC process is not ideal, explained a Lone Star lawyer, the agency is nonetheless very experienced with Latino claimants, has many Spanish-speaking/hearing officers, and has a generally good reputation for pursuing wage claims even for undocumented workers. After arming workers with the relevant information, this lawyer would do what he could to equip undocumented claimants to approach the agency on their own. He would always gently remind them, however, that they should be prepared, as unrepresented workers, to face an array of challenges.[27]

Without the benefit of strong state protections and lacking access to legal counsel, for years undocumented workers in Houston had nowhere to go for help outside the formal bureaucracy. This gap became crucially apparent among the city's day laborers, who were experiencing an alarmingly high level of labor abuse. Home to nearly thirty recognized day labor corners, Houston has the largest concentration of urban day laborers after Los Angeles.[28] In response, a group consisting of the City of Houston's Mayor's Office of Immigrant and Refugee Affairs, the Harris County AFL-CIO, immigrant rights organizations, and the Metropolitan Organization (the local Industrial Areas Foundation Affiliate),[29] formed the Day Labor Taskforce at the request of then-mayor Lee Brown. Following recommendations by the task force, two Houston nonprofits secured Community Development Block Grant contracts to operate day labor centers.[30]

Public opposition to the centers was always strong, as described in the previous chapter, coming even from Houston's established Mexican American population, which was "one of the most organized voices of opposition," according to the director of MOIRA.[31] The downtown day labor center was eventually defunded in 2006 and, after a one-year resurrection with private funds, shut down (Pinkerton 2007a; Pinkerton and Carroll 2007). Its sister center, the Oscar Romero Day Labor Center, was operated by the Central American service agency GANO-CARECEN in the immigrant-dense Southwest of Houston. This center moved several times and at one point lost its city-funded space to a trash recycling project. Its visibility eventually declined, the center stopped drawing both employers and contractors, and the project was suspended when funding dried up.[32] Since then, the only nominally organized day labor site in Houston has been operated through the Catholic ministry Casa Juan Diego, which receives no public funding, citing a desire to avoid directives from the city. It relies overwhelmingly on support from Catholic parishioners and is an icon of the Catholic Worker Movement (Zwick and Zwick 2005, 2011).

Casa Juan Diego's director, Mark Zwick, said of the day labor situation in Houston: "Day laborers *are* the source of some of our [community] problems. Just today a woman just really raised hell with us about some guys across the street . . . about the way they were treating women. And you know, she really was correct, they weren't treating the woman with respect." On the other hand, he acknowledges that this behavior is by no means typical of all laborers, and he argues that the problem is twofold. There are legitimate public concerns about day laborers' presence, but at the same time these workers' ubiquitous exploitation is also unacceptable. For the last quarter century, the center Zwick runs with his wife, Louise, has struggled to help day laborers who come to him when they are cheated:

It's common that a guy will come and say, "You know, my *patrón* [employer] has cheated my wages." Okay, if they can find where the *patrón* is, [identify] the guy who hired them, we'd go there right away with them . . . to see what's happening. But these contractors are smarter than I am, and sometimes . . . if they're at a building site where the supervisor is present . . . okay, we'll get that money because we know that's their contractor [and] he's worried about his reputation. But so often, you can't find the *patrón*.

Zwick explains that it is particularly hard to keep track of mobile undocumented workers: "Everything adds up in favor of the *patrón* who cheats them, . . . [and] in favor of the traditional prejudices against immigrants. This certainly colors the response that comes from the community. . . . The traditional biases against immigrants make it hard for us, because they [workers] are not so eager to collaborate."[33]

Over the years, the need for something more to address the needs of the city's day laborers, as well as other Latino immigrant workers, became palpable. The answer advocates rallied around was the Justice and Equality in the Workplace Program (JEWP). The official mission of JEWP was to reach out to the city's growing Latino workforce. Unofficially, it aimed to address the specific challenges undocumented workers in Houston were experiencing. JEWP emerged after the Harris County AFL-CIO's Building and Construction Trades Department presented a white paper to the Equal Employment Opportunity Commission in 2001. The exposé, entitled "Houston's Dirty Little Secret," detailed the prevailing wage violations that were rampant among those employing Latino workers. The JEWP initiative, kick-started by the EEOC, eventually gained the support of a long list of government agencies and community leaders (Karson 2004). JEWP has become the primary resource that community leaders like Casa Juan Diego use to advocate for Latino workers, and in particular for those who are undocumented.[34]

Day labor politics in Houston, as well as the statewide debate over the efficacy of the Texas Workforce Commission (TWC), shaped the creation of JEWP. Critics charged that the TWC was doing a poor job of serving workers, and the San Antonio–based Lawyers Committee for Civil Rights even led an effort to sue the state of Texas and introduce reform via a legislative proposal.[35] A community leader involved in this campaign recalled that "there was barely any relief for workers" in the TWC process, a problem that the state itself admitted.[36]

The level of exploitation of undocumented workers in Houston was also a major impetus for JEWP, even if the public campaign did not acknowledge this. Though federal agencies had publicly declared their willingness to serve all workers, and despite a series of outreach campaigns targeting the Latino immigrant workforce, advocates understood the likely reluctance undocumented workers would feel about paying a visit to a federal building to sit down with a government employee. As a result,

JEWP became just as much a resource for federal agencies struggling to reach out to Latino immigrant communities as it was for workers seeking assistance.

While the list of official signatories has changed over time, steadfast supporters of JEWP have included the Harris County AFL-CIO's Central Labor Council, the Mayor's Office of Immigrant and Refugee Affairs, the Equal Employment Opportunity Commission, the U.S. Department of Labor's Wage and Hour Division, the Occupational Safety and Health Administration, the Mexican American Legal Defense and Education Fund, several religious organizations, the Mexican consulate, and the consulates of Colombia, El Salvador, and Guatemala (Karson 2004). Following the opening of an Interfaith Worker Justice affiliate in Houston after hurricanes Katrina and Rita, this organization also became a core JEWP participant. Notably missing from the coalition is the Texas Workforce Commission, which was invited to join but has not had sustained participation.[37] Efforts to substantially involve the National Labor Relations Board have also failed.[38]

To formalize the coalition, JEWP member agencies signed an accord, to be renewed annually by all participating signatories. According to the outreach manager for the EEOC, the vision of the group is to "create many forms of outreach, including videos, town meetings, and public events, in order to show people how to file a complaint, and to raise awareness about their rights."[39] To start, JEWP launched the ¡No Se Deje! (Protect Yourself!) campaign. The JEWP hotline was advertised through community events and ethnic media outlets, as well as via a large billboard installed above the Mexican consulate building and through flyers distributed by community organizations. Groups such as Casa Juan Diego regularly direct workers to call for help. The hotline was initially hosted by MOIRA, then later moved to the Mexican consulate. Staff were trained by each federal agency to evaluate a caller's issue, assess which referrals were needed, and direct the case to the appropriate agency. All claims were cross-filed with participating signatories so that the various components of claims could be simultaneously addressed. The intake staff would then act as bureaucratic brokers to follow up on each case.

One of the newest participants in JEWP is Houston Interfaith Worker Justice (HIWJ), which has also developed a parallel set of mechanisms to serve workers through the initial leadership of both Rick Shaw of the

AFL-CIO and Kim Bobo, the dynamic director of the National Interfaith Worker Justice organization. Its stated mission is to provide "a safe space for low wage workers to gather and learn about their rights in the workplace, network for various social services, file complaints with government agencies, meet with attorneys and connect with community allies" (HIWJ 2008). The 501c(3) organization started with a skeleton staff and funding from the Houston Endowment during the summer of 2006; it was drawn to the area in large part due to the effects of Hurricane Katrina. According to its ally at the AFL-CIO, the group filled a gap left by a weak union movement and the lack of a strong social service network for workers. It played a particularly essential role following the "hibernation" of the AFL-CIO's now defunct Community Service Program, which was originally funded by the United Way to provide a food pantry and social service referrals. When the Harris County AFL-CIO tried to shift toward a worker center model, funding dried up, and the council was unable to support it.[40]

When Houston Interfaith Worker Justice first arrived, it spent several months working out of an office provided by Catholic Charities and teamed up with a disaster relief group affiliated with the Mennonite Church. The long-term need for HIWJ soon became apparent. In the lucrative rush to rebuild following the devastation of hurricanes Katrina, Rita, and later, Ike, contractors were coming to Houston seeking labor from the plentiful pool of day workers (Rhor and Prengaman 2008). Yet, many workers were tragically misled. The director of the Houston Initiative on Worker Safety, which collaborated with Interfaith Worker Justice on this issue, explained the scene that awaited workers in New Orleans: "When they would arrive, their wages were either withheld, they lived in miserable, dismal living conditions, many were living out of their cars or vans, [the contractors] were not feeding them, not paying them, and not [providing] safety equipment. They also ended up going into these basically hazardous waste sites with no respiratory devices, no gloves, nothing."[41] Because the vast majority of these workers actually lived in Houston, it was to Houston that many initially returned seeking help when things went awry—or in many cases in Houston that they were abandoned and disposed of by contractors at the end of a job.[42]

In the midst of the post-Katrina chaos, advocates like Houston Interfaith Worker Justice also had to contend with groups like the Minuteman

Project, an anti-immigration group that, in cooperation with sympathetic forces within the Houston Police Department, began to initiate vigilante campaigns targeting laborers headed to Louisiana. One interviewee described these campaigns:[43]

> They [the Minutemen] dressed up as regular contractors and started driving around the areas like Washington and Shepherd [key day labor sites] . . . and wooing these people [with promises] that they would get like ten dollars an hour to do painting [in Louisiana]. They get them in their truck, but they brought them to a paint store parking lot, where there were [police] paddy wagons. . . . Then they [officers] would demand their documentation, which of course these people didn't have on them, and then haul them to jail. But it was a jail way down in the south part of Houston, miles and miles away from any kind of bus rides. And of course we all tried to demand *habeas corpus*, and they finally let them go without charges.[44]

In the short time since it was created, HIWJ has become one of the most prominent allies for immigrant workers in the city. The vast majority of workers that come to the center have wage theft cases, though the center also deals with small numbers of injury and discrimination issues. Houston Interfaith Worker Justice has received training from all JEWP agencies, including OSHA, the EEOC, the DOL, and even the Social Security Administration, enabling its staff to refer cases to the relevant agencies.[45] For those workers who wish to proceed with a formal claim, staff can either shepherd them through the process or attempt to refer them to a legal advocate from a small network of attorneys willing to offer pro bono or contingency assistance.

In other cities where Interfaith Worker Justice has a presence, and especially where there is a broad network of other worker centers (including day labor centers), outreach to low-wage workers is less cumbersome. In Houston, however, HIWJ is the only holistic resource of its kind for workers. A wide range of workers approach HIWJ, including but not limited to workers in construction, domestic work, home health care, restaurants, and even factories. The vast majority of workers who seek assistance through HIWJ are Latino immigrants, but the center has also worked with native-born workers and is embarking on outreach to the African American community. Though Fine (2006) has chronicled the singular importance of IWJ in several cities, as of this writing no comparable model has emerged in San Jose.

Given the individualized attention it offers, HIWJ's approach to direct service is similar to what legal advocates provide in San Jose, but the group's ultimate goal of educating and empowering workers makes it distinct. Upon first coming to HIWJ, a worker is required to attend an introductory orientation. Once the worker's case has been accepted, a staff member or volunteer places a call to the offending employer to verify the facts of the case. In a handful of cases, the center is able to arrange payment with the employer right away. Most cases do not go this smoothly, and both the worker and the center have to dig their heels in and decide on a next step. The choice of what to do next is ultimately left up to the worker, the center's director explained: "The worker really makes the decisions; we're accompanying them through the process." A worker may ask HIWJ to send the employer a certified letter declaring the worker's intent to amicably resolve the matter: as one HIWJ worker told me, "We explain to [the employer] what laws they're breaking . . . and give them a deadline of ten days to make a payment." Alternatively, a worker may choose to go through another JEWP partner, small claims court, or file a theft-of-services claim with the Houston Police Department.

The centralized nature of Texas agencies has led HIWJ, like other JEWP affiliates I spoke with, to conclude that the state claims system is an "ineffective" agency for workers to use. The HIWJ director recalled a recent case: "We sent a claim to the Texas Workforce Commission in May 2008. It wasn't until November that they called the workers (involved) and told them that they were going to start working on the case."[46] The TWC eventually ruled in the workers' favor, but the extent of its enforcement efforts consisted of a letter sent to the employer alerting him of his responsibility to pay. Conversely, going through the federal bureaucracy is also an option for some. Yet many of the workers who come to Houston Interfaith Worker Justice are not covered by federal law (as described in chapter 1). Day laborers, for example, often work for small businesses that gross less than the $500,000 required to be covered under the Fair Labor Standards Act, or for companies that employ fewer than the fifteen employees required to be covered under the 1964 Civil Rights Act.

The Houston Police Department is another potential alternative to the state and federal bureaucracy, but it too can be a challenging bureaucracy to navigate. "The only way that the Houston Police Department will get involved [in a wage theft case] is if the worker hasn't been paid at all, and in many cases a worker will receive a small portion of what they're owed, and in those instances they are unable to file with the police department," explained the HIWJ director. The police department also traditionally lacked the ability to effectively force an employer to pay restitution: penalties are lax, and the police department has few incentives to make such cases a priority.[47] Houston Interfaith Worker Justice also spearheaded an effort to form a task force within the police department that would assign dedicated officers to work on the issue of wage theft. In the interim, the center has settled on educating workers on the provisions of the theft-of-services mandate and on developing close working relationships with sympathetic officers. In 2011, it also launched a campaign to pressure the city council to directly address the wage theft epidemic with local resources (Down With Wage Theft Campaign, 2012).

Finally, HIWJ also encourages workers who do not wish to pursue a police claim to consider filing in small claims court. Counseled by a justice of the peace who serves on the center's advisory board, advocates have learned how to advise workers to apply for a waiver of the court filing fee (usually $85); once the plaintiffs have filed and received a court date, an HIWJ advocate will accompany them through the trial. Houston Interfaith Worker Justice has had "surprising success" with this route, though it can sometimes take months to get a hearing. The director explains why the approach has been effective: "They [employers] see that we've taken it this far . . . they know we're serious. . . . They know that we're going to continue to pursue the case . . . and sometimes it doesn't take us going to court. . . . Getting a letter from an organization that's supporting the worker [shows] that the worker isn't alone. . . . They know that this guy's not by himself!"[48]

What makes Houston Interfaith Worker Justice distinct from its legal services colleagues in San Jose, and even from the typical JEWP approach, is the choice it offers workers to completely opt out of the formal state and federal bureaucracy, which has primary jurisdiction over workplace enforcement. In addition to directing workers toward the various local claims processes, the center also encourages workers to consider direct action. Strategies may include leafleting outside restaurants to publicly air the employers' dirty laundry. This unconventional approach is not seen as simply ancillary symbolic protest, but rather as a legitimate route to seeking recourse given the inadequacy of state protections. The director explained, "We can't depend on laws to protect us like in [other] states. Texas is the only state in the union that doesn't require employers to cover workers' compensation insurance. . . . [Here,] an employer is not required to give you a break unless you need to go to a bathroom, so you can work a twenty-three-hour shift and not get a break, and that's totally legal! The laws are all in favor of business, . . . and not of protecting workers."[49]

If an employer agrees to settle, either through a formal claim or direct action, the center asks the employer to sign a form detailing the terms of the agreement. With a worker's consent, HIWJ then sets up a payment plan with the offending employer and upon full restitution will issue a "release form" to confirm the case has been closed. The process is not foolproof, and the center has seen several reoffending employers in its short time in Houston. "Once we had an employer who owed a couple thousand dollars, and had been diligent about stopping by and dropping off payments," explained the director. "Then, at the next week's *charla* [workshop], another worker from the same employer [who had no knowledge of the previous case] filed a similar claim." The center contacted the employer again, and the employer reluctantly agreed to start another payment plan. In 2008, HIWJ recovered approximately $95,000 for workers, followed by close to $70,000 in the first half of 2009.[50]

Immigrant worker advocates are providing direct services to aggrieved claimants in San Jose and Houston, albeit through very different channels. In addition to acting as bureaucratic brokers, civil society groups in both cities are also involved in the long-term process of mobilizing workers to demand their rights collectively. In the following section, I examine what organizing strategies the political fields in San Jose and Houston have produced. I argue that while direct action is a key strategy in both cities, the agendas and actors involved are very different. As I will show, there is an apparent delineation between groups focused on direct service and those dedicated to mass mobilizations in San Jose, where union-led campaigns dominate efforts to organize workers. Conversely, civil society in Houston lacks the luxury of such exclusive specialization, and even the Harris County AFL-CIO must wear a number of hats to fulfill its mission. The central labor council has collaborated with other groups to address a range of issues outside of union campaigns, and organizing itself is understood as an enforcement strategy for basic workplace rights.

Advocacy through Organizing: Rallying for Immigrant Worker Rights

Unions operate essentially as local organizations influenced by the specific politics and economies of the cities and regions that house them (Sellers 2007). While national leadership can dictate the broad direction of labor organizing, the constraints and opportunities unions face "increasingly have to do less with national differences than with the particulars of local politics and labor-business dependence" (Greer 2007, 193). In today's progressively de-unionized workforce, moreover, worker centers also play an important role in organizing workers. For immigrant workers in particular, this new form of organizing has become one of the only avenues of worker support (Fine 2006; Gordon 2007; Milkman, Bloom, and Narro 2010). Worker centers' collaborations with community organizations have become essential not only to promote unionization but also to advance broader causes that support working people everywhere.

In both San Jose and Houston, the central labor council has been a key leader in "rallying for immigrant rights" alongside a coalition of allied local representatives, faith leaders, and immigrant rights organizations (Voss and Bloemraad 2011). Yet the distinct political fields of San Jose and Houston have given way to divergent strategies to organize immigrant workers in each city, as well as distinct leadership roles for each central labor council. In the section that follows, I contrast the goals of immigrant worker organizing in each city and the particular coalitions that have evolved to advance immigrant worker rights.

Unions Organizing at the Vanguard in San Jose

The rights of immigrant workers are integral to the mission of the South Bay Labor Council, which has developed a long legacy of support. One of the most prominent victories in the early 1990s, for example, was the Justice for Janitors campaign (R. Preston 2004; Zlolniski 2006). Today, the Service Employees International Union continues to fight for more than twenty thousand janitors through Justice for Janitors and is one of many SBLC affiliates mobilizing to organize workers and negotiate better working conditions for members (Staff 2008b; SEIU 2010).[51] In the two decades since Justice for Janitors, the SBLC has also supported new worker mobilizations such as the UNITE HERE Hotel Workers Rising Campaign.[52] The national campaign, which has targeted Hyatt, Hilton, Sheraton, and Marriot hotels, follows a classic "top-down" approach with the goal of attaining a card-check neutrality agreement. In California, organizers can build on a legacy of 160 unionized hotels, while the parallel campaign in Texas has only three past victories to work with.[53]

Struggling for public support in a recessionary climate, organizers from these and other Silicon Valley campaigns have relied on a broad base of political support. UNITE HERE's Rising Together supporters for the Hyatt Santa Clara campaign, for example, included Santa Clara City Council member Jamie McLeod and State Assembly member Paul Fong (District Twenty-two). Similar campaigns at the San José McEnery Convention Center and Doubletree drew political support from top San Jose leaders such as vice-mayor Dave Cortese. These and other organizing drives have convened a wide cross-section of allies across "the boundaries of color, occupation, gender, sexual orientation, religion, employment, and immigration status" (Rising Together 2009). Rising Together steering committee members include the central labor council and affiliated unions, representatives from a wide range of community organizations—including housing and homeless services organizations, LGBT leaders, peace advocates, student activists, and immigrant rights organizations—and a number of faith leaders who represent the "moral voice" of the campaign.[54]

The South Bay Labor Council has also worked with its community research arm, Working Partnerships USA (WPUSA), to advance campaigns. The WPUSA Interfaith Council on Race, Religion, and Economic and Social Justice, which has been extremely active on the labor and immigrant rights front, serves as the local affiliate of the national Interfaith Worker Justice coalition. Led by a Presbyterian minister and longtime community leader in Silicon Valley, this association of more than four hundred clergy members and laypersons defines its mission as "[to] address the crisis of working poverty and provide a moral framework for the public dialogue regarding race, religion, [and] economic and social justice" (WPUSA 2008b). The Interfaith Council director frames the council's goal as bringing "people of faith into action alongside and with worker justice issues . . . to use our authentic, moral, religious voice . . . to challenge corporate managers to do the right thing."[55]

Collaborations between organized labor and faith-based groups, like Houston Interfaith Worker Justice and Casa Juan Diego, have grown in Houston and other cities through the AFL-CIO Labor in the Pulpits program (AFL-CIO 2009a). What is innovative about the Interfaith Council in San Jose, however, is the direct sponsorship it receives from the WPUSA, the South Bay Labor Council's "think and act" tank (SBLC 2009; Dean and Reynolds 2010). Through their support of campaigns such as SEIU's Justice for Janitors, UNITE HERE's Rising Together! and UFCW's Justice for Mercado Workers, immigrant workers have been integral to the mission of the Interfaith Council, and that of the South Bay Labor Council more broadly. Reflecting on the work of her colleagues in other cities, the head of the SBLC Interfaith Council admits the opportunities provided by working in the "more liberal" context of San Jose, where many residents "appreciate diversity."[56]

The South Bay Labor Council has also invested in organizing beyond union campaigns. In 2006, the Interfaith Council was a pivotal player in historic immigrant rights marches. Key actors from previous immigrant-rights victories, including SEIU Local 1877's Justice for Janitors campaign and the San Jose Coalition for Driver's Licenses, came together to mobilize against the controversial HR 4437. The council took the lead in the formation of the San Jose Immigrant Rights Coalition, which included over seventy civil society groups in Silicon Valley and turned out 25,000 marchers on March 25, 30,000 on April 10, and an estimated 330,000 on May 1, 2006 (Vital 2010).[57]

Apart from this rich history of supporting union campaigns and immigration reform, the direct actions sponsored by the South Bay Labor Council have for the most part focused on collective bargaining campaigns. Individual aggrieved workers, as explained in the previous section, are usually directed toward legal advocates who can help them file a formal claim with the appropriate state agency. Aside from the legal aid clinics discussed above, nonunion action-oriented worker centers are also relatively absent from Silicon Valley. In her inventory of worker centers, Fine (2006) lists two in San Jose: Filipino Community Support–FOCUS (a Filipino community-based organization) and the Temporary Workers

Employment Project at Working Partnerships USA. As of this writing, FOCUS no longer works specifically on workplace issues in Silicon Valley,[58] and the Temporary Workers Employment Project has become the Contingent Workers Project at Working Partnerships USA and now focuses on producing high-quality, action-focused research rather than providing services to or organizing workers (WPUSA 2009). Each of these organizations does critical work on behalf of low-wage immigrants, but neither is a bottom-up, member-driven group focused on direct action.

This is not to say that worker centers have no history organizing in San Jose. Several centers were propelled into existence by a 1997 anti-loitering city ordinance targeting day laborers (City of San Jose 1997). Two faith-based, service-oriented centers were established in the city's dense immigrant Eastside neighborhoods (Alindor 2007) yet struggled in the last decade to stay afloat. The only member-driven organizing group in Silicon Valley, by the definition I am proposing here, is a day labor center located in the northern suburb of Mountain View. The Mountain View Day Labor Center, an affiliate of the National Day Labor Organizing Network, serves a mostly residential employer base in the tightly bound regional area of Mountain View and its more affluent neighbors, Palo Alto, Los Altos, and Los Altos Hills (DeBolt 2010).

Outside Silicon Valley, several innovative worker centers have emerged in San Francisco with the support of local unions. For example, Young Workers United is known for launching grassroots-based direct actions to pressure (mostly restaurant) employers to comply with state and city laws and provide better working conditions (Asher 2007). Since it was founded in 2002, Young Workers United has garnered thousands of dollars in victories for workers in San Francisco (YWU 2009). In San Jose, however, direct labor actions are led mostly by traditional unions, and worker-focused community organizations have concentrated on funneling even undocumented claimants through state agencies.

Considered broadly, then, the South Bay Labor Council has fomented considerable regional power and political capital, making it the primary powerhouse for worker organizing in San Jose. Organizing and direct-action efforts have focused primarily on waging top-down union campaigns and pushing for key policy reforms. While coalitions abound, they have not adopted direct action as a salient solution for addressing basic workplace violations. Far from being an oversight on the part of the Silicon

Valley labor movement, this focus represents a strategic division of labor that capitalizes on a political field characterized by a well-honed enforcement bureaucracy and a labor- and immigrant-friendly political culture. In the next section, I contrast this approach to the more intertwined and decentralized use of "lawyering" and "organizing" in Houston. In this decidedly more hostile context, organizing is used not only to fill the void of legal services but also to mobilize workers poorly served by traditional unions.

Divided Unions Partnering with Progressive Allies in Houston

Efforts to organize immigrant workers in Houston face an uphill battle, both in terms of the weak labor standards that govern the workplace and of the strength of opposition groups. Within this political field, the local labor council has had to do double duty with fewer resources. For the last fifteen years, the Harris County AFL-CIO Council has been led by the powerful duo of President Dale Wortham and Secretary-Treasurer Richard Shaw. Yet aside from two administrative staff, Shaw fills the only full-time leadership position for the organization. From this post, he has spearheaded efforts to make the council more inclusive of African Americans, women, and immigrants. One of the most dramatic changes the council has made in recent years has been to "integrate worker rights issues into the immigrant rights struggle in Houston" (Karson 2004, 212).

The inclusive vision advanced by the Harris County AFL-CIO, however, has met with significant resistance from some of its affiliated unions, particularly within the building trades. Among these locals, the specter of Houston's entrenched pro-business lobby and the competition posed by "illegals" has sparked fierce tensions. One business manager I spoke with grudgingly approached the politically charged issue on the condition of anonymity: "It's a huge challenge . . . a never-ending pool of cheap people that come through Houston daily. Our biggest competitors here are former union contractors that broke away and used cheap labor to have a competitive advantage." He and others are frustrated by the changing demography of their industry, yet they are also cognizant of the need to organize the growing number of Latino and Vietnamese immigrant workers:

> Do we organize Hispanics, Latinos and Asians? You bet! Our president's from Mexico . . . and we have many members here that are from Mexico.

> They make good union members . . . [but] they're just hard people to get to. They're hard to talk to. . . . I mean, they're scared, it's obvious. They've been led to believe by other people, by the company, that when you talk to union guys . . . you're gonna be terminated. I mean, these people, they're here to work, they have a family to support, and they're gonna take what they can get. They don't want any trouble. They just want to work.[59]

Other union leaders voiced similar anxieties, but in less forgiving terms. One said: "I would like to see our government stop the illegal immigration and deal with the people that are here illegally now, and figure out some sort of solution. . . . We got to shut the border now and deal with the people that are here illegally and work out something with them so that they can become good citizens here . . . and not feel threatened by these contractors that are just abusing them for minimum wage with no benefits." He acknowledged that immigrants are simply "here to work," but he argued that they create "a burden on society because . . . they undermine the standards of living" and drain public resources. He concluded: "They're taking a lot out and not putting a lot back in. They go and send a lot of their money home. I mean, it's just a bad situation. I don't know what the answer is."[60]

Many Houston union leaders, even in the building trades, are keenly aware of the unsustainability of these tensions and describe a slow change happening. An organizer with Carpenters Local 554 explained, "Well, you know, twenty years ago 'we,' the AFL-CIO, was against the illegal. And then they kind of made a 180-degree shift."[61] From his perspective, this shift was the result of the declining strength of unions nationally and the demographic transformation of the Houston workforce. Even moderate union leaders I spoke to felt disconnected from the more radically nativist perspective espoused by anti-immigrant groups and conservative politicians like Republican congressman John Culberson, who in 2005 pushed for public funding of civilian border patrols. One reason, the Carpenters Local 554 organizer explained, is that a new generation of unions now emphasizes the struggles all workers face rather than the differences of race and immigration:

> Whether you're white, black, Hispanic, Asian . . . if you can go out and produce on the job, you show up every day and you got a work ethic, that's

how you gain respect at the Carpenters. . . . Since unions are a minority in
Texas—white, black, I mean all of us union guys are a minority—we got
to kind of stick together. This is our turf, you know, we're like a family, so
we're trying to battle to keep our turf as a union more so than worrying
about whether the brother's black, white, or a Hispanic.[62]

The ambivalence some Houston unions feel toward immigrant workers
is not unique. San Jose Building Trades leaders I spoke to also expressed
similar challenges. One Carpenters representative recalled the tensions
during the 1980s when the Mexican population started to grow within the
industry. While these tensions have eased substantially, he still urges some
members to remember that "no matter color, age, or country they're coming from, we're all in this together."[63] His colleagues at the Laborers' Local
270 recounted similar tensions that have surfaced during recent business
manager elections. Latino immigrant members I spoke to in that local recounted fierce debates over the use of Spanish-language translation during
meetings, grievances that went unanswered, and ongoing mistreatment.[64]

What makes the tensions in Houston distinct from those in San Jose is
the slower pace at which immigrant incorporation is taking place, a consequence of broader anti-immigrant sentiments in the city. Though the Harris County AFL-CIO has declared its commitment to bringing immigrant
workers into the fold, some labor unions are struggling to follow suit. This
is the case not only in the building trades, which have a storied history of
racism, but also in emerging service-industry locals. One UNITE HERE
organizer I spoke with in Houston candidly recounted a refrain he heard
often from his mostly white colleagues in the region: "Why would we support those illegals?"[65] Beyond internal divisions, all workers in Houston
face the same "business-friendly" environment. In this David-versus-
Goliath context, which chips away at protections for nonunion members
especially, unions and other organizations advocating on behalf of immigrant workers have few options other than to band together.

One avenue for coalition building that the Harris County AFL-CIO
has pursued is the Justice Bus. This self-professed "Michael Moore–style"
campaign was launched in 1998 by the central labor council and its allies to shame abusive employers into compliance—and at times even to
praise exemplary ones. One of the most memorable targets of the Justice
Bus was Quietflex. In 2000, this manufacturing plant was the subject of

an employment discrimination case involving the segregation of Spanish-speaking and Vietnamese workers. Latino workers labored in more dangerous and lower-paid areas within the plant and were routinely prevented from ascending into better positions. In response to these conditions, the Justice Bus rolled through filled with community organizers, religious leaders, and local officials to pressure plant managers to conform to fair labor practices (Karson 2004). Other Justice Bus targets have included a poultry processing plant accused of withholding bathroom breaks and imposing forced overtime on workers and to contractors at public-works projects who regularly misclassify workers, most of them Latino immigrants, as independent contractors to avoid paying thousands of dollars in compensation (Sixel 1998, 1999). According to Shaw, these public shamings are an essential vehicle for building labor power in Houston and a powerful tool for addressing pervasive workplace violations.[66]

Houston Interfaith Worker Justice has been a key proponent of the Justice Bus and the Harris County AFL-CIO. HIWJ is also one of a growing number of grassroots worker centers affiliating with central labor councils across the nation (AFL-CIO 2006). In addition to the technical assistance HIWJ provides to workers via the Justice and Equality in the Workplace Program, the center also regularly refers workers to their industry's respective unions, and it has worked with building trades unions on prevailing wage issues at large government job sites.

Perhaps the biggest component of Houston Interfaith Worker Justice's grassroots organizing involves day laborers. The organization provides basic services and resources to these workers who often fall outside the reach of formal protections and beyond the scope of traditional union organizing. The day I visited, the director was busy coordinating a twenty-five-person church youth group that was headed to a local Home Depot to distribute water and worker-rights manuals. The center also regularly sends representatives to community events like health fairs and back-to-school forums. However, the group's most effective form of organizing, the director explained, is led by "work leaders" who reach out to workers in their own communities. These "steward-like" leaders are selected from the series of monthly meetings (or *asambleas*) and weekly *charlas* (talks) that the center holds. The *charlas* follow a popular education model to train workers about their rights and responsibilities and teach them about the benefits of being organized.

Charlas are also used to organize direct actions on behalf of workers who have opted to bypass the formal bureaucracy to resolve their workplace violations. Houston Interfaith Worker Justice has used direct action not only to recover lost wages for workers but in some cases even to demand jobs back for workers who have been fired. While technical assistance is a key part of what the group provides, according to the HIWJ director the power of direct action is to persuade employers who otherwise are confident that the formal system will work in their favor: "[Employers] know that there's a backlog . . . so sometimes you have to humiliate someone, in a very public way." Workers vary in their willingness to participate, and some prefer to make use only of the center's direct services. Yet the director explained that a minority prefer direct action to the administrative and judicial process, which they find threatening. Direct actions are never conducted without the consent and direct involvement of the worker bringing the claim. They can entail tactics such as leafleting outside restaurants and talking to clients about the employer's violations. On actions, aggrieved workers are accompanied not only by fellow workers but also by a delegation of interfaith representatives the center coordinates.

My aim here is not to highlight HIWJ as a unique model for worker advocacy. The organizing approach that worker centers like HIWJ and its allies have taken has been successful in cities across the country (Fine 2006; Gordon 2007; Bobo 2008; Milkman, Bloom, and Narro 2010). What seems exceptional in Houston compared with San Jose, however, is the simultaneous integrated relationship HIWJ has developed with not only the Harris County AFL-CIO but also the Justice and Equality in the Workplace Program, which brings together the central labor council, immigrant rights organizations, several Latin American consulates, the major federal labor standards enforcement agencies, and local bureaucracies. Unlike the specialization approach in San Jose, where unions have primarily directed worker "organizing" and most worker centers promote "lawyering," HIWJ has directed efforts toward both.

A key partner for the organizing advanced by both the Harris County AFL-CIO and HIWJ is the Centro de Recursos Centroamericanos (CRECEN). Founded in the early 1980s at the height of the exodus of migrants from Guatemala and El Salvador, CRECEN has been at the center of every immigrant rights mobilization in Houston.[67] Located in the immigrant-heavy Gulfton neighborhood in close proximity to other immigrant-serving organizations, CRECEN and its affiliated group, America Para Todos, are known for their grassroots immigrant organizing. CRECEN has been a member of the Justice and Equality in the Workplace Program from the beginning. Before JEWP, community-based groups like CRECEN worked with the Mayor's Office of Immigrant and Refugee Affairs and a small network of sympathetic police offers and private attorneys to help aggrieved workers who came to them for help. A lead organizer recalled the situation before this integrated network existed:

> In the pre-JEWP era, it was very difficult. It was the same complaints, you know, lack of payment of wages . . . and it was in all industries, construction, restaurants and service industry. . . . We would call up a group of Latino police officers [that we knew] . . . and they would call the employer. They would report them to the IRS if they didn't pay, and sometimes it worked, and sometimes it didn't. When they had time, they would actually go see the employer. . . . Now, I've been impressed that [JEWP] has managed to actually reclaim . . . just tons of complaints.[68]

Though JEWP has by no means been a panacea, and has received mixed support from immigrant rights groups, through organizing, it exists alongside efforts to strengthen the safety and well-being of Houston's immigrant communities. CRECEN's hallmark actions have included a delegation sent on the 2003 Immigrant Workers Freedom Ride and ongoing mobilizations in support of the Dream Act.[69] In 2006, CRECEN also joined forces with Justice for Janitors' SEIU Local 199 and ACORN as key conveners of the May 1 march to oppose the passage of HR 4437. Every year since, organizers have continued to march in support of comprehensive immigration reform. In 2010, they convened a demonstration in the heart of Gulfton to demand "the right to be acknowledged, 'to come out of the shadows,' through a just immigration reform for all the contributions immigrants make" (La Nueva Raza 2010).[70] Today, CRECEN is a key member of the coalition Houston Unido (Houston United), which bills itself as "Houston's grassroots coalition for immigrant rights."[71]

Facing a decidedly more hostile climate for immigrant worker organizing, then, advocates in Houston have diversified rather than specialize. In addition to its work with JEWP, the Harris County AFL-CIO focuses most of its union organizing on traditional sectors while collaborating with Houston Interfaith Worker Justice to educate and organize workers in new sectors. Such coalitions in Houston pool resources and influence to pursue the common goal of supporting the rights of undocumented workers at the same time that the member organizations work toward their individual objectives. The collaboration is a strategy of necessity rather than simply solidarity.

In addition to providing direct service to individual workers and organizing workers through direct actions, a third tool for advancing immigrant worker rights is public policy advocacy. In the following section, I assess the distinct ways immigrant worker advocates have approached policy reform in San Jose and Houston.

Advocacy through Lobbying: Leveraging Political Capital on Behalf of Immigrant Workers

This final section contrasts the actors, goals, and strategies of policy reform in San Jose and Houston. I contend that a strong labor history and legal tradition in San Jose has catapulted unions, immigrant advocates, and lawyers to the forefront of major lobbying efforts to improve workplace standards, promote programs to support working people, and endorse progressive immigration reform. Conversely, an entrenched business lobby and vocal anti-immigrant coalition in Houston has led advocates to forge unlikely alliances to affect policy change. In this case, the central labor council and key immigrant rights groups have combined efforts, sometimes uncomfortably, with well-funded business elites and faith-based groups in an effort to appeal to the unique political culture of the Bayou City.

Standing Their Ground: How Unions, Nonprofits, and Lawyers Lobby in San Jose

A quick read through the speakers at past city council and county board meetings reveals two frequent attendees: the South Bay Labor Council and the leading immigrant rights group, the Services, Immigrant Rights and Education Network (SIREN). Regarding the former, the number of SBLC-backed candidates who have garnered key city and county seats is undeniable, as is the inability of any political hopeful to ignore the council's power. Through its Committee on Political Education, the SBLC endorses a slate of candidates every election season, while also promoting a wide range of national policies, including immigration and health care reform and the stalled Employee Free Choice Act (SBLC 2010a). Though it does not actively endorse any particular candidate, SIREN has supported many of the SBLC's organizing campaigns, spearheaded the San Jose May 1st Coalition to support comprehensive immigration reform, and in 2008 deployed the South Bay Rapid Response Network in part to "STOP Immigration Raids and Enact Just and Humane Immigration Reform" (SIREN 2011, 2012b). These are not the only advocates of immigration reform policy in San Jose, however: the category also includes several prominent lawyers and industry watchdogs working behind the scenes to propel legislative change at the state and national level. I will address the efforts of each in turn.

While I have already profiled the work of the South Bay Labor Council's Working Partnerships USA, perhaps the most significant aspect of WPUSA's fifteen-year legacy in San Jose is the policy reforms it has achieved.[72] Much has been written about the power WPUSA has fomented in Silicon Valley and California as a whole (Brownstein 2000; Benner 2002; Byrd and Rhee 2004; Rhee 2007; Rhee and Sadler 2007). The 501(c)3 organization defines itself as first and foremost a "public policy and research institute that builds partnerships with community groups, labor unions, and faith based organizations to improve the lives of working families in Silicon Valley" (WPUSA 2010a). First, in conjunction with community organizations like People Acting in Community Together, the local affiliate of the PICO National Network of faith-based organizers, it fought for and won the creation of the Santa Clara County Children's Health Initiative through a combination of research-based advocacy and public pressure.[73] In January 2001, the initiative, which was supported with state tobacco funds, became the first children's insurance program in Santa Clara County.[74] It has provided health care to an estimated 71,000 uninsured children in the county, including many who are undocumented (Children's Health Initiative 2010).[75]

Working Partnerships USA has also been active on redevelopment issues in an effort to save the San Jose region from falling into the urban sprawl patterns that are characteristic of other Sunbelt cities, such as Phoenix and Houston, where poor people are priced out of prime neighborhoods and live far from services and jobs (Byrd and Rhee 2004).[76] In 2001, unions collaborated with environmental and social justice groups to advocate for "smart growth with equity" while providing high-wage jobs and affordable housing in Coyote Valley, a vast redevelopment area in southern San Jose. The Coyote Valley redevelopment plan laid out an urban reserve development program that would provide twenty-five thousand affordable housing units and two public health clinics (Auerhahn and Brownstein 2004a). Working Partnerships USA went on to hold a permanent seat on the Coyote Valley Specific Plan Task Force, which proposed recommendations to city council on the area's long-term development plans in April 2008 (City of San Jose 2008). Other WPUSA victories include the creation of San Jose's living wage ordinance, a campaign to regulate the installation of "big box" stores, efforts to make public transit in San Jose more affordable, and several green jobs initiatives. In the words of Byrd and Rhee (2004, 131), Working Partnerships' "aggressive political program" has kept "politicians responsive to the needs of workers."

Working Partnerships and the SBLC have also been at the forefront of every local effort to advance the rights of undocumented workers in San Jose over the last decade. Together the central labor council and the immigrant rights community in San Jose have endorsed the passage of the California Dream Act (Senate Bill 1301), as well as passage of the national Dream Act, while also denouncing draconian immigration laws such as Arizona's SB 1070 and ongoing ICE operations throughout the country. In 2004, Working Partnerships published a report on the economic effects of immigration that debunked several of the myths associated with immigrant labor and assessed the fiscal impacts of immigrants in the county and state (Auerhahn and Brownstein 2004b). In 2007, the SBLC issued its "Principles on Comprehensive Immigration Reform," which opposed the expansion of any guest-worker program and encouraged binational cooperation with sending countries and the strengthening of state and national labor laws (SBLC 2007).

On the immigration front, the most prominent and active immigrant rights organization in San Jose has been the Services, Immigrant Rights and Education Network. SIREN's history in Silicon Valley dates back to the organizing drive that followed the passage of the Immigration Reform and Control Act in 1986. In addition to SIREN's invaluable immigrant hotline and the technical assistance to naturalization applicants, the group has been at the head of every immigrant rights march the city has seen in the last twenty-five years. For example, SIREN has been a critical leader in support of the Dream Act and against the introduction of Secure Communities. It has also worked closely with the Silicon Valley Alliance for Immigration Reform, which was a coalition formed in 2008 whose "membership consists of leadership from labor, non-profits, faith-based groups, educational systems, agencies, grassroot groups and individuals from the community that are passionate advocates for human rights" (SVAIR 2012).

Many of the organizers I spoke to affirmed that SIREN's primary strength is policy advocacy to advance reforms that improve the lives of immigrants. It does so by monitoring and evaluating policies at all levels of government, providing updates and advocacy training to community leaders, and using its well-honed communication networks to rally support around pending legislation (SIREN 2012a). As a member of the California Immigrant Policy Center (formerly known as the California Immigrant Welfare Collaborative), SIREN works alongside three other immigrant rights advocates in California: the Coalition for Humane Immigrant Rights of Los Angeles, the National Immigration Law Center, and the Asian Pacific American Legal Center. Through the California Immigrant Welfare Policy Center, SIREN "works to restore and preserve health and social services programs in addition to addressing barriers faced by immigrant communities in accessing services, including citizenship assistance" (CIPC 2010).

In addition to the efforts of the SBLC and SIREN in San Jose, a number of other lawyers and industry watchdogs quietly lobby for policies to improve the lives of immigrant workers. Immigrant rights per se have remained an ever-present policy concern, though a mostly latent campaign focus. According to one of the founders of the Santa Clara Center for Occupational Safety and Health (SCCOSH) and Silicon Valley Toxics Coalition (SVTC), "Immigration status was never brought up as an issue," even though these organizations lobbied on behalf of a workforce composed of mostly immigrant women.[77] Similarly, while many of its training efforts are directed specifically at immigrant workers, the central focus of WorkSafe!—an occupation health and safety advocacy group—is vulnerable workers, broadly defined to include a number of categories, according to a former director. She explains, "You're an immigrant working, English is not your first language, you're a young person, you're a woman, or you're working in an industry where there's no union. Any of those things means you're more vulnerable than somebody who isn't."[78] Groups like SVTC and WorkSafe! which initially emerged out of the same effort, see their work as officially distinct from that of immigrant rights groups such as SIREN. Yet their efforts inevitably intersect.

One of the clearest intersections of immigrant and worker rights policy advocacy in San Jose was the environmental justice movement that emerged in the peak years of the electronics industry in Silicon Valley. Pellow and Park (2003) trace the creation of SCCOSH, which was formed in 1978 as an outgrowth of a national effort to implement the 1970 Occupational Safety and Health Act. Since then, twenty-nine Committees on Occupational Safety and Health (COSH) "committed to promoting worker health and safety through training, education, and advocacy" have sprung up across the nation (NCOSH 2009). When SCCOSH was originally created, one of its main outreach efforts was the largely female Vietnamese, Filipina, and Latina workforce in the "electronics corridor" centered in San Jose, Palo Alto, and the surrounding suburbs of Sunnyvale, Santa Clara, and Mountain View (Matthews 2003). Workers filled both the vast electronic assembly plants and "flexible" home-based businesses making circuit boards, cables, and other electronics components at piece-rate pay (Chun 2001). According to Pellow and Park, these workers "labored sometimes twenty-four hours straight at poverty wages with no benefits, and the ever-looming possibility of dismissal," for which they were sometimes "paid as little as a penny for each component produced" (2003, 158). Women who worked in the ironically labeled "clean rooms" at companies such as IBM were also developing a wide range of illnesses. SCCOSH's Project on Health and Safety in Electronics (PHASE) operated a hotline to field questions about chemical hazards and referred residents and workers to local medical and legal resources, and it also started a support group called Injured Workers United and launched the Working Women's Leadership Project (Hawes and Pellow 2006; Pellow and Matthews 2006).[79]

From the beginning, however, SCCOSH, whose founding members were a core group of dedicated lawyers, gravitated toward policy advocacy. The first of their successful campaigns instituted a ban on toxic chemicals that wreaked havoc on workers' reproductive health. Together, both SBLC and SCCOSH lobbied the state legislature for better regulation (SCCOSH and SBLC 2000). SCCOSH also worked diligently to push OSHA, which one worker advocate described as "always so far behind the curve,"[80] to eliminate a long list of hazardous chemicals from the electronics industry. This posed a challenge for SCCOSH leaders. Unlike with most industrial injuries, company liability for illnesses resulting from chemical exposure is exponentially harder to prove. Despite previous successes with asbestos lawsuits, the effects of other chemicals were little known even to the scientific community, and lacking major epidemiological studies, causation is notoriously difficult to establish. The legal process for environmental injury and illness claims is also very expensive, privileging high-profile class-action lawsuits.

A recurrent target of the group was the heavy-hitting Semiconductor Industry Association, which had significant support from local officials and had successfully influenced state policies in its favor. Local municipalities saw the electronics industry, despite the many documented hazards facing workers and residents in its shadow, as an important "cash cow," which in turn made it immune to political pressure.[81] In response, SCCOSH partnered with the Silicon Valley Toxics Coalition, which emerged in 1982 to pressure government agencies to address the residential hazards of the electronics industry. The SVTC director explains the strategy the advocates took:

> Governmental agencies tend to make a major distinction between the jurisdictions of environment and labor. Local governments have responsibilities to their entire residency, not just labor. . . . As a worker, your only recourse is to go through Cal/OSHA, but as a resident you have many other options, including local environmental and public health agencies. So to the extent that [we] could link a company's practices to the health of the surrounding community, [we] can be more successful in addressing the issue.[82]

By creatively allocating various industries to their respective agencies, SVTC was able to pressure agencies outside the typical labor standards enforcement apparatus, such as the Santa Clara Valley Water District and the California Environmental Protection Agency, to effectively improve conditions for workers in the industry. The group was ultimately successful in passing several local laws, which served as model ordinances for other cities and counties (Byster and Smith 2006). These include the nation's first community "right-to-know" law via the Toxic Release Inventory (a hazardous materials model ordinance) and the Toxic Gas Model Ordinance. In 1990, Silicon Valley Toxics also created the Campaign for Responsible Technology, whose goal was to raise public awareness of the impact of the electronics industry. It later collaborated with similar organizations to launch the Electronic Industry Good Neighbor Campaign, "a community-based, multi-racial, collaborative effort to strengthen the work of local organization in high-tech communities" (Byster and Smith 2006, 115). Together, through these efforts, SVTC and SCCOSH eventually also created the International Campaign for Responsible Technology, which has gone on to become a "globally relevant clearinghouse and resource center of technical advice, organizing strategies, and information" (Byster and Smith 2006, 118).

Over the last decade, electronic assembly has followed the familiar pattern of globalization, lured abroad by cheaper labor and weaker environmental and labor standards (Smith, Sonnenfeld, and Pellow 2006). In response, SVTC has continued to advocate for environmental justice in the San Jose region while also adopting a global focus on workplace health and safety in China, where much of the electronics assembly industry has moved. The coalition now partners with international groups such as Power in Asians Organizing, a project of the Asian Pacific Environmental Network, to hold companies accountable (SVTC 2009). Other organizations that were also once active in advocating for worker health and safety in the electronics industry, such as Asian Immigrant Women's Advocates, now work on other regional industries, such as garment assembly, which is concentrated primarily in nearby Oakland's immigrant-dense Chinatown (Lashuay et al. 2002).

In 2004, SCCOSH officially ended its formal work.[83] One of the group's founders, a dynamic and dedicated lawyer in San Jose, now advocates via WorkSafe!, which serves as California's official Committee on Safety and Health. A registered nonprofit that operated without paid staff for twenty-five years, WorkSafe! emerged out of the Bay Area Committee on Safety and Health, a key supporter of efforts to reinstate the Cal/OSHA program after it was dismantled in the 1990s by then-governor George Deukmejian.[84] Today, the group is supported by several paid staff and the assistance of affiliated volunteer lawyers who advocate for laws that protect the health and safety laws of workers, and for effective remedies for injured workers. Their primary work is focused on holding government accountable to enforcement goals, engaging in impact litigation, and providing training and support to other legal advocates "who serve low wage and immigrant workers."[85] They have also participated in campaigns "in coalition with other unions, workers, community, environmental and legal organizations, and scientists to eliminate hazards and toxic chemicals from the workplace" (WorkSafe! 2012).

Like direct service providers and organizers, then, policy advocates in San Jose have carved out a precise division of labor that relies on the specialized leadership of various experts. Unions, nonprofits, and legal teams collaborate through coalition building where their interests overlap but mostly rely on one another to refine their lobbying targets.

Strange Bedfellows: Leveraging Big Business and Faith in Houston

While unions, nonprofits, and lawyers wield significant political capital in San Jose, the same is not true in Houston, which has neither the institutional density nor the political culture to support a specialized approach to promoting legislative change via unions and immigrant rights groups. Union leaders and immigrant rights organizers, while equally dedicated, have relatively fewer resources to lobby and lack access to the same networks of influence. What has emerged, therefore, in this politically conservative climate is a peculiar coalition of unions, immigrant rights advocates, and business elites driven by a Catholic social justice ethic.

Several institutions in San Jose and Houston actively advocate for immigrant worker rights, albeit through different channels. The Houston Initiative on Worker Safety (HIWS), for example, is the only Committee on Safety and Health (COSH) group in the state of Texas—and one of only three in the South (NCOSH 2009). As such, HIWS plays a role significantly different from that of its COSH counterpart in San Jose. While SCCOSH has focused overwhelmingly on high-profile lawsuits and legislative lobbying, HIWS mostly provides direct services to immigrant and other low-wage workers. In 2003, HIWS received training from the Labor Education Program of the University of Arkansas and the Committee on Safety and Health unit in Arkansas to gain formal recognition as a COSH group. Its main collaborators have included the Harris County AFL-CIO, a social justice program of the Dominican Sisters of Houston, and the Mayor's Office of Immigrant and Refugee Affairs.[86] While the parallel COSH group in Silicon Valley (SCCOSH and now WorkSafe!) was formed nearly two decades ago and today focuses almost exclusively on policy advocacy, Houston COSH was not formalized until 2003 and engages largely in direct service. Its outreach efforts include "Know Your Rights for a Safe Workplace" seminars and referrals through the Justice and Equality in the Workplace Program. Compared with WorkSafe! the Houston COSH operates in a much more isolated context, with few allies that can help facilitate regional or state-based lobbying efforts.

Consequently, efforts to advocate for labor-oriented policy reforms in Houston have fallen largely to the Harris County AFL-CIO, which, like the South Bay Labor Council, has a long tradition of policy advocacy. Lacking the link between research and organizing that Working Partnerships USA provides the SBLC, the Harris County AFL-CIO has nonetheless spearheaded many efforts, including living wage campaigns, corporate subsidy accountability reforms, and smart growth measures. However, a divided member base presents challenges to conducting union-led policy advocacy in Houston. Major ideological division between the building trades and service sector unions persist, particularly on the issue of immigrant worker rights, while internal union squabbles mean that the consensus needed for policy advocacy remains elusive.[87]

Nonetheless, the Harris County AFL-CIO does indeed lobby for immigrant worker rights. It has done so primarily through local advisory boards like the Mayor's Advisory Committee on Immigrant and Refugee Affairs (MACIRA), which also includes several prominent immigrant advocacy groups and community organizations. For example, both The Metropolitan Organization (TMO) and the (now restructured) Association of Community Organizations for Reform Now (ACORN), which have been key supporters of the Justice for Janitors campaign and the Justice Bus, have also worked with the Harris County AFL-CIO to lobby the city for housing reform and corporate responsibility policies. In the past, ACORN also mobilized families to lobby both in Houston and in Washington on issues related to immigrant rights. This was not without its challenges, as one ACORN leader explained to me: "Since [immigration] is a very controversial topic, even though we have [some political power], we can really only get support from our politicians in small groups, and not always publicly. . . . We just know that politics is politics and they [politicians] also have to keep in mind what might cost them their office."[88] Even before an election-timed right-wing campaign cast a national shadow over ACORN, the Houston chapter faced a decidedly hostile climate at both the local and state level.[89] Today, the Texas Organizing Project, which was formed as an independent organization by former ACORN leaders, continues to organize with low-income and minority communities in Houston, and has been very active in recent campaigns in support of immigrant worker rights.

In recent years, the central labor council has also pushed back against punitive local policies that would endanger the security of immigrant workers. Here, the line between organizing and lobbying becomes hard to distinguish. When the Ellis Resolution was being hotly debated, for example, key MACIRA member organizations, including the Harris County AFL-CIO and CRECEN, gathered resident testimony to present to the city council. The resolution, which aimed at eliminating the Mayor's Office of Immigrant and Refugee Affairs and eradicating the city's "sanctuary" label, was met with equally vocal support from nativist groups in the city. More recently, the central labor council and MACIRA have pushed for improvements in relations between police and immigrant communities and has lobbied against the proposed 287(g) program and the national Secure Communities rollout. While several states are actively pushing to limit the program, Texas is poised to expand Secure Communities' reach (Buch 2011).

Though organized labor and nonprofits have a strong legacy in Houston, perhaps the most effective immigration reform efforts emerging from Houston in recent years hail from the business community. Though it is traditionally right of center, some moderate countercurrents flow in Houston's business community. Longtime construction magnate and Catholic philanthropist Stan Marek, for example, has done an impressive job of rallying his colleagues around the economic rationale for federal action on undocumented immigration and has even argued for the importance of such action for building power in the Republican Party. A descendent of Czechoslovakian immigrants, Marek comes to the immigrant rights movement with a dual commitment to "good business sense" and Catholic social justice. He and his colleagues have launched a state initiative called Texans for a Sensible Immigration Policy (TX-SIP 2009), as well as a savvy federal campaign launched through the Greater Houston Partnership called Americans for Immigration Reform (AIR 2009).

Marek explains the organizations' approach to the conundrum illegal immigration poses in the United States:

> What we've been advocating all along is *not* deportation. That won't work. You can't round up 12 to 20 million people. You've got three and half million American-born kids with undocumented parents, probably more than that. That's not going to work. And you can't give them all amnesty like '86. The public would have your head. You [just] can't create that many voters. So you need to find that middle ground. And what we are advocating is first of all, let's ID who's here. Let's find out who's in our country, and let's get them in a taxpaying role . . . and of course, securing the border. We have to secure the border. We have to know who's coming and going. We have to stop the flow of drugs, and the flow of weapons out. . . . We gotta talk about the economic realities, the way people are being exploited, human trafficking, all these things that are a result of a broken immigration system.[90]

Supporters of Texans for a Sensible Immigration Policy and Americans for Immigration Reform are skeptical of initiatives that place the onus of enforcement on employers through programs such as E-Verify and the notorious no-match letters. TX-SIP supported the Kennedy-McCain bill in 2007, the most recent attempt to advance comprehensive immigration reform in Congress, which was never allowed to go to a full vote. In hopes of resurrecting the issue, the group has strategically chosen to continue working with Senator John Cornyn, rather than his more extreme colleagues in Congress. The Greater Houston Partnership—the major chamber of commerce in Houston—even met with then–Department of Homeland Security director Michael Chertoff. TX-SIP and AIR also lobby alongside immigration advocacy groups inside the beltway, such as Immigration Works and the National Immigration Forum. Their goal, according to Marek, is to "to bring business, faith, advocacy groups all together to form a huge lobby."[91]

The group has nonetheless been able to rally significant support, enough even to commission a 2007 analysis of the contribution of immigrant workers to the Texas economy (Pipes and Rodriguez 2007). In 2009, the Greater Houston Partnership sponsored an immigration forum that brought to town high-profile speakers such as Geraldo Rivera, who spoke out against the increase in ICE enforcement (Carroll 2009a). In conjunction with other Republican supporters, a campaign was launched in cyberspace via

TexasGOPvote.com to counter the extreme views of constituents supporting zero population growth and the "hate media," as Marek referred to it, of Lou Dobbs and other conservative commentators: "We're having these little battles all over this website in cyberspace. We've got a thousand Twitter followers. We've got two thousand Facebook followers. And all of a sudden we are a major force in the Republican Party when it comes to the primary vote."[92] By 2011, with the prospects for movement toward immigration reform in Congress, the group turned its energies toward support efforts to combat wage theft and the misclassification of independent contractors on the grounds of unfair business practices through the group Construction Citizen (Construction Citizen 2011), and toward a proposal for state-level immigration reform (TX-SIP 2011).

While Marek admits he does not agree with union and immigrant rights advocates on everything, he has continued to foster a close relationship with them. Why? For Marek and his colleagues, it's an issue rooted in both social justice and good business sense. As he explained, this is not a matter of lobbying politicians but of organizing supporters on and across the fence. This collective effort is also necessary, he argues, to counter the apathy of most other business groups, as well as the blatant racism of more extreme groups: "The trade associations aren't getting it done. . . . They're all lobbyists. This is a grassroots issue. It has to be solved with the grassroots organizations. And that's where the opposition has been so effective in getting the faxes and the e-mails out. You know, when you hate something, when you're a Ku Klux Klan member or John Birch Society or a hate group, you're a lot more active."[93]

Many more conservative leaders are also driven by a commitment to social justice. In addition to his work with business leaders, Marek has built a close relationship on the issue of immigration reform with the Archdiocese of Galveston-Houston and the Catholic Worker movement. He is a regular donor to Casa Juan Diego and Catholic Charities, two organizations that provide direct services to immigrants in poverty. Americans for Immigration Reform has also become a supporter of the Houston Coalition for Immigration Reform, which brings together current and former elected officials, immigrant rights groups, and many faith-based organizations and social service agencies in Houston.[94]

Over time, the Harris County AFL-CIO and CRECEN decided to collaborate with business leaders dedicated to reinvigorating progress toward

immigration reform. A CRECEN leader acknowledged the tension between the attraction of the resources the business community have on the
one hand and the differences of philosophy that threaten to make collaboration impossible on the other. Referring to the business community's support of guest worker programs, which CRECEN does not support, one
longtime organizer recounted a recent meeting she attended: "I could have
stood up and blasted them any time I wanted to, but I've been refraining
myself because, even though we don't like their plan, they are targeting
congressional districts around the country and putting a lot of publicity to
get the iffy congressmen to vote, so in a way they're still creating a sort of
pro-immigrant sentiment, and they have a lot of resources."

In the meantime, this support is a welcome diversion from the broader
apathy in the business community. The Harris County AFL-CIO's
secretary-treasurer reflects on his struggle reaching out to the business
community directly in the past:

> When the Immigrant Workers Freedom Ride came around, I thought:
> "Well that's a great chance for them [employers]!" . . . So I wrote all the big
> employers in this town explaining how this is going to help, "You're em-
> ploying all these people, if they become legal, you won't have to worry any-
> more. . . ." I didn't get one single dime from them! So the employers . . . are
> content to exploit the workers and are content with the status quo.[95]

The different goals, social networks, and tactics of these grassroots
leaders and the business lobby are evident. In a context in which access to
power and influence is closely guarded, however, most any collaboration is
full of promise. "We're not sure at what point we'll really have to say, 'You
go your way. We'll go ours,'" explained one immigrant rights leader, but in
the meantime they continue to try to work together.[96] As of 2012, however,
these three powerful sources of leadership in Houston—organized labor,
the immigrant rights community, and the business community—continue
to collaborate in innovative and sometimes surprising ways on issues ranging from wage theft to the proposals for immigration reform in Texas.[97]

Overall, in contrast to the broad policy campaigns led by organized
labor and employment attorneys in San Jose, policy advocacy in Houston has focused on countering imminent threats to the safety and security of immigrant workers. To this end, Houston's most effective voice for

immigration reform has been a coalition of moderate business actors and Catholic leaders who delicately negotiate the politics of legislators on both sides of the aisle with the reluctant support of organized labor and immigrant rights groups. Each party knows it needs the other to achieve its goal, be that to establish legitimacy with their opponents, to gather the resources to beat them, or both.

Specializing versus Diversifying: The Division of Labor for Defending Immigrant Worker Rights in San Jose and Houston

Throughout this chapter, I have painted two portraits of how civil society groups are supporting immigrant worker rights. San Jose and Houston inhabit very different political fields, which have shaped the strategies that each set of actors has adopted. In San Jose, well-resourced and influential labor and immigrant rights groups focus on organizing and policy advocacy, while accessible state agencies and legal advocates provide direct services for undocumented workers. Within this context, worker centers tend to specialize in "lawyering" in order to shepherd workers through the process of filing a claim with the relevant state agency. Meanwhile, the central labor council has focused its efforts on launching successful organizing campaigns and advancing local policy agendas. A regional consortium of legal advocates has also pushed to improve industry standards for workers and compel state agencies to provide better oversight. A separate set of immigrant advocacy organizations and their allies, in turn, works toward comprehensive immigration reform. Key participants in these efforts include a coalition of interfaith leaders, elected officials, and union leaders. Through a system of referral and outreach, these groups are able to concentrate on their goals while also providing solidarity when needed.

In Houston, by contrast, a hostile political culture for labor and immigrants has led civil society groups to wear many hats and come together in order to gain political power. Through a strategy of diversification, groups in Houston have tried to surmount their opponents by drawing on a menu of options to advance undocumented worker rights. In a city where undocumented workers have limited access to legal counsel and approach federal agencies with apprehension, civil society groups partner to refer aggrieved workers to the appropriate agencies and collaborate directly with those agencies to facilitate a holistic response to workers' needs. The central labor council and affiliated worker centers fill multiple roles in order to both coordinate direct service to workers and support worker organizing. As civil society groups in Houston dedicate the majority of their energy to these grassroots goals, fewer resources are available for policy reform. Through a fusion of business interests and a vision of faith-based social justice, this role has been filled by a well-resourced coalition of political moderates focused on advancing state and federal efforts at immigration reform. In the case of Houston, then, collaboration has taken some interesting turns that at times require negotiation and compromise.

This chapter's comparison of San Jose and Houston suggests that the strategies and tactics civil society groups adopt across different contexts become relevant as a means to attaining goals dictated by the logics and opportunity structures in which they exist. In the chapter that follows, I move beyond local governments and civil society to introduce a lesser-known actor in the process of advocating for the rights of undocumented workers in the United States: the Mexican consulate. Drawing on the cases of San Jose and Houston, as well as eight other cities, I demonstrate how the Mexican consulate adopts hybrid approaches similar to those of local government and community advocates, using outreach and advocacy in some places and going beyond this model to provide direct technical assistance and bureaucratic brokering in others. In this final case study, I also use the Mexican consulate as lens to assess the institutional dynamics of organizational mission, leadership preference, and resource capacity in the process of advocating for immigrant workers.

5

ADVOCATING ACROSS BORDERS

Consular Strategies for Protecting Mexican Immigrant Workers

In the last three chapters, I have examined the position and influence of myriad actors in the political field of enforcing immigrant worker rights. Chapter 2 examined the statutes that labor standards enforcement bureaucracies carry out and the role professional missions play in promoting a status-blind approach to protecting even undocumented workers. Then in chapter 3, I looked beyond federal and state governments to examine how local elected officials shape the political culture and institutional landscape for the implementation of these protections at the city and county level. Chapter 4 moved beyond the government apparatus to examine how civil society groups—including unions, nonprofits, faith-based groups, and even business associations—divide up the work of serving, organizing with, and advocating for immigrant worker rights. In this chapter, I add a fourth actor to the political field of immigrant worker rights: the Mexican consulate. Long known for advocating on behalf of its nationals living abroad on issues ranging from health to criminal justice, the consulate today is also active in helping Mexicans—who constitute the largest share of immigrant and undocumented workers—access their legal workplace protections.

Like the other actors I have discussed, however, the Mexican consulate has not carried out its mission identically in all the cities where it is located. Its approach is shaped by the needs of the particular communities where it operates, and it too has had to make tough choices about how to invest its political and economic capital. Given this scenario, in this chapter I present the Mexican consulate as an important actor in the process of enforcing immigrant worker rights, but also as a case study for examining the key factors that shape organizational strategies. After tracing the Mexican consulate's history of transnational advocacy in the United States, I discuss the role of the consulate in enforcing the rights of its nationals in San Jose and Houston. I then reflect on what the Mexican consulate's work in these two cities, as well as others I have examined, reveals about how an organization's regulatory context, the preferences of the organization's leadership, and an organization's resource constraints can shape how it engages in rights advocacy. I end by considering the advantages and liabilities of consular efforts to promote immigrant worker rights and the long-term viability of consular involvement.

Transnational Actors and Labor Rights: The Mexican Consulate

In an era of globalization, bureaucratic institutions and their intermediaries have come to play an increasingly important transnational role in enforcement of international standards.[1] This advocacy has found many outlets. For example, the human rights paradigm has been leveraged to advance the rights of children (Mundy and Murphy 2001), women (Sperling, Ferree, and Risman 2001), indigenous communities (Oliart 2008), and migrants (HRW 2005a, 2005b; Paoletti et al. 2006).[2] Less attention has been paid, however, to how "diasporic bureaucracies" collaborate in enforcing rights in host societies.[3] As the representative of the largest migrant group in the United States, and given its institutional reach and Mexico's strong binational relationship with the United States, the Mexican consulate is arguably the most relevant of these overseas institutions. The Mexican consulate has become crucial to implementing the rights provided to immigrant communities in recent decades, especially to those who are undocumented (Laglagaron 2010).

The mission of the Mexican consulate, handed down by the Mexican secretary of the exterior, is to address the needs of Mexican nationals abroad. González Gutiérrez (1993) articulates an important paradox of consular behavior in the United States: "Why should the Mexican government, with so few resources and so many domestic problems, feel obligated to address the concerns of a Mexican population that has decided to leave the country and settle permanently in the United States?" The answer lies in the Mexican government's "vested interest in maintaining and improving its relations with the Mexican diaspora," which it must balance against the constraints of U.S. law. González Gutiérrez explains: "Most consular protection is done silently, both because it serves a community of first-generation Mexicans with little clout in the political system, and also because there is a conscious attempt on the part of the consulate to avoid any unnecessary publicity concerning its protection services. When dealing with local authorities, the trick is to be effective without appearing confrontational, since every hostile encounter jeopardizes the long-term relationship that the consulate needs to cultivate with immigration, police, and civil authorities" (227). Deploying its political influence and institutional resources judiciously while taking care not to step on the toes of its American host, the consulate can operate as an effective advocate and service provider for Mexican nationals in the United States.

The consulate's presence in the United States can be traced back to the period following the 1848 Treaty of Guadalupe Hidalgo, in which Mexico lost a vast territory to the United States. Thousands of Mexicans found themselves displaced. Balderrama (1982) documents the consulate's establishment and its growth in Los Angeles during the Depression and argues that a lack of detailed regulations gave consuls "wide latitude in implementing policy" (9). In traditional destinations for Mexican migrants, consular advocacy efforts ranged from intervening during deportation-repatriation campaigns to providing resources and support for charitable organizations and even to leading the legal battle against school segregation. The Mexican consulate has also been influential in nontraditional migrant destinations, such as the rural South during the early part of the twentieth century, where, Weise (2008) argues, the consulate represented "the only formal structure for collective activity among Mexican immigrants" (760).

Today, there are fifty consular offices in the United States concentrated in major population centers for Mexican immigrants. These offices fall into three leadership categories: The *consulados generales* (consulates general) tend to have more political weight and are more likely to have available resources to provide services to their emigrants. The *consulados de carrera* (career consulates) are located at smaller field offices. The third group, *cónsules honorarios*, are not official diplomats but do offer services to Mexican nationals, though their functions and access are more limited (SRE 2012). In addition, the mobile consulate program rotates to outlying areas that have less access to offices in central cities.

The consulate plays complex and varied roles for Mexican immigrants in the United States, more than half of whom are estimated to be undocumented (Batalova 2008). One of the most high-profile campaigns that the Mexican consulate promotes is Bienvenido Paisano (Welcome Countrymen), which coordinates with various Mexican government agencies to provide migrants traveling to and from Mexico with information during their journey. The program coordinates with the National Institute of Migration to manage return migration during heavy travel periods (such as during Holy Week and the Christmas holiday), regulate goods that are transported, and promote safe travel routes. The program's familiar *Guía Paisano* (Guide for Countrymen, an eighty-page travel guide) is ubiquitous in consular offices. In 2005, the Mexican Foreign Ministry received substantial attention (including denouncements from anti-immigrant activists) for publishing the *Guía del Migrante Mexicano* (Guide for the Mexican Migrant) (Gómez 2005). This comic-book-style pamphlet detailed various survival tips and cautionary tales for would-be undocumented migrants in an effort to prevent border deaths and to warn migrants of unscrupulous *coyotes*, or *polleros* (human smugglers). Once migrants have settled, the Mexican government actively promotes the financial investment that many of them make in their country of origin and has challenged the usurious transaction rates that are often charged to remitters (IME 2012c, 2012d). The consulate has also been an instrumental resource for those who wish to be posthumously repatriated to Mexico (Félix 2011).

Perhaps the most high-profile service the Mexican consulate has provided in recent years is the provision of millions of *matrículas consulares*. Typically required to attain basic services from the consulate or to vote abroad, these consular ID cards have become supremely important in domestic affairs as well. Following the implementation of the federal REAL ID program, almost all states have stopped issuing driver's licenses to undocumented individuals (Johnson 2004). Yet driver's licenses are not simply necessary to legally drive: they are the form of identification Americans rely on for all sorts of official business, from signing a mortgage to filing a claim with a government agency. Since most of the undocumented lack access to government-issued identification in the United States—with the very small exception of those who live in the few areas where municipal ID cards are available to all residents regardless of immigration status (de Graauw 2009; IME 2012f)—the *matrícula consular* has become a crucial tool for immigrant incorporation and rights enforcement. In some states, migrants who are unable to provide official government-issued identification have been caught in dragnets of detention and eventual deportation following routine car stops (Armenta 2012). Businesses such as Wells Fargo Bank have also capitalized on this new resource by accepting *matrículas* as legitimate identification to open accounts. Massive campaigns have been launched to lure the market share that the roughly twelve million undocumented immigrants in the United States represent (Dávila 2001). As of November 2005, approximately four million cards had been issued to Mexicans in the United States, and they were accepted by 178 financial institutions, 1,204 police departments, 293 cities, and 168 counties (Varsanyi 2007).

Another well-known area of consular outreach area is health advocacy via the Ventanilla de Salud (health window) program (IME 2009g; Ventanilla de Salud 2010). The target population for the program is the largely uninsured Mexican immigrant population, as well as those who have access to medical benefits but are reluctant to use them due to their immigration status. This program conducts health education outreach for Mexican immigrants via public service announcements and community events. Its objective is to distribute information about resources for accessing routine health care (through networks of community-based service providers), as well as to provide material on particular health issues, such as breast cancer prevention, promoting child vaccination, and occupational health. These efforts culminate every year in the Binational Health Week, a massive outreach effort concentrated in California and coordinated between community-based organizations, universities, public foundations, and various local, state, and federal agencies (Semana Binacional de Salud 2005).

Consular offices also often network with various representatives of Mexican immigrant civil society, including the *clubes de oriundos*, or hometown associations. Though these groups tend to be diffuse and informal, research has shown that they are growing and are often incredibly well resourced and organized, even if only a small percent of migrants actively participate in them (Orozco and Rouse 2007; Waldinger, Popkin, and Magana 2008; IME 2012b). Their activities range from coordinating cultural festivals to organizing fund-raising drives to support infrastructure building projects in their communities of origin. Many do so with the assistance of the Mexican government's Tres Por Uno (Three for One) and Dos Por Uno (Two for One) federal and state funds-matching programs, which the Mexican consulate helps facilitate. The consulate also frequently gets involved in cultural and recreational events in the communities where it operates, such as promoting soccer tournaments, in an effort to develop social capital in immigrant communities (IME 2012a). It is then able to leverage these networks to disseminate information about its resources and services. In addition to providing mundane services, such as issuing birth certificates, conducting marriages, and facilitating the repatriation of the deceased, consular offices also promote educational initiatives for both children and adults (Laglagaron 2010), and many local offices hold weekly *charlas* (talks) on issues such as immigration, civil disputes, criminal law, and, increasingly, workplace rights.[4]

To be sure, relations between the Mexican immigrant community and the consulate have not always been positive, and the consulate has had to fight to counter its well-entrenched reputation of corruption and racism. In the revolutionary period, consular offices provided key information on the activities of exiled opposition leaders and were complicit during the period of repatriation (González Gutiérrez 1993, 227). The consuls have also drawn protests from Mexican nationals for corrupt church-state relations, as well as for failing to support the goals of organized labor (Balderrama 1982; Gonzalez 1999). These tensions continued throughout the century and followed the consulate's expansion across the United States. Pitti (2002) describes the trouble in Silicon Valley during the early chapters of union organizing, where "in the name of Mexican patriotism, the Mexican consul openly discouraged some Northern and Southern Californians from joining the CIO [the dissident union, the Committee for Industrial Organization], and officials rarely if ever intervened on local Mexicans' behalf in complaints about living or working conditions" (119). Years later, union organizers picketed the consulates to protest the "sale of cattle at ten dollars per head" (145), referring to the $10 the Mexican government received for each contracted bracero it sent to the United States.

Even today, the Mexican consulate in the United States has a reputation for being a behemoth of red tape—and in some cases corruption (Corchado 2009). In response to a recent article praising the outreach activities of the Chicago office, one community member remarked lividly about the poor service he received from the consulate and indicated his preference for the help of other nonprofit community organizations to that of the "parasitic" consulate (Staff 2009). In my conversations with outreach staff, many echoed the difficulty they faced in shifting the reputation the consulate had earned over the years and combating the persistent classist and racist organizational culture in many offices. One consul anonymously explained that Mexican migrants who visit consular offices "to get their documentation and papers in order" are often "turned off by how they are treated by many staff that are whiter and richer than they are." As a result, they have little to no desire to linger in the office longer than they have to, even if their extended stay would mean getting access to one of the many outreach programs available.

Although many Mexican immigrants are often skeptical of the character and efficacy of the Mexican immigrant bureaucracy back home, the consulate nonetheless remains one of the few allies undocumented immigrants have in many U.S. communities (Fitzgerald 2008). Especially for immigrant workers who have experienced a workplace violation and lack the protection of a union, the Mexican consulate has evolved into an important broker for accessing what would be an otherwise inaccessible set of rights. In the context of the consulate's long tradition of advocacy, its recent foray into labor standards enforcement stands out, for it entails not only implementing directives from the Mexican government but also helping aggrieved workers access their rights under U.S. law. In this role, foreign consulates act as hybrid institutions. They have the relative legitimacy of nonprofit community organizations, but they also have the resources (staff, funding, and stability) of a typical government institution.

Efforts to assist workers fall naturally under the consulate's Área de Protección (Department of Consular Protection), a consular program that provides legal assistance to nationals residing abroad. This legal counsel is meant to help immigrants with family law, criminal law, and in some instances even immigration law. The program serves Mexican nationals generally through three routes. In the first, the consulate simply refers clients to the appropriate outside resource, whether that be an agency with which the immigrant should file a claim or a lawyer who is willing to take the case. In these instances, as one consul explained, "They don't need us."[5] In the second route, the consulate may connect a client to an attorney who works directly with the consulate on a pro bono basis. Third, if a case is complicated enough to necessitate legal counsel, and a pro bono attorney is unavailable, the consulate may choose to provide assistance under the Programa de Asesoria Legal Externo (Program for Legal Counsel in the Exterior). Under this program, a consul may refer a client to a lawyer who has contracted directly with the consulate on a prepaid basis. These attorneys provide assistance mostly with more-complex cases that cannot be addressed under the first model; the category tends to include high-profile cases, such as those that address human rights or involve women or children.

In recent years, the Área de Protección has increasingly addressed workplace rights. This initiative began informally in cities across the United States and was formalized in April 2002 when the U.S. secretary of labor, Elaine L. Chao, and Mexican secretary of labor and social welfare Carlos Abascal Carranza signed an agreement reaffirming "their commitment to the effective enforcement of labor laws by their respective labor departments" (DOL 2002c). As part of this symbolic accord, the secretaries formed a Binational Occupational Safety and Health Working Group, and several Mexican state agencies agreed to undertake outreach efforts to inform members of the public about their workplace rights under both U.S. and Mexican law.[6] In addition, the U.S. Department of Labor agreed to develop informational materials addressing the workplace rights of migrant workers and to train consular staff on federal and state laws concerning workplace rights. Examples of efforts already under way in Los Angeles and Houston were hailed as models when a joint declaration was signed on June 11, 2002 (DOL 2002a). The declaration eventually led to a formal 2004 binational accord not only to reach out to and educate workers about their rights, but also to collaborate in the actual claims process. The express purpose of partnership was "to improve compliance with and awareness of workplace laws and regulations protecting Mexican workers in the United States" (DOL 2004b). The dedication to cooperation between the two governments has maintained momentum through changes in administrations, as evidenced by a May 2010 meeting between Mexican ambassador Arturo Sarukhan and President Obama's newly appointed secretary of labor, Hilda Solis, to reaffirm the joint declaration on labor rights (Embajada de México en Estados Unidos 2010).[7]

A 2004 memorandum from the Mexican Foreign Ministry's Institute of Mexicans in the Exterior codified the consular relationship with U.S. labor agencies. It states: "The U.S. Department of Labor, local governments and community organizations, with the collaboration of Mexican consulates in Houston, Dallas, and Colorado, launched the 'Justice and Equality in the Workplace Partnership.' These initiatives are aimed at informing migrant workers about their rights and responsibilities, as well as offering mechanisms for those who do not speak English to report labor violations of laws administered by the Occupational Safety and Health Administration, the Wage and Hour Division, and the Office of Federal Contract Compliance of the U.S. Department of Labor. During 2004, considerations for launching similar initiatives in other regions of the United States are taking place" (SRE 2004). The accord standardized piecemeal alliances that had emerged in some cities such as Houston, and it allowed both the Wage and Hour Division and the Occupational Safety and Health Administration to formalize their collaborative relationships with the Mexican consulate. This led to many collaborations in cities from Seattle to Kansas City, where OSHA, for example, regularly participates in joint radio and television appearances with the consulate to promote worker health and safety (OSHA 2007b, 2008a).

In 2009, the collaboration led to the first annual Semana de Derechos Laborales (Labor Rights Week). During Labor Day week, consular offices helped to coordinate a packed outreach agenda in Atlanta, Chicago, Dallas, Fresno, Los Angeles, New York, Phoenix, Sacramento, Salt Lake City, San Diego, San Jose, San Francisco, and Washington. Though approaches varied from office to office, the general purpose was largely the same: to raise awareness about rights and resources available to workers. Labor standards enforcement agencies and other labor advocates were invited to distribute resources and speak to individuals while they waited for their consular transactions to be completed. Local ethnic media outlets promoted the week's events widely. During my visit to the consular office in San Jose during the Semana de Derechos Laborales, I stopped by several tables staffed by representatives from unions, labor standards enforcement agencies, community organizations, and local law firms that were scattered throughout the office waiting room. I also listened in a packed room to a representative of the California Department of Occupational Safety and Health describe the system of filing a complaint with the agency. Next followed an organizer for the Building Trades Council, who rallied the audience to exercise their rights. He spoke about their understandable fear and the complicated system of rights in this country. He then ended with a rallying cry of "¿A que venimos, a trabajar? ¡OK, pues no se dejen a la pobreza!" (What do we come for, to work? OK! so don't let yourself be taken advantage of!). The session ended with a speech by the head of the Department of Consular Protection, who repeated emphatically that each of the labor rights that had been discussed was available regardless of immigration status. In 2011, the third annual event had the theme "Woman in the Workplace" and involved nearly every Mexican consulate office in the nation, as well as their counterparts at the consulates of El Salvador, Guatemala, Nicaragua, Honduras, Dominican Republic, and Costa Rica (Consulado General de México en San José 2009).

National Vision, Local Innovation

Within the context of the binational agreement to collaborate on worker rights, local innovation has emerged as local offices respond to the particular needs of their communities. In Denver, for example, OSHA worked with the Mexican consulate in partnership with other community-based organizations to bring "hard-to-reach Mexican workers" the necessary information and help to prevent violations of their rights (OSHA 2004b). This alliance has also partnered with the Department of Labor's Wage and Hour Division and the EEOC to focus on protecting workers in the construction, migrant agriculture, and meat and poultry processing sectors. In other places, including Utah, Iowa, and Nebraska, health and safety alliances with the consulate also include the participation of state agencies (OSHA 2003c, 2007a, 2008b, 2009a), which sometimes even cooperate across state lines, as is the case between Tennessee OSHA and the Mexican consulate in Atlanta (OSHA 2003c).

Depending on the lead agency in each city and the occupational makeup of the immigrant workforce, certain industries may be emphasized over others in these consular partnerships. The OSHA–Mexican Consulate Alliance in Atlanta targets Latino construction workers and collaborates with the Health and Environmental Division at Georgia Tech University to develop worker education programs. Construction workers are also the intended audience in Albuquerque (OSHA 2003d), Austin (OSHA 2005c), Dallas (Delaney 2002), Houston (OSHA 2006), San Antonio (OSHA 2005b), and New York (OSHA 2005a).[8] In San Francisco and San Jose, by contrast, the local Mexican consulate partners with the EEOC on a broad campaign to combat the sexual harassment of Latina agricultural workers all over Northern California.[9] The Department of Labor's Wage and Hour Division in Los Angeles has also fought an aggressive battle against minimum wage and overtime violations, particularly in cleaning services and the garment industry (DOL 2004a, 2007a). And though he believes this to be a phenomenon unique to his office, a consul in Las Vegas recounted the huge outreach efforts he and his staff have deployed to serve the mostly undocumented Latino men who distribute publicity for unscrupulous escort services.[10]

Not only do the collaborations the Mexican consulate forges with government and community partners vary, but the advocacy strategy a local consulate adopts may also diverge substantially. Services range from providing educational material from U.S. labor standards enforcement agencies to the community and offering referrals, to assisting claimants directly with the claims-making process. The consular offices in Houston, Atlanta, and Los Angeles, for example, have established help lines to process the complaints they receive from the community, in effect functioning as deputized information and assistance officers (DOL 2002a; OSHA 2007c). Following the launch of the 2009 Semana Laboral, Chicago even established its own Ventanilla Laboral (Education Window), with staff dedicated solely to processing labor claims (Consulado General de México en Chicago 2010).

What accounts for this wide variation? In the following sections, I compare the two distinct consular models in San Jose and Houston to highlight the way two local political fields have shaped the Mexican consulate's varied initiatives in promoting the labor rights of its emigrant workforce across the United States.

The San Jose Model: Advocacy via Outreach, Resources, and Referral

In San Jose, where the formal claims-making infrastructure has significant legitimacy and the norm is to refer even undocumented workers directly to the relevant labor standards enforcement agency or to an appropriate legal advocate, the aim of consular assistance is to empower workers with the knowledge necessary to access state bureaucracies and local legal resources. The consulate has played a mostly ancillary supportive role, and labor rights are incorporated as one of several program areas that the Área de Protección directs. The San Jose consul for this area says of the office's approach, "We are convinced that preventative protection is fundamental to prevent labor abuses."[11] Such consciousness-raising is no doubt an important element of any legal mobilization paradigm, and is foundational to an aggrieved worker's ability to name, blame, and eventually claim (Felstiner, Abel, and Sarat 1980).

The consulate coordinates its efforts in part with volunteers from local labor unions, who visit the office regularly to give worker-rights workshops. In conjunction with union representatives, the consulate also sponsored the development of a pamphlet containing information about workplace protections, union contacts, and a list of local resources for filing workplace claims. The pamphlet reads, "IMMIGRANT WORKER RIGHTS! In the United States, many immigrants suffer workplace abuses because they don't know their rights and don't know where to seek help. LEARN THEM AND EXERCISE THEM TO LIVE A BETTER LIFE!"[12] It highlights important protections such as the right to form a union, to receive minimum wage, and to not be discriminated against, and it lists three state agencies as resources to file claims. The pamphlet also provides contact information for major unions, including SEIU, UNITE HERE, UFCW, and the various building trades. In addition to this informational brochure, the Mexican consulate, in conjunction with the Santa Clara and San Benito Counties Building Trades Council, funded a small workweek calendar that workers can use to keep track of their hours worked and record other vital information that is necessary for filing a claim. This material is distributed at weekly *charlas* given in the lobby of the consular office where union representatives address a captive audience of individuals waiting to process their requests for government documents.

Given the close working relationship between the consulate and labor unions, the consulate has had to be careful to maintain its neutral position, particularly on the topic of labor organizing. The consul emphatically explained: "Of course we don't refer them [to the union] or tell them to go. We think that labor freedom should be respected. Since we are a consulate that is part of the Mexican government, we have to be neutral, and we only inform them of the possibilities at their disposal." Instead of advocating for unions, the consulate concentrates on what it calls "preventative efforts." The consul explains that this outreach is "not a spontaneous response to the demand of workers" but rather "one additional option we have" to serve the needs of their nationals. It is seen as a natural outgrowth of the consulate's existing legal advocacy program: "Prior to this collaboration [with unions], we always provided legal counsel to people. . . . Now our approach is simply more public."[13] Only a select few cases become direct beneficiaries of the consulate's "corrective" efforts, which provide hands-on legal services through the legal assistance program. From the consul's perspective, educating the Mexican immigrants in the United States about their rights and the various resources at their disposal is the main goal.[14]

While the consulate must maintain its neutral diplomatic position, it simultaneously acts as a watchdog to ensure that migrant rights are respected. The consul explains: "Immigration authorities here in San Jose have been quite clear on what their role is and what jurisdictional problems can arise. Consequently, we are confident about [the immigration authorities'] purpose, and in what capacity they can act."[15] Like the legal advocates discussed in chapter 4, consular staff look to the formal labor standards enforcement bureaucracy as a reasonable avenue for claims-making and the best solution for workers who request assistance.[16] As such, the Mexican consulate's Department of Consular Protection in San Jose has invested substantially in educating workers, with the assistance of key union volunteers, and in referring workers to legal advocates who can help them navigate the claims-making process. They also regularly invite labor standards enforcement agencies to conduct on-site outreach. On a recent visit, for example, representatives from the California Division of Workers' Compensation, the Division of Labor Standards Enforcement, and Cal/OSHA were all present in the lobby and available to speak with community members. If the consulate chooses to assist with a case, the process is fairly simple: It begins when the Mexican citizen first meets with a staff member in civil legal affairs, who then listens to the worker's complaint and takes down information on an intake form. Based on this information, the consul may refer the individual directly to the relevant agency or to a local law clinic.

The consulate in San Jose will, however, make a point of following up with workers it has referred. The office maintain contacts with labor standards enforcement agency staff whom consular staff can contact for follow-up assistance, ensuring that claimants are able to access the appropriate compensation. They may also help identify concerns the worker may have that are unrelated to the specific workplace grievance, as one consular staff member explains:

> A case that starts out as a labor issue could have other larger, or even additional simple, problems. Maybe a person reaches a favorable result. The boss pays them, gives them the required compensation. But then maybe the individual is unable to cash that check because they don't have identification. In that case, the consulate can provide a form of support, such as issuing a passport or *matrícula consular*. But maybe that person doesn't even have the documents to get [one]. . . . Well, in such a situation, we can check in with the appropriate offices in Mexico to have them send us their documentation, and in the end issue them [one], and see how we can help them from there.

In other, more complicated cases, if the consul deems a simple referral to the relevant government agency inadequate, or the case involves a more complicated issue that the local workers' rights clinic cannot handle, the consulate may refer the claimant to JURIMEX, a consular service that operates a toll-free hotline serving individuals seeking legal counsel. The Mexican consulate in San Jose participates in the Northern California JURIMEX program, which is also supported by consular offices in San Francisco and Sacramento. The head of the Department of Consular Protection in San Jose explained the utility of the program: "Think about a hotline administered by a [U.S.] authority. It's not likely that a *paisano* will have the trust to dial . . . they are more likely to use a hotline run by the Mexican consulate. Therefore, we saw there was a need, and that is why we created the program."[17] Depending on the claim, the migrant may be referred directly to the Department of Consular Protection, which works with consulting attorneys who visit clients at the office on a weekly basis for counseling in a range of legal arenas, including civil, administrative, human rights, and labor law. For indigent claimants with complicated claims, the Legal Assistance Program may also have funds to provide direct legal representation, though this is the exception rather than the rule for workers' rights claims in San Jose.

The role of the Mexican consulate in San Jose, then, can broadly be described as an ancillary one that capitalizes on the existing labor standards enforcement bureaucracy. Legal advocacy for workplace claims is integrated into existing programs and referred out to specialized legal advocates when necessary. Representatives from labor standards enforcement agencies are invited to do outreach in the lobby on a regular basis. Well-established lines of communication with organized labor, low-cost legal clinics, and state offices in particular allow the consulate to provide personal connections between aggrieved workers and what is otherwise an intimidating and complex bureaucracy. In this sense, the San Jose consulate sees itself as only one of many nodes of support in the specialized field of immigrant worker rights.

This advocacy model stands in stark contrast to the consular approach adopted in Houston, where the decidedly more hostile political culture for workers and immigrants, as well as a woefully undeveloped state administrative process and lack of affordable legal counsel, has made the Mexican consulate's advocacy role more multifaceted.

The Houston Model: Beyond Advocate to Transnational Bureaucrat

In the decidedly more worker-hostile context of Houston, the need for alternative claims-making channels has become more urgent, and the Mexican consulate has emerged as a key partner in providing them. The Houston consulate was an early signatory to the Justice and Equality in the Workplace Program, taking a distinctively proactive role compared with consulates in other cities. The most obvious manifestation of this advocacy is the consulate's investment in the JEWP hotline. Initially located at the Mayor's Office of Immigrant and Refugee Affairs, the JEWP hotline's staffing and maintenance was eventually transferred to the Mexican consulate. Flyers advertising the hotline were distributed, and a large billboard was installed over the consular office advertising its services.

In addition to sharing the responsibility of running the hotline with MOIRA, the Mexican consulate in Houston has also established relationships with federal agencies in JEWP (most notably the EEOC and the DOL's Wage and Hour Division) that allow workers to file claims directly through the consulate. Consular staff in Houston are trained to take and process claims, which are then cross-filed with all relevant signatories in

JEWP.[18] The Houston consul explained the model: "The worker program is one of the most promising that we have undertaken, because it combines various elements and is a coalition between various agencies. . . . Since this program was signed, the agencies get together once a month and discuss the programs and the common interest we all have of promoting justice and employment at the workplace. . . . The consulate serves like an intake point for claims, and then the Department of Labor, etc., are able to work together [to process them]."[19]

By running and staffing a workers' rights hotline, the consular office in Houston functions as more than simply an advocate: it is a transnational bureaucrat that fills an acute need in a bureaucratic vacuum of worker rights enforcement. Unlike community organizations, which have distinct missions and often face significant resource constraints, the consulate has the administrative capacity to undertake broader endeavors, is motivated by its commitment to serving and protecting its nationals living abroad, and is held accountable by its binational accord with the United States. Consular offices in other cities have assumed similarly engaged roles (OSHA 2003b; DOL 2006; OSHA 2009a), but arguably none to the extent that Houston has over as long a period.

According to the consul in Houston, "What is novel about this hotline [compared with other offices] is the central role that the Mexican consulate plays. In this jurisdiction, the hotline is maintained and administered by the Mexican consulate. Calls arrive here, this is the number that we put on our flyers, and here we have control of all the calls we received, and are able to explain to callers what they need to do."[20] Not all calls the consulate receives are for workplace claims. The consul estimates that close to half of the individuals who call the hotline are seeking broader assistance with consular documentation or other services. Furthermore, not all workplace claimants the consulate serves are undocumented, though the consul I spoke to estimates that most are. When the hotline receives an actual workplace claim, consular staff proceed in some ways similarly to the protocol their colleagues in San Jose follow. They assess the case, provide general information about the legal protections the person is entitled to, and may set up a time for the worker to visit the office.[21] However, the direct ties that have been established between the consulate and federal bureaucracies in particular, and the extent of the consulate's involvement in the claims process after this initial assessment, are what make the approach in Houston distinctive.

In order for claimants to receive administrative or legal assistance from the Mexican consulate, they must be Mexican nationals. Yet many of the callers that use the JEWP hotline are not Mexican. Nonetheless, the Mexican consulate acts as an entry valve for many other Latino workers seeking assistance: "We explain what they have to do, tell them what paperwork is necessary, and what agency would pertain to their case . . . just as we would with a citizen of any other country that participates in the [JEWP] alliance."[22] In fact, many of the other workers who utilize the hotline are Central American immigrants, and they often choose to work directly with MOIRA instead. The head of MOIRA, Benito Juárez, is a Guatemalan immigrant and longtime leader in the Central American community in Houston. He and his staff have been authorized to directly process claims, as does the Mexican consulate. Both agencies have also developed a follow-up system with the Department of Labor (which receives the vast majority of referrals) to help track the progress of claims.

Some claims involving a legitimate workplace concern are not eligible for a referral to the Department of Labor. This is often the case for individuals working for small employers. In cases such as these, the consulate may refer the worker directly to a local agency, such as the police department or small claims court, for assistance. In some cases, further referral may not even be necessary after some direct intervention. The consul gave a recent example:

> Say a person comes who is owed $600. . . . They come here, and I get in touch with the person who owes him. I'll tell him "Hey so-and-so person, look, Ramon is here with me, and says you owe him $600. Well, I just want to know what's up. . . . So we'd like to come up with a settlement . . . find out why you owe him this money." Then they might respond, "No, no, no, I'm sorry. I'm not sure what happened. Tell him to call me, and I'll get him the money." . . . So in that case, a referral wasn't even necessary. . . . For a lot of people, a call from the consulate carries a certain amount of weight. In reality we're nothing, this is out of our jurisdiction . . . but it does help . . . and the worker then understands that we are a place that can protect him, and where he can ask for assistance.[23]

Prior to the formal creation of JEWP, there were no formal structures in place that facilitated claims processing at the Mexican consulate in Houston. The consular office at that time was characterized by "*muchas ganas y poca estructura*" (lots of passion and little structure), according to a representative I spoke to. With training, consular staff are now able to more precisely identify whether claims are legitimate and to refer claimants to relevant resources. They have also learned to educate workers about the broader network of advocates in the community. The consul said: "I see the consular program as being in the center, with the other agencies surrounding us. . . . It doesn't necessarily mean that the problems we might encounter with a case will always require another agency to intervene. But, if the consulate can't solve a case, they can refer it out. Or, and this has sometimes happened, if a case [at another agency] requires some official document, we can also intervene. . . . So we all have a particular synergy."[24]

Similar to the Department of Consular Protection in San Jose, the program in Houston also works with a broad network of lawyers to provide counsel to workers unable or unwilling to go through the normal administrative channels. In a city where policies favor business interests, where worker-friendly employment lawyers are few and far between, and where pro bono counsel of any sort is severely lacking, this consular resource is particularly significant. When asked to identify other legal resources in the community, the consul identified several legal clinics at local universities, but he also lamented that most do not take employment cases. This lack of legal representation is particularly problematic for workers with grievances that do not admit alternatives to going to court, such as stalled workers' compensation cases.[25] The relatively few lawyers in Houston willing to take such cases do so largely based on the merit of the case and the eventual damages they may be able to collect. The relatively weak labor laws can also affect cases involving wage and hour violations. "It can cost more to go to court [than the final penalty is worth]," explained the Houston consul. "This has created a space where companies habitually abuse workers and are not sanctioned by the law." Relying on a private network of attorneys, the Mexican consulate in Houston has even supported several class-action suits.

While the approach of the Mexican consulate in Houston is, in the consul's own words, "no panacea" for the broader structural problems facing the workers it serves, the office provides a unique and integrated approach to the problem of workplace violations facing immigrant and undocumented workers in Houston. Its work with JEWP has been hailed as an exemplary model for implementing the landmark agreement reached in 2004 between the United States and Mexico (DOL 2004b). Yet rather than characterize the consulate's approach in Houston as exemplary and that of the San Jose office as lacking, I would argue that in fact each office has adopted a strategic response to the political, economic, and bureaucratic reality in the city in which it operates. The following section explores some of the key factors shaping consular approaches in each city and draws on the example of other consular offices to highlight which factors shape how consulates choose to advocate for immigrant worker rights.

Key Factors Shaping Consular Strategies

Based on the approaches the Mexican consulates in San Jose and Houston have adopted, three main factors emerge as key elements shaping the strategy a consular office may undertake to advocate for the workplace rights of its emigrants: the regulatory context, the preferences of consular leaders, and basic resource constraints. In some regards, the Mexican consulate is a hybrid institution: it possesses the legitimacy and resources of a government agency, as well as the dedication to protecting Mexican immigrants and the access to do so, yet often there are wide gaps between the goal that is formally decreed and the particular steps the staff take to fulfill that mandate. In the case of worker rights, no consular office is required at present to adopt any particular outreach model. Though the 2004 binational accord facilitates bureaucratic cooperation with federal agencies, whether and how an office has chosen to respond depends substantially on what role the consulate plays in the enforcement process vis-à-vis other agencies. While the binational accord paves the way for potential cooperation between the Mexican consulate and the Department of Labor, how developed this relationship becomes at the local level also depends on how federal protections shape up against state and local ones.

Other factors that influence consular behavior include the particular preferences of consular leaders, who turn over regularly, and the ties staff are able to forge with partner agencies. While bringing in new leadership regularly may mitigate corruption and complacency, it also stymies the creation of deep relationships with not only government agencies but also local partners that have extensive knowledge of and access to the community. Furthermore, the economic and political capital available to a consulate will also shape its priorities. Large consular offices with extensive staff have the luxury of expanding their programming more than do their smaller counterparts.

In this section I draw on the examples of the Mexican consulate in San Jose—where the consulate operates minimally in a specialized political field of worker rights—and that of Houston, where a diversified political field has made room for more expansive and hands-on involvement. I pair these findings with evidence from other cities where the Mexican consulate is active, as well as the activity of other-country consulates in San Jose and Houston. Together I use these examples as a way to understand what drives consular behavior, and in doing so I provide some insight into the importance of the regulatory context, leadership preferences, and resource constraints the other organizational types heretofore discussed likely also face.

Regulatory Context

As the previous chapters have demonstrated, San Jose and Houston represent two distinct political fields for immigrant worker rights. San Jose represents what Ray (1999) refers to as a "pluralist" field that encompasses a variety of immigrant worker advocates who nonetheless inhabit a homogenous political culture that promotes a singular solution for addressing the claims of aggrieved immigrant workers. In this well-coordinated but crowded field of advocates, claimants are encouraged to seek out legal counsel in order to file a claim with the formal state labor standards enforcement apparatus. Within this context, the Mexican consulate in San Jose has opted to invest resources in funneling claimants into the formal state system through an active outreach program and engaged referral process that nonetheless stops short of directly processing claims.

In contrast, the Mexican consulate in Houston operates in what Ray (1999) describes as a "fragmented" political field. Here, a robust coalition of immigrant worker advocates also exists. However, in contrast to the singular and specialized approach promoted in San Jose, Houston advocates instead inhabit a heterogeneous political culture that encourages a wider variety of solutions. As such, a more diversified approach to claims-making has distributed the leadership for enforcing immigrant worker rights across several stakeholders in the Justice and Equality in the Workplace Program. With Texas agencies relatively absent from Houston, federal agencies are overburdened and face significant barriers to gaining the trust of undocumented workers, particularly in the city. Within this context, the Mexican consulate has taken a lead role alongside several federal agencies, the Mayor's Office of Immigrant and Refugee Affairs, and the Harris County AFL-CIO.

In both San Jose and Houston, the Mexican consulate, like the other actors discussed in chapters 2 through 4, has had to assess how much room it has to maneuver and innovate in the political field of immigrant worker rights. Offices in both cities have incorporated worker rights into their community outreach agenda, but each has also chosen to do so according to the solutions that make sense in their city. The head of the Department of Consular Protection in San Jose explains:

> We have some programs that are institutionalized, and handed down from [the secretary of] Foreign Affairs, and these are carried out in all consular offices. . . . And then each consulate also has their specific programs as well. Ours focuses on worker rights, and we work with the unions. It all depends on what is going on in the city where you are located. . . . In this part of California, we have more ways to serve the Latino population than [consulates in] other states do.[26]

The Mexican consulate in Houston, conversely, relies on a broader patchwork of solutions to addressing workplace violations, which are coordinated through JEWP. With state agencies mostly absent from this partnership and city resources for immigrants embattled by constant public opposition, the Mexican consulate in Houston fills a pressing demand for institutional support.

Beyond San Jose and Houston, the example of other cities highlights other potential configurations of outreach. The Mexican consulate in Denver, for example, has had to negotiate not only the state policy context and the local politics of sixty-four counties in Colorado but also an expansive consular jurisdiction that includes Utah, Idaho, Montana, Nebraska, North and South Dakota, and Wyoming.[27] In 2003 the Mexican consulate in Denver signed an agreement with the state of Colorado, as well as the Department of Labor, the Equal Employment Opportunity Commission, and the Occupational Safety and Health Administration (OSHA 2003a). As a part of this agreement, these state and federal agencies exchanged information with the consulate, provided training, and gave regular out-reach talks at the consular office. In exchange, the consulate agreed to refer cases to the appropriate agencies but stopped short of directly processing them as Houston does. This local accord was renewed after two years, but in 2008 the challenges of bringing four large bureaucracies together proved too complex, and the struggle over details derailed the renewal of the partnership. The consul of political affairs explained: "It was very complicated. It took a lot of time [to negotiate], and in the end we decided not to waste any more time, and that it would be better to continue collaborating on issues that didn't imply any big compromise for either party. So in 2008 we decided to just sign individual agreements with each agency."[28] The consulate continues to work with the Colorado Department of Labor and Employment, which enforces a minimum wage that is nominally higher than the federal one,[29] but coordinates more directly with federal agencies.

As the examples of these cities have shown, the regulatory partner a consulate chooses to work with is shaped not only by the regulations in place at each level but also by the scope of the jurisdiction in which the consulate operates. In the case of San Jose, direct relationships with state agencies make sense given the more comprehensive protections and agency presence provided by the State of California. In Houston, weak state protections and an absent Texas bureaucracy promote working with the federal government. Denver represents a third model, wherein slightly better state protections cannot counterbalance the size of the jurisdiction, which encompasses seven other states that have wage protections little better (or no better) than those of the federal government (DOL 2011a).

Leadership Preferences and Tenure

In addition to providing guidance amid the regulatory context of workplace rights, the priorities a consul sets can also shape which relationships he chooses to nurture with enforcement agencies and how. Both the consul general and the consul for the Department of Consular Protection have significant discretion in this regard. Only a small fraction of consular offices in the United States have chosen the path Houston pioneered of direct involvement. For those consulates that have, the passions of the respective consul general were paramount. For example, Enrique Buj Flores, who was the Mexican consul general of Houston for less than a year from July 2001 to May 2002, became a forceful proponent of the Mexican consulate's involvement with JEWP. The EEOC deputy district director remembers:

> He was a very dynamic personality. . . . He's a career diplomat, and he knew how to work the crowd. . . . I mean he was unbelievable . . . [and] exceptionally supportive in everything we [JEWP] did. We used to do joint interviews together . . . and we would do radio talk shows. Now if you don't call that outreach I don't know what is. At the inaugural event for JEWP we had about eighteen *television* stations there. . . . So, the involvement of the first consul general [with JEWP] was unbelievable. He had a lot of heart and wanted to make it happen and make a difference.[30]

The departure of Buj Flores, as well as the subsequent shuffling of his staff, led to a significant weakening of consular involvement in JEWP, according to other stakeholders. The problem became, from the EEOC director's perspective, how to get his new consular colleagues "enthusiastic about something they have no ownership in." What followed was decreased enthusiasm from consular representatives at monthly JEWP meetings and less outreach to Spanish media. Such priority shifts can create challenges not only for propelling new initiatives but also for maintaining relationships with outside agencies. The tension became evident at one JEWP meeting when a stakeholder invited a major news station to a partnership meeting in an effort to renew outreach to the community. Though he had done this freely and regularly when the previous consul was in place, this time, rather than welcome the attention, consular staff "politely advised" the proactive member that JEWP was *a collaboration* and that he did not have the authority to invite the media without prior approval from the consul general's office.

The sustained work of the head of protection and legal affairs at the Mexican consulate in San Jose has conversely proven vital. During his tenure, he has spent several years cultivating relationships with union leaders who provide weekly outreach at the consulate.[31] Because of this consul's relatively long-lasting tenure, he has also developed outreach paradigms for the mobile consulate program, which serves agricultural communities

in the consulate's outlying jurisdiction. Along with his colleague in the Department of Press Affairs, he has been able to develop community education campaigns in partnership with local media outlets. The consulate has
even attained free reserved space on the network Telemundo one Monday
each month.

On the flip side, the short tenure of most consular staff can present challenges for sustaining the relationships and the resource base fostered by
previous administrations. The recently appointed head of political and
legal affairs in San Francisco, for example, contrasted his office's approach
to that in Houston, where he also spent time: "Our model is more diffuse,
and we rely mostly on personal relationships." The consulate's liaison at the
San Francisco Workers' Compensation office, for example, is an information and assistance officer (one of only three Spanish-speaking officers in
all of Northern California) who conducts outreach via the consulate for the
state agency's monthly injured worker workshops geared toward Spanish-
speaking claimants. Yet other agency connections established by previous
consuls had been lost. When I spoke to the consul in spring 2009, the relationships with the EEOC and the California Division of Labor Standards
Enforcement had stagnated, and the consul had no active contact with the
San Francisco Office of Labor Standards Enforcement, which enforces the
substantially higher minimum wage for San Francisco. With only seven
months behind him, however, the consul vowed to continue to improve
these connections.[32] On my visit to Houston in January 2012, several advocates confirmed that the Justice and Equality in the Workplace Program
had once again become a core focus for the Mexican consulate. The head
of Hispanic Outreach for OSHA in Houston, also the current chairman
of JEWP, reiterated that his role was simply to facilitate the partnership,
while "everything else is driven by the consulate."[33]

Certain consuls, however, may simply arrive with particular passions.
After serving as consul in Los Angeles, director of community affairs for
the Mexican Ministry of Foreign Affairs in Mexico City, director of Latino
affairs at the Mexican Embassy in Washington, D.C., and most recently
as director of the newly formed Institute of Mexicans Abroad, the Sacramento consul general spoke to me enthusiastically about his passion for
prisoner advocacy. Most recently, this has included lobbying the California Department of Corrections and Rehabilitation to change its rules to
allow undocumented immigrants to visit their loved ones in prison (Smiley

2010). Worker rights, though important to him, have simply not been as pressing.[34]

Consuls also attempt to transfer their successes from previous posts to new ones. In New York City, for example, consul general Rubén Beltrán (previously consul general of Los Angeles) has taken the lessons of his hugely successful worker rights program, EMPLEO, to start a similar program in the tri-state area. EMPLEO, which along with JEWP is heralded as a model consular worker rights program, also maintains a toll-free hotline. It coordinates with both federal and state agencies, as well as Mexican consulates in San Bernardino, Oxnard, and Santa Ana, and the consulates of five Latin American countries. The largest immigrant rights organization in Southern California, the Coalition for Humane Immigrant Rights of Los Angeles, is also involved. Now that he is in New York, Beltrán's vision is to create a "one-stop shop" in the form of a dedicated *ventanilla* (consular station) to receive and process claims, which would augment the weekly outreach presentations the DOL already provides. He also looks forward to replicating the close relationship he had with the mayor's office in Los Angeles with Mayor Michael Bloomberg of New York City and integrating worker rights outreach into both the mobile consulate and his newly created "consulate on wheels" program.[35]

Priorities and time matter for how any organization articulates and deploys its mission. As an extension of a foreign government, the Mexican consulate is already further removed from the local community, making the experience and relationships of its staff all the more important for the creation of viable outreach. This is particularly important for surpassing the generalized fear consuls often have of overstepping diplomatic protocol and being labeled "interventionist." The particular rhythm of foreign service makes long tenures uncommon, and consuls—not unlike nonprofit leaders—often come and go before they can institutionalize relationships with outside agencies. Yet as the examples of the several consuls profiled here reflect, the circulation of consular staff may also promote a diffusion of innovation.

Relationship and Resource Constraints

Finally, in addition to the regulatory context and leadership preferences, a consulate's role in the process of enforcing worker rights is also shaped by basic resource constraints. These resources are a reflection of both the size of the population the consulate represents and the share this population constitutes of the broader population. Due to the sheer number of Mexican immigrants in the United States and the geographic and political history the two countries share, no other country has had as significant a diplomatic presence in this country. The Mexican consulate therefore represents a "best-case scenario" in terms of its institutional capacity to help the Mexican diaspora realize its rights under U.S. law. In metropolitan areas like the San Francisco Bay Area and Southern California, some Mexican consular offices are even able to pool resources to deploy regional programs.

Yet, clearly, not all Latino immigrants are Mexican. Though Mexicans constitute the majority of undocumented immigrants in the United States (59 percent), as well as 30 percent of all foreign-born residents, another 22 percent of undocumented immigrants hail from other Latin American countries (Terrazas and Batalova 2009). As such, the Mexican consulate is by no means the only relevant diasporic bureaucracy for Latino immigrants. The second- and third-largest sources of undocumented migration, respectively, are El Salvador and Guatemala (U.S. Census Bureau 2010), and immigrants from these two nations have a significant presence in many traditional gateway cities. Nationally, Salvadorans constitute only 3.9 percent of all immigrants (4.9 percent of the undocumented), yet more than half of Salvadoran immigrants in the United States reside in California and Texas. A full quarter of Salvadoran immigrants live in the Los Angeles metropolitan area, and over 8 percent of immigrants in the Houston metropolitan area are Salvadoran (Terrazas 2010). Reflecting this demographic concentration, the Consulate of El Salvador has sixteen offices across the nation, three of them in California (Los Angeles, San Francisco, and Santa Ana) and two in Texas (Dallas and Houston). Similarly, Guatemalans constitute 2 percent of all immigrants and 3.7 percent of all those who are undocumented, yet over a third of Guatemalans reside in California (PHC 2009). Two of the eight Guatemalan consulates are in California (San Francisco and Los Angeles), with a third located in Houston.

It should not be surprising, therefore, that the consulates of Colombia, El Salvador, Honduras, and Guatemala are all formal signatories to the Justice and Equality in the Workplace Program in Houston. Yet due to their small institutional capacities, they play a relatively smaller role. In other places, coalitions aimed at promoting worker rights have evolved further:

the Guatemalan consulate has a relationship with OSHA in New York and New Jersey (OSHA 2005e, 2005f), for example, and OSHA works with the Salvadoran consulate on Long Island (OSHA 2005d). In Chicago, the Department of Labor has reached out to a wide array of consular offices, including those of Mexico, Brazil, Colombia, Costa Rica, Ecuador, El Salvador, Guatemala, Honduras, Peru, and Uruguay (OSHA 2009b). The Southern California alliance in Los Angeles, EMPLEO, works with the consulates of Mexico, El Salvador, Guatemala, Honduras, Nicaragua, and Costa Rica (DOL 2005), producing many high-profile victories for Latino workers. Yet lacking the same level of resources, these other consulates play a decidedly smaller role, which, as one JEWP member explained, is "mostly symbolic." The Mexican consul I spoke to in Denver recounted a similar dynamic in his city:

> It's because of the size of our community. The services we are able to offer are completely distinct from what other [consulates] have the capacity to offer. Here [in Denver] we have six consulates [Peru, Guatemala, Mexico, Japan, Canada, and the United Kingdom]. Of those six, the Mexican consulate is obviously the biggest, and we have thirty employees. . . . The next largest is Canada, with like twenty employees or less, and Peru and Guatemala have maybe six or seven each. So, they simply aren't in a position to offer the same services we are. So I don't really know if they have attempted to garner agreements on worker rights like we have.[36]

As a result, the Mexican consulate is often called upon to respond to the general needs of the Latino community and account for that population's actions in the public sphere. The head of legal and political affairs in Houston recounted how this unfolded following the recent shooting of an officer in his city: "Whenever something happens, it could involve a Colombian, a Salvadoran, etc. . . . Everything below Mexico is considered Mexico. They see everything as Mexico, so when they see our Mexican flag flying off the side of the freeway, right next to a billboard advertising our hotline . . . they contact us [to complain]."[37]

The specific relationship between some diasporas and their country of origin also influences consular actions and can determine how prominent a role consulates may play in enforcing the rights of their diasporas. In Houston, for example, the EEOC, which spearheaded the JEWP coalition, tried to launch a similar program for the sizable Asian American population. The Information Group for Asian American Rights works with key Vietnamese and Chinese advocacy organizations and focuses on challenges facing the diverse Asian workforce (DOL 2003). Yet the troubled relationship between China and Vietnam and their respective emigrant populations has made building a parallel relationship with these consulates impossible. Instead, civic groups play the major liaison role with their respective communities. As a result, labor standards enforcement agencies have found it much harder to cater to the "Asian" workforce as a whole due to its relatively more diverse cultural and linguistic repertoire. Questions such as what language to produce outreach material in, and where to hold outreach events, prove more troubling than the question of which consulate to involve.[38]

Consular action is shaped by the regulatory context in which consulates operate, the preferences and tenure of consular leadership, and the relationship between foreign governments and their emigrants and the basic resources at their disposal. Consular involvement in advocating for the workplace rights of their nationals living abroad has taken the form of dozens of different initiatives, collaborations, and programs. In the following section, I evaluate the benefits that this advocacy presents for both the consular offices involved and the communities they aim to help. In doing so, I consider the long-term viability of consular involvement in this arena.

Benefits and Long-Term Viability of Consular Involvement

There is no doubt that consulates are an important bureaucratic intermediary between their diaspora and often-overburdened enforcement bureaucracies. Other community-based organizations have long filled a similar brokering role, but consulates have unique linguistic and cultural access to the communities they serve. Undocumented immigrants in particular often view their consulate as a preferred ally over U.S. government institutions. "Each agency attracts their own audience," explained the consul in Houston. "For example, if the U.S. Department of Labor holds a community meeting, no one will attend. [The community] sees the INS [now the CIS] as government and synonymous with all other government agencies. But if the Mexican consulate brokers the deal and hosts the event, there will be a better turnout."[39]

In addition to providing an effective channel to contact an otherwise hard-to-reach population, the Mexican consulate possesses key qualities that even the best-intentioned U.S. agencies often lack. The San Jose consul explains: "There are two types of barriers [we see]: one is language, and the other is cultural. In terms of language, it is not just a matter of whether the person speaks Spanish but whether they speak Spanish with the particularities of Mexico, or that maybe someone who learned Spanish in school, or from another country, may not understand."[40] As migrant-sending regions shift to include more indigenous areas, there is an increasing need for agencies to include linguistic diversity beyond Spanish. In collaboration with community organizations, Mexican consulates across the country coordinate outreach to indigenous communities such as the Maya, Mixtec, Triqui, and Zapotec, who often have a multitude of unique needs beyond language barriers. While community-based organizations are well organized in these largely agricultural indigenous immigrant communities and have established impressive ties to the Mexican government in Mexico (Fox and Bada 2008), they too often lack access to U.S. bureaucracies and the institutional capacity to do sustained outreach on the issue of worker rights.

By working hand in hand with labor standards enforcement agencies, the consulate can also help legitimize the formal process of legal mobilization for an otherwise skeptical community of Mexican immigrants. At a 2004 DOL meeting on health and safety in the construction industry, a top OSHA administrator was questioned by a union leader regarding the agency's efforts to communicate with the Latino immigrant community. The union leader pressed the official to clarify whether OSHA's functions were indeed distinct and separate from those of immigration authorities. In his defense, the administrator cited the alliance OSHA has with the foreign ministry of Mexico and its fifty consular offices in the United States:

> The thinking here is that if you're a Mexican worker in the United States and you're not sure who to talk to, or [wonder if] I can trust these people . . . there may be a reason why they may not trust some people. But they'll trust the consulate, because it is the only connection they have. Through this agreement with the consulates, we'll get information to them so they can communicate to that worker, and maybe even help them make the call, or make the referral, or fill out a complaint, or whatever the issue might be . . . so they can be our go-between, they can be our broker, if you will, [especially] for the Mexican workers. (OSHA 2004a)

Clearly, the involvement of consular institutions is a boon to labor standards enforcement agencies.

Beyond helping their diasporas, consulates can also relieve some of the burden U.S. bureaucracies must bear. Prior to either referring a potential claimant to the relevant agency (as the San Jose consulate does) or starting a formal claim that will be cross-filed with the federal system (as the Houston consulate is equipped to do), consular staff will often conduct preliminary investigation work to evaluate the validity of a claim. Sometimes, a simple call from the consul is enough to resolve the process then and there. Consular involvement "can give more seriousness to the case," explained the San Jose consul. "It's not the same if an employer were to receive a demand from a worker who went to them alone, than if they show up with the support of their consulate."[41] A call from the Mexican consulate carries greater legitimacy than a similar call from a nonprofit, particularly when the call is made to a Spanish-speaking employer.

Last, the Mexican consulate's core mission to "protect and serve their emigrants living abroad" creates a unique set of institutional incentives to invest resources into worker rights outreach. While civic groups have a long legacy of this type of advocacy, community organizations can be short-lived and face substantial resource constraints.[42] Federal and state agencies committed to "serving all workers regardless of immigration status" are nonetheless also subject to the whims of policy change. For example, the EEOC director in Houston explained, "If tomorrow a new administration or Congress were to require that investigators check the documentation status of potential claimants, we would be obliged to do so."[43] Though consular posts are relatively short-lived (two to four years) and turnover makes coalition-building difficult to sustain, the core mission of the consulate will always remain the same.

Despite these advantages, there are a number of reasons to still be cautious about fully endorsing consular leadership in the process of enforcing immigrant worker rights. First, bilateral agreements have costs as well as benefits. For example, the formal 2004 accord signed by Elaine Chao and Luis Ernesto Derbez formalized many long-standing local collaborations and even effectively spurred new collaborations and legitimated existing ones. Yet the accord has also simultaneously—and perhaps unintentionally—narrowed the scope of the consulate's official arena of labor standards enforcement involvement. This has in turn complicated community partnerships in some cities, such as Houston.

As the excitement of the initial JEWP signing wore off, and once a new consul general arrived, tensions arose when the JEWP hotline's quality of service began to decline. Complaints rolled in about unstaffed phone lines and unreturned calls. Understandably, the consulate—which was never meant to be a labor standards enforcement agency or an employment rights center—had started to run up against its own limitations. In the face of these complaints, however, the consular office repeatedly insisted that, due to its unique authority under the formal accord with DOL, it alone had the right to run the hotline and field formal claims. Meanwhile, when in 2006 the new Houston Interfaith Worker Justice affiliate was established, the center offered to help staff the hotline. This led to tensions as the consulate insisted on maintaining sole responsibility for the hotline, citing its ultimate responsibility for this role under the 2004 accord.

It is unclear, moreover, what the ultimate impact of consular involvement will be on the development of robust domestic labor standards enforcement bureaucracies. Will consular offices continue to complement the functions of these agencies, or will they become replacements for the investments of resources, staffing, and cultural literacy that U.S. bureaucracies should be compelled to make? As the consul in Houston said, "If an agency changes leadership, or focus, and they want to concentrate on something else . . . they might choose to either become *more involved* . . . or [instead] suspend their involvement in the program."[44] Three years after I originally spoke to individuals in the JEWP collaboration, the tenacity of the consulate's involvement had waned, and many JEWP affiliates spoke with great skepticism about the consulate's role. One immigrant rights advocate whose organization is a JEWP signatory joked, "The Mexican consulate is the last place I would refer a worker today!" Overreliance on consular involvement can perhaps, then, be just as problematic as overreliance on a civic group.

Finally, the very features that have facilitated the Mexican consulate's relationship with the U.S. government may ultimately hinder its ability to advocate for Mexican immigrant worker rights in the way that other nongovernmental civic groups can. While consulates possess the stable infrastructure that many nonprofit organizations lack, and they have the unique strength of diplomatic influence, as diplomatic institutions they must also follow a strict "noninterventionist" policy. For this reason, they are limited in their ability to advocate for meaningful policy change in the host country; at best, they offer resources and influence to implement existing rights. The Mexican consulate in Houston has been able to leverage its influence to benefit Mexican immigrant workers, but its role proscribes other specific forms of outreach that community organizations such as worker centers are able to provide. While the consulate in San Jose works with the only designated day labor center in the city to do outreach, it cannot do the same at the many more informal corners across the city due to concerns over "propriety." "We don't go there, because that is not the appropriate venue or climate to do outreach," the San Jose consul explained.[45]

It follows, therefore, that the worst-case scenarios of employer intimidation that can spur the involvement of immigration authorities are difficult cases for consular offices to assist with. In massive raids in which hundreds of suspected undocumented workers are arrested, the consulate's ability to display indignation in the court of public opinion is tightly bound. The San Jose consul explained:

> If there were to be a raid, we can't, obviously, stop it. Nevertheless, we would monitor that the rights established under the law are followed for the people who have been taken by immigration authorities, and that are facing deportation proceedings . . . [but] the consulate is not going to interfere in the deportation, or stop it, or accelerate it either. We are simply going to monitor that the legal steps provided under the same law are followed for our co-national that is being deported.[46]

The Mexican consulate is a hybrid institution with unique qualities that allow it to reach out to its ever-growing diaspora. Unlike U.S. agencies, it is relatively isolated from domestic politics and is not beholden to the same political pressures that circumscribe the action of federal agencies charged with protecting worker rights. Yet it is also a formal government institution with a diplomatic relationship that must be maintained, nurtured, and negotiated. As partnerships between U.S. enforcement agencies and consular offices proliferate across the nation—a development likely to be spurred by the appointment of Hilda Solis to head the Department of Labor—it remains to be seen what role the Mexican consulate can play and what impact it will have in helping Mexican workers in the United States realize their rights.

Conclusion

Making Rights Real for Immigrant Workers

This book has offered tools for understanding the process of enforcing rights. There is often a wide gap between formal protections and the experiences of rights holders, and as Tilly (1990) argues, in the absence of effective enforcement, rights cannot be said to exist. Despite the firewall between immigration enforcement and labor standards enforcement in the United States, the mere *possibility* of collaboration between agencies is enough to foil well-meaning attempts to protect immigrant workers. As I have shown, each member of a wide network of advocates in local government, civil society, and consular offices plays a role in bridging the gap. The strategies of these advocates, however, are influenced by the particular needs of the communities on whose behalf they operate, and by the strength of their opponents. Together, the political culture and distribution of power shapes how advocates navigate the political field of immigrant worker rights.

When compared with the national landscape, San Jose and Houston are two cities with a strong history of immigration, and both have in many ways successfully incorporated immigrants into the fabric of their city. Yet, as I have also shown, not all traditional immigrant destinations are created equal. While San Jose is no racial utopia, Houston, in comparison, is a place where anti-immigrant forces are well resourced and enjoy significant political support. In combination with relatively weak Texas labor protections and stronger business interests in Houston, this creates a very different set of priorities and strategies that advocates of immigrant workers must adopt. In San Jose—where unions have power, local officials are supportive of immigrants, and legal counsel is readily available—formal claims-making remains the primary strategy for addressing immigrant worker rights. In Houston, by contrast, business interests dwarf the power of unions, the anti-immigrant constituency is strong, state workplace enforcement is minimal, and consequently a range of alternative solutions have emerged.

In this concluding chapter, I examine what lessons San Jose and Houston provide for our understanding of how immigrant worker rights are enforced and what best practices emerge. I caution against reactionary conclusions that privilege one model over another and argue instead for the continued importance of local innovation alongside federal reform. To this end, I focus on examining relationships within a political field, the factors that shape organizational behavior, and the processes of rights enforcement. I end by addressing the implications of this study for democracy in America and considering the potential effects of changes on the horizon.

Expanding the Political Field of Immigrant Worker Rights

Throughout this book I have focused on several actors that shape the enforcement of immigrant worker rights. Government enforcement bureaucracies are the most obvious of these, as they are charged with carrying out the letter of the law. Yet in a complex federalist democracy, no single agency is typically solely responsible for any one arena of rights. For example, environmental justice advocates often alternate between mobilizing city public planning ordinances, state public health regulations, and federal conservation protections. Similarly, immigrant worker rights traverses not only the minefield of federal—and increasingly state and local—immigration enforcement but also provisions at all levels of government intended to protect workers. Local governments are influential in channeling both immigration and labor standards enforcement efforts. As of 2011, forty-seven states had enacted or passed laws or resolutions related to immigration enforcement (NCSL 2011), and the country remained divided over state oversight on workplace protections in areas ranging from the minimum wage (DOL 2011a) to discrimination (EEOC 2001), health and safety (OSHA 2011), and collective bargaining (NRTWO 2007).

Even in instances in which state and local governments cannot or will not create new standards for immigration, labor, or both, they may offer resources and political capital to legitimate existing ones. This may come, for example, in the form of community development grants to build day labor centers or to support other advocacy organizations. City staff may even be devoted to addressing the needs of a particular population and developing relationships with state and federal entities to better serve them.[1] Sometimes the support is simply symbolic, as is the case with the resolutions passed in support of immigrant worker rights after the failed attempt to pass HR 4437 or the presence of individual elected officials at organizing drives. Conversely, benign neglect of—or direct opposition to—the presence of immigrant communities can widen the gap between immigrants' formal rights and the rights they are actually afforded, and in this way further marginalize them.

Beyond the government apparatus, civil society also plays a crucial role in enforcing immigrant worker rights. As with the process of enforcing the rights of other populations, such as the rights of women (Ray 1999), LGBT individuals (Andersen 2006), and the homeless (Noy 2009), labor standards enforcement agencies are constantly challenged by—and sometimes work hand in hand with—a broad network of advocates who aim to keep them accountable. Organizations ranging from unions to community-based organizations, legal clinics, faith-based groups, and activist research groups all influence the process of rights enforcement in distinct ways. There are many opportunities for intervention, including direct service, organizing, and policy advocacy (Fine 2006). The relationships between these groups and the strategies they adopt depend largely on the broader political field in which they exist.

In San Jose, I uncovered a specialized division of labor, with legal advocates focusing on direct service to individuals, while Silicon Valley unions lead some of the most aggressive organizing campaigns in the country.

Houston advocates, conversely, have adopted a more "all hands on deck" approach to confront their long list of opponents. Meanwhile, advocates in each city have also honed their approach to policy change. In San Jose, the charge has been led by the central labor council's progressive research arm, a statewide initiative for worker safety headed by labor attorneys, and a consortium of immigrant rights groups. Conversely, lacking resources and political capital, labor and immigrant advocates in Houston have cautiously joined efforts with a well-resourced consortium of business groups focused on leveraging economic arguments for congressional reform. In both cities, faith leaders are core allies in each aspect of immigrant worker rights.

Last, in this volume I have also widened the scope of consideration of immigrant rights enforcement beyond the domestic sphere to include transnational actors. Though substantial scholarship has focused on the interventions of nongovernmental organizations across borders (Keck and Sikkink 1998), national governments themselves also play an active role in enforcing the rights of their diasporas. To this end, I have examined the Mexican consulate's role as it shifts from a legacy of "limited engagement" to a more engaged approach. While the Mexican consulate in San Jose has built on resources already in place for referral, its counterpart in Houston has taken the lead in the Justice and Equality in the Workplace Program, which allows it to directly process claims in conjunction with several federal agencies. Consular advocacy is not without its limitations, but it brings a powerful combination of resources and political legitimacy to the table.

From Rights to Claims: Evaluating the Process of Enforcement

After surveying the political field of immigrant worker rights in San Jose and Houston, we are compelled to ask, "What works? Which model is best?" We know that workplace violations are ubiquitous, and claims-making remains universally difficult (Bobo 2008; Bernhardt et al. 2009). The challenges of "living in the shadows" further discourages undocumented workers from coming forward when violations occur and often pushes them to make calculated, risk-averse decisions that prioritize stability and economic security over deferred, abstract notions of justice (Gleeson 2010). To be sure, then, immigrant workers and those who care deeply about the problems of these workers will wonder how San Jose's special-ized approach to worker rights compares with Houston's more diversified strategies.

Though this is a seemingly simple question, answering it raises a range of theoretical and empirical challenges. First, a particular outcome must be specified. What works for *what*? Felstiner and colleagues' now classic model of "naming, blaming, claiming" (1980) suggests there are various stages of claims-making that advocates can impact. Which one ought we to measure in determining what approach best protects the rights of im-migrant workers? Second, how do we compare two places with disparate policies, political cultures, and enforcement processes? Isn't this compar-ing apples and oranges?[2] Third, what is our evidence, and how should we interpret it? Do formal claims rates reflect the level of employer violations, institutional resources dedicated to enforcement, or the success of legal mobilization? Though survey and ethnographic data reveal an almost uni-versal experience of workplace abuse among vulnerable workers, institu-tional arrangements are critical to understanding how rights are mobilized (Edelman 1992; Hirsh 2008; Hirsh and Kornrich 2008).

Limited data make finding the answers to these questions difficult. However, if we turn to disaggregated administrative data, we can begin to establish some basis for comparison. Though wage and hour abuses are by far the most common type of violation (Bobo 2008), disparate policies and distinct administrative recording systems in California and Texas make triangulating wage and hour an incoherent task.[3] Evidence from discrimi-nation claims provides a sounder basis for comparison, since the federal Equal Employment Opportunity Commission cross-files all its charges with local Fair Employment Practices Agencies.[4]

If we focus specifically, then, on those violations that are most likely to affect foreign-born workers, claims of discrimination on the basis of na-tional origin, we find that 23.6 charges per 100,000 immigrants in the labor force were filed with the EEOC or the partner state agency in San Jose, compared with 60.9 in Houston.[5] While it may be tempting to conclude that these data provide proof of a more "effective" enforcement apparatus in Houston compared with San Jose, substantial caution should be used in drawing such a conclusion. In fact, if we assess the overall charge rate for each city, we arrive at similarly disparate levels: 78.2 and 131.2 for San Jose and Houston, respectively.[6] It seems unlikely, then, that the higher charge rates in Houston are solely the result of the decentralized and diversified interventions discussed in this volume.[7]

A more useful way to draw conclusions from this volume's case studies considers how rights enforcement operates, how and why organizations behave as they do, and what accounts for the relationships they develop with each other. To do so, let us consider the all-too-common case of an undocumented Mexican day laborer cheated of his pay. In this context, we should return to Tilly's definition of rights as "enforceable claims" in light of Felstiner and colleagues' (1980) model of legal mobilization. Two aspects of this definition are relevant. To begin, it is worth acknowledging whether a *claim* has actually been made to air the grievance. Many workers do not get even this far. Between the worker's return home without pay and his or her eventual filing of a claim, there are many steps, each of which requires intervention. To begin, it is relevant to ask whether the aggrieved worker knows what his rights are under the law. If so, he likely gained this information via social networks, previous workplace training, the ethnic media, or some other community outreach. Next, the worker must be willing to mobilize his legal consciousness. To do so, he must weigh the transportation and opportunity costs at stake, the risk involved, and his overall sense that the hassle will pay off. Further, how comfortable does this worker feel approaching a federal agency? Are there other alternatives? If this worker feels wary about the process, he may seek out support from a variety of bureaucratic brokers, such as a trusted lawyer, community leader, city worker, or even his consulate.

Viewed from the other end, what does it take to actually *enforce* this day laborer's claim? As the head of the federal or state agency in charge of upholding labor standards for this jurisdiction, I might be well aware of wage theft but nonetheless wary of my agency's ability to reach the worker. I might consult my counterparts in other offices, but my first order of business would be to learn about the needs of day laborers in *my* city and start to develop local contacts. If I'm lucky, there may be an existing relationship in place; but if institutional memory has been lost, I may have to start over. I might also reach out to my counterparts at other agencies, though— burdened by a lack of resources and staff—I may have few institutional incentives to do so. Driven by my professional mission, I would probably be full of good intentions to help this worker. I would also rely heavily on a series of bureaucratic brokers to bridge the deep divide that exists between this worker's construction site and my government office. Yet without credible evidence from this worker—a pay stub, a schedule of hours worked, and the name of an employer whom I can pursue for damages—my agency's hands might be tied.

What about these bureaucratic brokers? What do local governments, civil society, and consulates have to gain from this process? While local politicians represent the interests of their constituents, they also have an interest in maintaining the rule of law in their jurisdictions. Civil society organizations, too, though sympathetic to the pursuit of justice for workers like these, are also often driven by an independent interest in advancing broader missions and movements. For many, helping workers access their rights is a continuation of their original fight to get these protections on the books to begin with. Depending on their success at institutionalizing rights, advocacy groups such as these may then hand over the reins to the robust structures they helped create, like the Department of Labor, freeing them up to wage broader battles down the road. In places where victories are hard won and remain tenuous, groups may spend more time drumming up creative alternatives while pressuring the formal structures to further evolve. These are, of course, not mutually exclusive paths, but represent a series of decisions that any organization must make as it decides how to frame its goals and allocate resources.

Finally, how do we understand the role of foreign consulates? Driven by national interest, but bound by noninterventionist diplomatic convention, what incentive does the Mexican consulate, or any other foreign consulate, have in replicating the claims-making structures of the United States? The most instrumental interpretation of consular involvement recognizes the billions of remittances Mexican emigrants send home each year. Yet a more nuanced view of the consulate's role in enforcing the rights of its co-nationals recognizes that the offices spread throughout host communities confront an array of needs as diverse as the origin communities from which these emigrants hail. Within this context, consular staff must balance not only the allegiances tied to their professional missions but also the interests of their local posts. As such, the Mexican consulate acts as a transnational amalgam of the enforcement bureaucracies profiled in chapter 2 and the civil society groups in chapter 4; and like them, consular offices are influenced by the local regulatory context, the vision promoted by their leadership, and their basic resource capacity. This hybrid mission and infrastructure, as well as this locally crafted agenda, allow consular staff to provide a safe space for undocumented co-nationals in particular. Yet it remains to be seen how far consular efforts like those emerging in San Jose will go and how long engaged models of advocacy in Houston will persist.

Immigrant Worker Rights and Civic Engagement

Throughout this book I have presented two paths to enforcing the rights of immigrant workers in San Jose and Houston. While neither model should be understood as a universal template, each suggests some lessons about what spurs or stymies certain forms of civic engagement on the issue of immigrant worker rights. Skeptical scholars have argued that the creation of formal rights has simply appeased publics and consequently dampened social movements (Rosenberg 1991), while optimists have argued that institutionalized rights may in fact further spur individuals to organize (McCann 1994). While these debates rely on longitudinal comparisons over time or across different movements, the two case studies of immigrant worker rights advocacy presented in this book can provide some insight as well.

On the one hand, the specialized enforcement approach has allowed civic organizations such as unions, places of worship, and other nonprofits to rely on the administrative labor standards enforcement process to address the workplace violations that immigrants face. By strategically referring these workers to legal services, civil society has been freed up to mobilize political capital toward the achievement of goals such as union organizing and policy reform. On the other hand, the hostile political culture in Houston, an unengaged state labor standards enforcement apparatus, and the lack of viable legal resources for immigrant workers has motivated a much more involved coalition through the Justice and Equality in the Workplace Program. In both cases, immigrant worker advocates in San Jose and Houston are going far beyond what Amy Dean refers to as "transactional relations," or the "mutual backscratch" (Dean and Rathke 2008; Dean and Reynolds 2010). In fact there is evidence that immigrant worker rights have motivated deep coalitions in both places, albeit in different ways.

In San Jose, the South Bay Labor Council and its sister organization, Working Partnerships USA, have fomented significant relationships with community allies since Dean was at their helm. Unlike the direct role that the Harris County AFL-CIO has played in the Justice and Equality in the Workplace Program in Houston, the central labor council in San Jose has focused instead on union organizing and policy advocacy. In addition to the policy victories in health care, housing, and transportation, immigrant rights have been at the center of every major union-organizing campaign in San Jose, from janitors to hotel workers to, most recently, *mercado* workers (Mangaliman 2007). Working Partnerships USA and the Interfaith Council on Economics and Justice have also lent considerable support to every major immigrant rights action in the city, even creating a task force for immigrant rights that advocates at the local and national level. Its frequent ally, SIREN (Services, Immigrant Rights and Education Network), too, has promoted the work of local legal advocates to shepherd workers through the formal process while devoting organizational resources to other much-needed immigrant services, promoting immigrant leadership development and community organizing, and lobbying for policy changes at all levels.

Yet the Harris County AFL-CIO and its other allies on the Mayor's Advisory Committee on Immigrant and Refugee Affairs do not have the institutional resources or power to influence political elites on their own, nor the luxury of assuming that the official bureaucracy can successfully reach out to immigrant workers who need help. With decidedly smaller staffs and resources and significantly bigger challenges to their legitimacy, Houston unions, faith leaders, and immigrant rights groups like CRECEN (Centro de Recursos Centroamericanos) and America Para Todos (America for All) have built broad alliances out of necessity. Though the alliances have shifted over time,[8] together these coalitions have led direct actions for worker rights and immigrant-rights rallies. Dwarfed in size by even those in much smaller cities, these actions have grown successively over the years and suggest that labor and immigrant rights are building power in the city (Sarkar 2011). Further, by focusing not only on organizing and policy advocacy but also on the mundane work of processing individual claims, the signatories to the Justice and Equality in the Workplace Program—which also include the new worker center, Houston Interfaith Worker Justice, and the Mexican consulate—have not only expanded access to justice for aggrieved workers but also provided additional opportunities to fold immigrants into civic and political life.

There are several possible ways to interpret these two models. One can see the coalitions in San Jose as potentially more significant in the long run, given that the critical mass of civil society organizations allows allies to collectively attack the issue from all sides. In another sense, immigrants and their needs have been incorporated more successfully into the fiber of civil society in Houston. Almost every major progressive campaign in the city has found a way to frame the issues that integrates the mutual needs of the labor and immigrant rights communities. Yet Houston's slow but steady evolution should be watched carefully. The creation of new worker centers such as HIWJ and immigrant rights organizations such as the Alianza Mexicana, alongside important labor victories and transnational solidarity efforts (AFL-CIO 2010), all suggest that amid the antiunion fervor and vitriol against immigrants the immigrant worker rights community is standing strong.

Both models, to be sure, face challenges. San Jose will need to be careful to avoid redeveloping the "issue silos" that Dean warns us of (2011). Meanwhile, the advocates for immigrant worker rights in Houston will have to work to avoid being co-opted by their bureaucratic collaborators and business allies. As the current impasse over immigration reform lingers and unions take further blows during the recession, labor and immigrant rights will continue to be intricately linked. Not only can broad coalitions foster greater access to individual rights, but they may also provide additional opportunities for low-wage immigrants—whose voice is either formally excluded or disregarded—to be heard. The strengthening of these alternative avenues is vital to the future of organized labor. As Lichtenstein (2002) warns, the decline of the union movement has occurred in part because greater access to "rights conscious employment law" has become more attractive, and in many ways less cumbersome, than a union contract. Sustained mobilizing around immigrant worker rights should be seen as part and parcel of building a strong union movement, rather than as a substitute for it.

Toward the Future

Five summers after I started this project, there is evidence that local politics matter more than ever for immigrant worker rights. Despite several victories, many impasses remain. During his last year in office, Governor Arnold Schwarzenegger of California vetoed a bill that would have given farmworkers an equal right to overtime pay (Lagos 2010), and a year later Governor Jerry Brown rejected provisions that would have made it easier for them to unionize (McGreevy and York 2011). Meanwhile, despite signing a 2011 wage theft bill (J. Smith 2011), Governor Rick Perry of Texas still refuses to "overburden" his state by investing additional state resources in regulating the health and safety of workers. The national immigration debate continues to brew as well. Brown remains unresponsive to calls to reject the impending Secure Communities bill (Esquivel 2011), while Perry has called for its expansion in Texas (Buch 2011). Signs of economic recovery are scarce, immigrants remain a frequent target of public disdain and government cuts, and many civil society organizations struggle to stay afloat. To be sure, tough times are ahead, and the rights of immigrant workers remain vital.

Amid this turmoil, it is my hope that this book can leave us with at least three directions for public investment and scholarly thought. First, while significant resources have been expended by advocates trying to improve vital workplace protections, energy also needs to be spent determining how immigration restrictions prevent such improvements from taking full effect. Policy innovations such as the recent increase in the minimum wage, for example, are definitely needed and will likely alter employer practices. Yet the creation of such policies does not guarantee their implementation for all workers.[9] Any effort to enforce these rights on the ground must consider the broader political field in which they exist. The overlapping constraints of immigration enforcement—and restrictive immigrant policies in particular—in a given place will cast a shadow on even the most robust protections and shape the needs of that community.

Second, this research highlights the need to incorporate a wide array of nontraditional actors into the enforcement and outreach process. These stakeholders are needed not only to complement efforts by strained labor standards enforcement agencies but also to foster trust between different government jurisdictions and the marginalized communities they serve, including, but not limited to, undocumented immigrants. A multifaceted approach may prove fruitful far beyond the sphere of worker rights, including services for immigrant victims of domestic violence (Salcido and Adelman 2004; Fernández 2010), poor immigrants seeking help from the welfare state (Van Hook and Bean 2009), and efforts to bring community policing models to immigrant neighborhoods (Khashu 2009). Furthermore, policymakers should be aware of the limitations of claims-driven enforcement paradigms, which place the weight of enforcement on the victims of abuse. Budgetary constraints understandably limit the ability of labor standards enforcement agencies to take a more proactive enforcement strategy, and a wide array of other community concerns inevitably will draw away the attention of civic groups. Yet, when the entire onus of enforcement lies on the affected worker, no infusion of resources will ever be sufficient to completely eliminate workplace violations.

Last, as debate over potential immigration reform rages in Congress, it is vital to understand the inherent impact any legalization program is likely to have on undocumented-worker rights. At the collective level, any reform will undoubtedly affect immigrant-serving organizations. This was the case following the reforms of the 1986 Immigration Reform and Control Act, in which local governments, civil society, and foreign consulates became a crucial link between the policies handed down by legislators and the bureaucratic whirlwind that followed (Hagan 1994).[10] The networks currently in place to support immigrant worker rights will likely provide crucial infrastructure for reaching workers in the wake of future reforms.

Notes

Introduction

1. While the 2002 Supreme Court decision *Hoffman Plastics v. NLRB* has constrained the remedies available to undocumented workers, as I explain in chapter 2, several rights remain.

2. This precedent has been repeatedly upheld by lower courts. See for example a 2011 case where a Boston federal judge held that the immigration status of two undocumented workers was "irrelevant" to both their wage and hour claims under the Fair Labor Standards Act and their "suitability" to lead a class (*National Law Journal* 2011).

3. Prior to IRCA, provisions under the 1952 Texas Proviso held that employment was not considered "harboring" and was hence legal (Brownell 2005).

4. *Hoffman Plastic Compounds, Inc. v. National Labor Relations Board*, 535 U.S. 137 (2002).

5. One of the strongest declarations was signed on March 31, 2011, setting up communication capacity between the two agencies and establishing at least temporary protection to victims (ICE 2011b).

6. These workers were driven to the National Cattle Congress stables where they were charged with felony counts of identity fraud. Agriprocessors was ultimately charged with over nine thousand counts of child labor law violations and had $10 million levied in wage penalties (McCarthy 2009). Several staff were also indicted and convicted. Three years after declaring bankruptcy, Agriprocessors was sold, upgraded, and reopened under a new label, Agri Star, with the new ownership declaring a commitment to safer conditions and higher wages (Caspers-Simmet 2010; Henderson 2010). As for the workers caught up in the raid, most lost their job, served prison time, and were eventually deported.

7. According to a study conducted by the Pew Hispanic Center, the negative effects of enforcement go beyond individual undocumented migrants themselves. The study found that "over half of all Hispanic adults in the U.S. worry that they, a family member or a close friend could be deported" (PHC 2007).

8. As of July 1, 2009, four cities enforced municipal minimum wages: Albuquerque ($7.50), San Francisco ($11.54 for-profit, $11.03 nonprofit), Santa Fe ($9.85), and Washington, DC ($8.25) (Let Justice Roll Living Wage Campaign, 2009).

9. As of January 2011, "22 States and jurisdictions operating complete State plans (covering both the private sector and State and local government employees) and 5—Connecticut, Illinois, New Jersey, New York and the Virgin Islands—which cover public employees only. (Eight other States were approved at one time but subsequently withdrew their programs)" (OSHA 2011).

10. These include, for example, protections against discrimination on the basis of sexual orientation, status as a parent, marital status, and political affiliation.

11. This dynamic was prominent in the recent San Francisco Municipal ID campaign, in which advocates worked hard to frame the ID as a resource not only for undocumented residents (presumably the population with the fewest alternative options for obtaining U.S. identification) but also for other affected residents, such as the transgender community and any resident wanting to use the ID for discounts and regular easy access to city services (de Graauw 2009).

12. This was the case, for example, in a recent campaign by the UNITE HERE (a merger of the Union of Needletrades, Industrial, and Textile Employees and Hotel Employees and Restaurant Employees International Union) (UNITE HERE! 2009).

13. The Texas Workforce Commission has one central office in Austin that enforces the Texas Payday Law and civil rights protections. All claims are processed through a mail-in system that provides support over the phone.

14. Within California and Texas, I also aimed to compare two cities that were emblematic of the regulatory context of each state but not radically divergent in terms of local demographic or economic dynamics. While several excellent studies have examined the role of immigrant labor, they tend to focus on high-profile success stories in global cities such as Los Angeles and New York (e.g., Milkman 2000, 2006a). Noting the unique attributes of such cities, I also forwent state capitals (Sacramento and Austin) and border cities such as El Paso and San Diego, which have a distinctive demographic character. I settled on San Jose and Houston based on their similar economic profiles and immigrant histories.

15. The Federal Labor Standards Act states that "covered nonexempt workers are entitled to a minimum wage of not less than $5.15 an hour." In California in 2005, according to the California Industrial Welfare Commission (IWC) orders, the minimum wage was $6.75 an hour, increased to $7.50 in January 2007, and then to $8.00 in January 2008. California overtime provisions are stricter than the federal standard, requiring any time after eight hours in a day to be paid at a premium, compared with the forty-hour-per-week federal minimum.

16. In addition to protection from employment discrimination based on race, color, religion, sex, or national origin, as well as age and disability, the State of California provides protection from discrimination on the basis of sexual orientation.

17. The workers' compensation system provides a full range of benefits to the injured worker, including medical benefits and lost wages. This is a state-administered no-fault system in which the implicit agreement is that in exchange for these benefits, an employee cannot sue his or her employer if injured. If workers' compensation is not provided, employers are required to notify their employees, and if a worker is injured he or she has the option to sue the employer. However, a civil tort case such as this can be a lengthy and costly process that is likely prohibitive for most low-wage workers.

18. In "right to work" states, workers at establishments where a union has successfully gained recognition are not actually required to be members of that union or to pay union dues. Union

proponents argue that unions have fewer resources in these states, and gaining recognition is much more difficult. Note: unionization rates presented here are based on metropolitan statistical area data for San Jose–Sunnyvale–Santa Clara in California and Houston–Baytown–Sugar Land in Texas.

19. I also spoke with the Mexican consulate staff in San Francisco, Sacramento, Los Angeles, New York, Denver, and Chicago.

20. To establish a list of all nonprofits whose mission includes labor and employment issues, I used the premium search function provided by Guidestar, one of the leading organizations that compiles IRS database listings for charitable organizations. http://www.guidestar.org.

21. These included formal client-directed directories such as ImmigrantInfo.org, an online database of providers compiled by the Santa Clara County Immigrant Relations and Integration Services; referrals from the Houston Mayor's Office of Immigrant and Refugee Affairs; and community partners mentioned by each central labor council.

22. As noted, most respondents worked at well-known restaurant chains located near a heavily trafficked shopping center. These employment sites were middle-range "tablecloth" (i.e., dine-in) venues.

1. Work in Postindustrial America

1. The median annual family income in 1960 was $5,600 ($41,000 in 2010 dollars) (U.S. Census Bureau 1961), versus $62,000 in 2010 (U.S. Census Bureau 2011e).

2. When factored into official unemployment statistics, this involuntary part-time labor reveals a true unemployment rate that is well past what conventional figures might suggest (Haugen 2009). In October 2009, this rate—which included the unemployed, those working involuntary part time, and the marginally attached—stood at 17.5 percent (NELP 2009b). That same month, the *Wall Street Journal* reported that the number of people involuntarily working part-time jobs had more than doubled to 9.3 million over the previous two years, while the average workweek also fell to its lowest level in the post–World War II period at thirty-three hours (Dugan 2009).

3. This characterization of farm workers as low-skilled has been contested. Frank Bardacke, a long-time activist and scholar in the United Farm Workers movement, for example, has argued that agricultural labor is in fact highly skilled work that can take years to perfect, and should be treated as such in public discourse and the formation of immigration and labor policy (Bardacke 2012).

4. This has happened not just in the iconic "Rust Belt" regions of the United States but also in key cities in the West and South. The NUMMI auto plant, for example, was once the largest employer in Fremont, California, a suburb located at the northern tip of Silicon Valley, until it closed after fifty years in 2010. Though the plant has partially reopened under new contract, only a fraction of the originally thousands-strong workforce has returned (Kane 2010).

5. Today, preliminary evidence also suggests that the recent economic downturn has stalled migration flows. Yet other factors, such as the lack of opportunities in the country of origin and the difficulty of border crossing, have also kept many migrants from returning home (Meissner 2009).

6. H1-A visas provides "non-immigrant" entry for skilled professionals.

7. The United States is the prime destination for undocumented migrants worldwide. Large undocumented populations also exist in Europe and other advanced industrialized economies, though on a smaller scale (See also Calavita 2005; Willen 2007).

8. Under IRCA, amnesty was granted to two main groups of immigrants: those who had been present continuously in the United States since 1982 and certain agricultural workers. Three million of the estimated 3–5 million undocumented immigrants residing in the United States at the time applied for amnesty under IRCA, and ultimately 2.7 million adjusted their status. By 2001, one-third of the legal permanent residents who adjusted under IRCA had naturalized (Rytina 2002).

9. Employer sanctions have been concluded to be largely ineffective. See Brownell (2005) for a more detailed discussion.

10. Though Social Security "no-match letters" were halted in 2007, the E-Verify program that was originally required only of federal contractors expanded its reach, with several states enforcing, or considering, legislation that would require employers to use it (Wolgin 2011). This innovation was ruled constitutional in a 5–3 decision by the Supreme Court on May 26, 2011 (8 U.S.C. 1324a(h)).

11. These contemporary campaigns included Operation Hold the Line in El Paso, Texas (1993), Operation Gatekeeper in San Diego, California (1994), Operation Safeguard in Arizona (1994), and Operation Rio Grande in South Texas (1997) (Nevins 2002).

12. Through IIRIRA and the Anti-terrorism and Effective Death Penalty Act (also passed in 1996), Congress also further streamlined the deportation process by accelerating the removal of noncitizens with criminal records, restricting judicial review of administrative removal orders, and limiting alternatives to deportation (Aleinikoff, Martin, and Motomura 2008).

13. As of June 2011, UNITE HERE and the Laborers have reaffiliated with the AFL-CIO (AFL-CIO 2011).

14. Interview, Sheet Metal Workers Local 54, March 8, 2006.

15. Interview, Department of Labor Wage and Hour Division Houston Office, September 22, 2009.

16. A 2009 General Accounting Office report characterized the two-year statute of limitations as too short, given agency delays in processing time (GAO 2009a). Subsequently, House bill HR 3303 was introduced by Rep. George Miller (D-CA) on July 23, 2009. The bill, which did not pass, would have frozen the statute of limitations from the date an employer is informed of an investigation until the agency notifies the employer that the investigation has concluded (Govtrack 2011).

17. These figures are based on public records requests made to the Texas Workforce Commission and the California Division of Labor Standards Enforcement, submitted on March 6, 2007, and March 23, 2007, respectively. Note that the federal Department of Labor also processes claims, which are not reflected in these tallies.

18. Both California and Texas have added provisions to their labor codes in recent years regarding wage theft. In 2011, Texas Governor Rick Perry signed into law Senate Bill 1024, which made it easier for law enforcement to go after employers who had failed to pay wages in full. That same year, California Governor Jerry Brown signed into law Assembly Bill 469, which now requires employers to provide employees with specific information about rate and timing of pay, and increases penalties for non-payment of wages.

19. In 2006 dollars, the minimum wage established in 1968 ($1.60) would yield an estimated inflation-adjusted annual income of $19,115. Using the same set of assumptions, the $5.15 minimum wage would provide only $10,712, drastically less than the $35,693 that it would take to meet the basic needs of a one-parent, one-child family in a typical U.S. city (Sonn 2006).

20. The power for cities to create their own minimum wage varies from state to state, with ten states explicitly prohibiting the practice as of 2006 (Sonn 2006).

21. Interview, compliance assistance specialist, Occupational Health and Safety Agency, Houston South Area Office, October 11, 2006.

22. As of 2010, four state programs covered only public employees: Illinois, New York, New Jersey, and Connecticut.

23. Many of these critiques seem eerily reminiscent of those lodged decades prior. In a 1987 exposé, a *New York Times* reporter charged the OSHA office in Austin with failing to compel work sites to properly construct trenches in order to protect workers from the cave-in accidents that were killing ten annually in Texas alone (Glaberson 1987).

24. Interview, director, WorkSafe! April 25, 2006.

25. Interview, compliance assistance specialist, Occupational Health and Safety Agency, Houston South Area Office, October 11, 2006.

26. Interview, Santa Clara Center on Occupational Safety and Health, October 9, 2009.

27. A few states only provide insurance through state programs, while about a quarter of states have a state-run fund that insures state employees and regulates private insurance programs. In most states, however, programs are provided solely by private insurers (Fishback and Kantor 2006).

28. Interview, investigator, Equal Employment Opportunity Commission Houston District Office, June 23, 2006.

29. Interview, director, Equal Employment Opportunity Commission San Francisco District Office, August 4, 2006.

30. These figures are based on the author's calculations from data provided by the EEOC via a Public Records Act request.

31. The history of U.S. organized labor has been chronicled by countless labor historians (Brecher 1997; Murolo, Chitty, and Sacco 2001; Lichtenstein 2002).

32. The requirement to join a union before getting a job—i.e., "a closed shop"—has been banned for several decades, and union members are allowed to decide whether their dues are spent on political activities.

33. Within the private sector, these levels are starker: 6.9 percent of all private sector workers in the United States are unionized, compared with 3.2 percent in Texas, 9.3 percent in California, 3.6 percent in Houston, and 7.5 percent in San Jose (Hirsch and Macpherson 2009).

34. Some critics argue that the influx of undocumented immigrants in key union industries is what has led to the decline in union power, while other argue that the degradation of work standards preceded the huge demographic shifts in the 1980s and 1990s. Milkman, however, finds evidence of both trends (Milkman 2006a) and cautions against drawing absolute conclusions on either side.

35. Interview, director, Equal Employment Opportunity Commission San Francisco District Office, August 4, 2006.

36. These figures are based on data analysis of the Wage and Hour Investigative Support and Reporting Database, which I obtained through a Freedom of Information Act request.

37. Interview, Cal/OSHA, Oakland Office, November 21, 2006.

38. Interview, director, Mountain View Day Labor Center, September 6, 2005.

39. While recent evidence indeed suggests that the tide of undocumented immigrants has been stemmed somewhat in recent recessionary years (Passel and Cohn 2010), the overall size of the undocumented population has nonetheless grown substantially over the last several decades due to widening economic inequality, strengthening family ties, and the increased flow across borders of capital and goods, while legal channels for migration are closed off for most low-wage economic migrants (Massey and Espinosa 1997; Zolberg 1999; Massey, Durand, and Malone 2003).

2. Implementing the Legal Rights of Undocumented Workers

1. As stated in previous chapters, the Obama administration has avowed an infusion of resources for interior enforcement (Preston 2010), while an increasing number of states and localities have also created their own policies for policing immigrants (Pánuco 2008). Programs such as Social Security "no-match letters" and E-Verify have also placed enforcement power in the hands of employers (Chishti and Bergeron 2009).

2. *Sure-Tan, Inc v. National Labor Relations Board*, 467 U.S. 883 (1984).

3. *Hoffman Plastic Compounds, Inc. v. National Labor Relations Board*, 535 U.S. 137 (2002).

4. Federal agencies such as the National Labor Relations Board, the Department of Labor, and the Equal Employment Opportunity Commission administer different statutes, and thus their remedial authorities are also distinct. See Ho and Chang (2005) for a more nuanced discussion of the impact of *Hoffman* in these different arenas.

5. On November 17, 2008, the Supreme Court denied certiorari (refused to hear the case) in *Agriprocessors v. NLRB*, wherein previously both the NLRB and the DC circuit court had upheld

the definition of undocumented workers as employees under the National Labor Relations Act. The right of undocumented workers to organize has therefore been firmly upheld to date. However, more recently, the NLRB has maintained that undocumented workers are precluded from receiving back pay compensation, even in cases where the employer knowingly violated I-9 requirements and then proceeded to engage in unfair labor practices (NLRB 2011).

6. Among the most up-to-date sources on national public opinion toward immigration are polls fielded by media outlets. These are notorious, however, for relying on small and biased samples. See the Miller Center for Public Affairs (2010) for a useful compilation of such surveys, as well as the collection published by the Pew Hispanic Center (PHC 2006).

7. Under current employment termination law, it can be difficult for any at-will employee to prove unlawful termination and win reinstatement (Arnow-Richman 2010). In the case of undocumented workers, however, employer sanctions explicitly proscribe reinstatement under *Hoffman*.

8. Though the courts were certainly considering undocumented worker rights long before *Hoffman*, this case has reinvigorated the debate in the contemporary era (Brownell 2010).

9. *Flores v. Albertson's*, 2002 WL 1163623.

10. *Flores v. Amigon*, 2002 233 F.Supp.2d 462.

11. *Rodriguez v. The Texan, Inc.*, 2002 WL 31061237.

12. This sentiment was laid out in the minority opinion in *Hoffman*, penned by Justice Breyer, who argued that "[t]o *deny* the [National Labor Relations Board] the power to award backpay, however, might very well increase the strength of this magnetic force. That denial lowers the cost to the employer of an initial labor law [and] increases the employer's incentive to find and to hire illegal-alien employees. . . . [E]ven if limited to cases where the employer did not know of the employee's status, the incentive may prove significant—for, as the Board has told us, the Court's rule offers employers immunity in borderline cases, thereby encouraging them to take risks, *i.e.,* to hire with a wink and a nod those potentially unlawful aliens whose unlawful employment (given the Court's views) ultimately will lower the costs of labor law violations." *Hoffman Plastic Compounds, Inc. v. NLRB*, 535 U.S. 137 (2002).

13. *Hoffman Plastic Compounds, Inc. v. NLRB*, 535 U.S. 137 (2002).

14. 2003 658 N.W.2d 510.

15. Critics have also argued that by denying compensation for undocumented workers the court incentivized employers' use of Social Security "no-match" letters as a vehicle for strategic termination (Mehta, Theodore, and Hincapié 2003; NILC 2008a).

16. 2004 Kan. LEXIS 262.

17. This finding contradicted an earlier Tennessee case that found no issue with the use of fraudulent documents for the purposes of filing a workers' compensation claim. *Silva v. Martin Lumber Company* (2003, WL 22496233).

18. In an attempt to not entirely erase National Beef's responsibility in the matter, the court ultimately did order the employer to pay fees directly to a workers' compensation fund.

19. For example, in *Majlinger v. Cassino Contracting Corp.*, the court argued: "An undocumented alien performing construction work is not an outlaw engaged in illegal activity, such as bookmaking or burglary. Rather, the work is lawful and legitimate; it simply happens to be work for which the alien is ineligible or disqualified. Remedies have been awarded to individuals in analogous positions." The court mentioned the cases of a minor employed in violation of child labor law who obtained the job by misrepresenting his age but was entitled to workers' compensation benefits after sustaining a work injury, a truck driver awarded back pay despite his lack of a chauffeur's license, and a crane operator awarded back pay despite his lack of the engineer's license required by state law (Yale-Loehr 2006). (See *Majlinger v. Cassino Contracting Corp.*, 2005, 25 A.D.3d 14, N.Y. App. Div. 2d Dep't.)

20. *Fermin Colindres et al. v. Quietflex Manufacturing*, 2006 WL 846367.

21. Two sets of documents were produced. The first listed those plaintiffs who did not seek back pay for time lost (the "*Hoffman*" list"), and the second included documents, filed under seal,

showing the work authorization of those plaintiffs who were seeking compensation for lost wages (the "non-*Hoffman* list").

22. 768 N.Y.S.2d 556.

23. *Rosa v. Partners in Progress, Inc.*, 2005 868 A. 2d 994.

24. See summary in NILC (2005): "The court cited the following cases with this holding: *Veliz v. Rental Service Corp. USA, Inc.*, 313 F. Supp. 2d 1317 (M.D. Fla. 2003) (relying on *Hoffman*, the federal district court held that a laborer's undocumented status precluded an award of lost U.S. wages where the worker obtained employment by using fraudulent identification); *Hernandez-Cortez v. Hernandez*, 2003 U.S. Dist. LEXIS 19780 (D. Kan. Nov. 4, 2003) (disallowed undocumented immigrant's claim for lost U.S. earnings); *Majlinger v. Cassino Contracting Corp.*, 1 Misc. 3d 659 (Sup. Ct. 2003) (holding that the *Hoffman* decision would require the court to conclude that a plaintiff who cannot prove legal authorization to work cannot recover lost wages); *Sanango v. 200 East 16th Street Housing Corporation*, 788 N.Y.S. 2d 314 (App. Div. 2004) (court vacated a jury award for lost wages to an undocumented worker and remanded for a finding on earnings the plaintiff would earn in his country of origin)."

25. See summary in NILC (2005): "For example, in *Madeira v. Affordable Housing Foundation, Inc. and Mountain Developers Associates, LLC*, 315 F. Supp. 2d 504 (S.D.N.Y. 2004), the court, disagreeing with *Majlinger* and *Veliz*, upheld a jury's award of lost earnings to an undocumented worker. In fact, cases prior to the *Hoffman* decision have produced conflicting results, including *Rodriguez v. Kline*, 186 Cal. App. 3d 1145 (Ct. App. 1986) (undocumented plaintiff can only recover lost U.S. earnings if he can demonstrate he has taken steps to correct his "deportable condition"); and *Hernandez v. M/V Rajaan*, 848 F.2d 498 (5th Cir. 1988) (allowing undocumented plaintiff who was injured on the job to recover lost U.S. wages, unless the employer can establish that the plaintiff was about to be or surely would be deported)."

26. Interview, attorney, National Labor Relations Board, Region 20, December 6, 2006.

27. Interview, Department of Labor, Wage and Hour Division, Houston, October 17, 2006.

28. Interview, Equal Employment Opportunity Commission, Houston, June 23, 2006.

29. Interview, Equal Employment Opportunity Commission, San Jose, October 25, 2006.

30. Interview, Equal Employment Opportunity Commission, Houston, June 23, 2006.

31. Each of the federal agents I spoke to was also aware that some employers use the immigration status of workers to intimidate and control them, and on occasion as a defense for violating the law. In such cases, the director for the San Francisco District (which covers San Jose) sternly explained, "We charge them through retaliation [if they] try to get their undocumented status or if they threaten to report them to immigration. The only time it's relevant is if you're fighting back pay." Interview, Equal Employment Opportunity Commission, San Francisco, August 4, 2006.

32. Interview, Texas Workforce Commission, October 20, 2006.

33. Interview, Department of Labor, Wage and Hour Division, San Jose, December 12, 2006.

34. One explanation I was given for this deficit was that that language capacity, though a fundamental skill necessary to reach out to the highly vulnerable Latino immigrant population, was nonetheless not a prerequisite for advancement in these agencies. Consequently, non-Spanish-speaking candidates with superior educational qualifications, professional experience, and more seniority in the state system are given priority over those with poorer qualifications who speak Spanish.

35. Interview, Equal Employment Opportunity Commission, San Jose, October 25, 2006.

36. Interview, Department of Labor, Wage and Hour Division, Houston, October 17, 2006.

37. Interview, Cal/OSHA, Oakland Regional Office, November 21, 2006.

38. Indeed one conversation with an EEOC representative suggests that these fears are perhaps not completely unfounded. He explained reluctantly, "We're public servants, and if tomorrow Congress were to say that everybody has a role in looking at the immigration status of people, we will do that accordingly. But [currently] Title VII [of the Civil Rights Act] . . . and the laws that we enforce do not address that [immigration status]." Clearly, this ambivalence on even the part

of bureaucrats does little to foster trust in immigrant communities. Interview, Equal Employment Opportunity Commission, Houston, June 23, 2006.

39. While some research has found that Latino immigrants actually lose political trust over time (Michelson 2007), the specific concerns of undocumented immigrants seem imminent and distinct.

40. This is not to say that making claims on one's rights is antithetical to the ethos of a "good worker." However, here and elsewhere I argue that undocumented workers who are excluded from other bases of membership have many politically salient narratives that ascribe their belonging in society primarily to their labor function, thus potentially widening the chasm between workers and their rights (Gleeson 2010).

41. Interview, Equal Employment Opportunity Commission, San Francisco, August 4, 2006.

42. Interview, Texas Workforce Commission, October 20, 2006.

43. Ibid.

44. In 2011, workshops for injured Spanish-speaking workers, which were previously held in a local library, were moved to the Mexican consulate in San Jose and discontinued altogether in nearby Oakland.

3. Place Matters

1. Although federal poverty measures make the San Jose population seem almost doubly affluent, when the cost of living in Silicon Valley is factored in, this difference is dampened. A 2006 *Money* magazine report places the purchasing power of a San Jose family at $45,354, compared with the $53,233 of its Houston counterpart.

2. Amy Bridges describes *political* culture as "the practices, habits, and popular expectations of government and politics, as well as the words, values, and moralities ('publicly available symbolic forms') generally available for understanding and evaluating politics" (Bridges 1997, 23).

3. Based on the author's compilation of political histories for each councilor as of March 2010.

4. In 2010, twenty-two of Texas's thirty-four congressional representatives were members of the Republican Party. Sixty-five percent of Texas's congressional delegation were Republicans, versus only 35 percent in California. (Based on the author's compilation of congressional tallies for each state, Senate and House of Representatives, as of July 2010.)

5. Interview, South Bay Labor Council, April 20, 2006.

6. Interview, Service Employees International Union, Local 715, San Jose, May 31, 2006.

7. For an excellent account that chronicles the ascendance of the South Bay Labor Council, see Dean and Reynolds 2010.

8. Dean was not without controversy: many local opponents also criticized her leadership style and the management of the central labor council during her tenure (Hasan 2004a).

9. Interview, South Bay Labor Council, April 20, 2006.

10. Ellis-Lampkins had been a former summer intern for the SBLC and moved on from the SBLC to lead the high-profile environmental advocacy group Green for All, based in Oakland, California, and Washington, DC. Early in her tenure, Ellis-Lampkins had become a target in controversy over the organization's expenditures (Hasan 2004b), but she went on to spearhead many of the council's organizing and policy victories.

11. Interview, South Bay Central Labor Council, San Jose, April 20, 2006.

12. Interview, SEIU (Service Employees International Union), March 3, 2006.

13. Interview, WorkLife Institute, Houston, March 7, 2006.

14. Interview, ACORN (Association of Community Organizations for Reform Now), July 7, 2006.

15. Interview, Sheet Metal Workers, Local 54, March 8, 2006.

16. Tom DeLay was a member of the House of Representatives for twenty years, from 1985 to 2006, and was House majority leader for the last two years of his tenure. He eventually left

Congress the year following his indictment by a grand jury on criminal charges for violating campaign finance laws. He represented Houston's more affluent neighbor Sugar Land, which is in Fort Bend County. DeLay was known for his conservative leadership, alongside Newt Gingrich, on issues such as labor, environmental policy, and gay marriage.

17. For example, Culberson and Poe were members of the so-called birther caucus that challenged President Barack Obama's citizenship and opposed the Obama health care reform proposals.

18. Interview, Harris County AFL-CIO, March 3, 2006.

19. One of the largest immigration raids in history occurred on August 25, 2008, when Immigration and Customs Enforcement (ICE) arrested 592 suspected undocumented immigrants in Laurel, Mississippi, at the electronic products manufacturer Howard Industries. This followed three other major raids of the prior few years: one in Greeley, Colorado, on December 12, 2006, where 1,280 were arrested at the meat processor Swift and Company; one in New Bedford, Massachusetts, on March 6, 2007, where 361 were arrested at Michael Bianco Inc., a leather goods factory; and in Postville, Iowa, on May 12, 2008, where 389 were detained at the Agriprocessors meatpacking plant.

20. This legislation mandated that the Social Security Administration (SSA) implement and evaluate three employment verification pilot programs over a four-year period: the Basic Pilot / E-Verify, the Citizen Attestation Verification Pilot, and the Machine-Readable Document Pilot programs. The Basic Pilot / E-Verify program was deemed the most successful of the three and was expanded to all states on a voluntary basis. Participating employers enter prospective employees' I-9 information into a computer system that cross-checks it with an SSA database. Though initial evaluations found problems with erroneous nonconfirmation responses and data entry errors, the program appealed to many employers who feared sanctions for hiring undocumented workers and wanted to demonstrate that they act in good faith when refusing employment to workers they suspect are undocumented. This program also created an opening for states to adopt greater control over the regulation of immigration. In June 2005, the Social Security Number Verification Service was also made available in all states, allowing employers to verify Social Security numbers via the Internet. The program was intended to reflect whether the employer's records match Social Security Administration records, but employers were not allowed to use the program to pre-screen applicants or as a punitive device. However, immigrant advocates cite endless examples of manipulative uses of these searches (NILC 2009a; Wolgin 2011).

21. Immigrant worker advocates raised similar concerns regarding the SSA "no-match letter" program, which would send employers a letter of notification when the names or Social Security numbers listed on an employer's Form W-2 (an employee's IRS tax form) did not match SSA records. Savvy employers have been known to use these letters to intimidate workers. Often, they would hold on to the letters and produce them at opportune times, for example during a labor dispute or a union-organizing campaign (Mehta, Theodore, and Hincapié 2003). New rules were intended to go into effect in September 2007 that would have required employers to terminate workers who were unable to resolve a discrepancy within ninety days of an SSA no-match letter being sent. These rules were stalled, however, by a lawsuit filed in the U.S. District Court for the Northern District of California on August 29, 2007, to challenge them. Cosponsors of the suit included a wide range of civil society actors, including the AFL-CIO, the American Civil Liberties Union, the National Immigration Law Center, and the Central Labor Council of Alameda County, along with other local labor movement actors. As of November 6, 2009, the DHS—under the leadership of the Obama administration's appointee Janet Napolitano—had rescinded the program, leaving it unclear whether letters would be issued again (NILC 2009b). In 2011, the program resumed. The E-Verify program also emerged as a preferred employment-based program (Chishti and Bergeron 2009). See Lee (2009) for an alternative perspective on the utility of workplace screening.

22. For a more comprehensive overview of how this program is being deployed, see Armenta 2012, Coleman 2009, and Varsanyi et al. 2012. In early 2012, John Morton, director of Immigration Customs Enforcement for the Department of Homeland Security, announced that his office would not sign any new 287(g) contracts and will terminate the "least productive" of existing agreements. The focus instead will shift to the new Secure Communities Program, which has been rolled out nationwide (Gomez 2012).

23. As of July 2011, legal challenges to restrictive laws in Alabama, Georgia, Indiana, and South Carolina are pending.

24. According to the Public Policy Institute of California, there are an estimated 180,000 unauthorized immigrants in Santa Clara County, or an estimated 10.2 percent of residents (Hill and Johnson 2011). This makes Santa Clara the county with the fourth-largest proportion of unauthorized residents, behind Monterey / San Benito, Imperial, and Napa.

25. See also the San Jose Police Department Duty Manual, Section L 7911 (SJPD 2008).

26. A 2010 survey of residents in San Jose's Eastside confirmed this trend, and found that 35 percent of residents reported they had been stopped without cause (PACT 2010). A local news story also confirmed that the SJPD had investigated 150 case of racial profiling in the previous four years, without a single case of officer reprimand (Webby 2011a). The following year, under pressure from community groups and the independent police auditor, the new San Jose police chief Chris Moore specified further the prohibition against the practice (Hollyfield 2011).

27. While key aspects of SB 1070 have been rejected, such as a provision that would have made unlawful presence a state misdemeanor (*United States of America v. State of Arizona*, No. 10–16645, 9th Circuit, April 11, 2011), other provisions have been upheld as of June 2011, such as making it a misdemeanor to not carry proof of legal status, to aid unauthorized immigrants, and the requirement for all Arizona businesses to use E-Verify (*Chamber of Commerce of United States of America v. Whiting*, 558 F. 3d 856, May 26, 2011).

28. One of the goals of the program was to move redevelopment funds out of the business districts and into residential neighborhoods. It consolidated several initiatives, including Project Crackdown (focused on building community policing relationships between law enforcement and residents in high-crime areas) and the Neighborhood Revitalization Strategy (which instituted a deliberative planning approach to put neighborhood funding into action). To be chosen, neighborhoods have to meet the "blight requirement." Each of the areas is led by a Project Advisory Committee, composed of community members, that works with a city organizer to identify and implement a set of goals for the neighborhood. Interview, City of San Jose Strong Neighborhood Initiative, April 3, 2006. See also Larsen 2009.

29. Interview, City of San Jose Strong Neighborhood Initiative, July 12, 2004.

30. Ibid., December 11, 2008.

31. As of June 2011 the San Jose Redevelopment Agency (which housed SNI) was largely defunded amid California's budget crisis (City of San Jose 2010). Interview, former SNI organizer, June 22, 2011. Effective February 1, 2012, all redevelopment agencies in the State of California were dissolved, and the fate of the Strong Neighborhood Initiative remained indeterminate (City of San Jose 2012).

32. The event was at one time held twice yearly but due to budget cuts has been reduced to once a year.

33. Interview, Santa Clara County Office of Human Relations, April 24, 2006.

34. Personal Communication, Office of Human Relations, March 26, 2009.

35. Introduced by F. James Sensenbrenner Jr. (R-WI), House Bill 4437 was formally known as the Border Protection, Antiterrorism, and Illegal Immigration Control Act of 2005. The bill passed the House but not the Senate, and would have made illegal presence, and housing an undocumented immigrant, felonies, among other provisions (Sensenbrenner 2005).

36. In 2001, the *Houston Press*, Houston's alternative newspaper, awarded Juarez the title of "Best Activist." His achievements included brokering tensions between day laborers, property owners, and law enforcement in the affluent suburb of Kingwood (Houston Press, 2001).

37. Taken from MOIRA outreach material, summer 2005.

38. Personal communication, former MACIRA member, September 15, 2009.

39. Interview, Centro de Recursos Centroamericanos, Houston, July 1, 2009.

40. Interview, Neighborhood Centers Inc., Houston, March 9, 2006.

41. A key concession, however, required day labor staff to give potential employers an I-9 form, though it did not require day laborers to fill out the forms. At one point, the center also worked with the Hispanic Contractors Association and the Metropolitan Organization (the local affiliate of the Industrial Areas Foundation) to provide workers with a small ID card that listed their skills. Under pressure from opponents, however, it was forced to halt the effort. Interview, Neighborhood Centers Inc., Houston, March 9, 2006.

42. Interview, Dispute Resolution Center of Harris County, October 11, 2006.

43. These data were obtained via a Public Record Request, July 28, 2009.

44. Interview, Burglary and Theft Division, Houston Police Department, October 13, 2006.

45. The process of filing a claim with the Houston Police Department is quite simple. First, the case is reported to a patrol officer. It then goes to the Burglary and Theft Division, where it is assigned to an officer who will call the employer to compel him to pay. If the employer resists, the case is referred to the district attorney. Most cases, I was told, never go to court.

46. Though a public affairs officer I spoke to in July 2009 reiterated the Houston Police Department's commitment to enforcing the policy, many advocates were skeptical of the program's overall efficacy.

47. While Houston has a better track record than other cities in the state, a 2004 report commissioned by several Texas civil rights groups found that despite an explicit order prohibiting the practice, blacks and Latinos in Houston are consistently more likely to be stopped and searched (Steward Research Group 2004).

48. In another heated exchange, council member Addie Wiseman vigorously questioned a Spanish-speaking resident about her immigration status until she simply responded that she had the right to not respond. City Council records further summarize Wiseman as affirming the services immigrant workers provide, but also insisting that undocumented status constitutes commission of a crime, which should be scrutinized equally even in cases where undocumented immigrants call law enforcement for help (City of Houston 2005).

49. White, a Democrat, originally announced ambitions for the seat occupied by Republican Kay Bailey Hutchinson, whose sights were set on the governorship in 2010. White went on to run against incumbent Rick Perry for the governorship (Staff 2008a; Olson and Ratcliffe 2009).

50. Local 287(g) agreements have risen steadily since 2002, when the Department of Justice reversed its position and announced that states have the "inherent authority" to enforce civil provisions of immigration law (Khashu 2009).

51. A Harris County AFL-CIO representative told me in 2006 that the mayor and chief of police were committed to the 1992 Houston Police Department policy (HPD 1992). He said of the possibility of the policy's being rescinded: "The chief of police and the mayor are so committed to it [the 1992 HPD policy] that I don't think it's going to change. When we showed up to city council on the Ellis Resolution, I and the others [at MACIRA], they [the city council] let it die. It's not gonna happen, and now we have the majority of progressive people. The police don't want it, no one wants it, other than a few right-wing nuts who don't really understand it." Interview, Harris County AFL-CIO, March 3, 2006.

52. In July 2010, President Obama appointed Hurtt as director for the U.S. Immigration and Customs Enforcement's Office of State and Local Coordination.

53. See also a report by the Police Foundation titled, "The Role of Local Police: Striking a Balance between Immigration Enforcement and Civil Liberties" (Khashu 2009).

54. Though the Houston Police Department chose not to sign a 287(g) agreement, Harris County did so and was first in the nation to institute the Department of Homeland Security's biometric identification system IDENT (ICE 2008b; ICE 2008c; Carroll 2009b). Other surrounding cities, such as Pasadena, have also been criticized for having de facto programs and have worked with immigration authorities during raids in the city.

55. Interview, City of Houston Mayor's Office of Immigrant and Refugee Affairs, March 6, 2006.

56. Today the newly dubbed Office of International Communities focuses on international relations more broadly, including international students, international investments, and maintaining relationships with Houston's large consular corps (interview, Director, Office of International Communities, January 11, 2012).

4. Beyond Government

1. In July 2011, Assembly Bill 889 passed the California Senate Labor and Industrial Relations Committee. If the bill were to become law, it would remove exemptions for an estimated 200,000 domestic workers under Wage Order 15. Though federal law does not explicitly exclude undocumented workers from protections, like New York's recently passed Domestic Workers' Bill of Rights, California's coverage would go significantly further (Legislative Counsel of California 2011).

2. Interview, South Bay Labor Council, April 20, 2006.

3. Outside San Jose proper, a wealth of legal aid resources are available for low-wage workers in the greater San Francisco Bay Area. These include two other clinics run through the Employment Law Center at Hastings Law School in San Francisco and at the East Bay Community Law Center in Berkeley. Others include La Raza Centro Legal, whose long history of organizing day laborers and domestic workers in San Francisco is legendary; the Golden Gate University Women's Employment Rights Center, which works with low-wage female workers in San Francisco; the Centro Legal de La Raza, which serves the largely Latino Fruitvale district in Oakland (Alameda County); and the California Legal Rural Assistance and Watsonville Law Center clinics (Santa Cruz County), which serve the largely agricultural regions south of San Jose.

4. According to the American Community Survey, over a third of residents in San Jose—the largest Bay Area city—commute more than thirty minutes to work (U.S. Census Bureau 2009a). In 2000, over a third of residents in Santa Clara County, for which San Jose is the county seat, commuted to another county for work. Of all the workers in Santa Clara County, almost a quarter commuted *from* another county, most significantly San Mateo and Alameda (MTA-ABAG 2011).

5. Interview, Legal Aid Society of San Mateo, May 12, 2006.

6. Interview, Katharine and George Alexander Law Center, April 18, 2006.

7. Ibid.

8. Ibid.

9. Interview, Stanford Community Law Center, April 17, 2006.

10. Interview, Katharine and George Alexander Law Center, April 18, 2006.

11. The legal fees these organizations are able to garner during a successful case do go back to support clinic activities but in no way cover the full institutional costs incurred.

12. Interview, Katharine and George Alexander Law Center, April 18, 2006.

13. Ibid.

14. Ibid.

15. After extensive conversations with the Santa Clara County Dispute Resolution Program, also housed within the Office of Human Relations, I confirmed that workplace disputes were

infrequently handled by this agency, and those that it did handle typically involve employment discrimination mediation. The vast majority of work-related cases, however, are referred to state agencies instead. Interview, Santa Clara County Dispute Resolution Program, October 26, 2006.

16. Interview, Katharine and George Alexander Law Center, April 18, 2006.

17. Interview, Carpenters' Local Union 405, May 24, 2006.

18. Interview, Service Employees International Union Local 715, April 24, 2006.

19. This is not to say that union members face no issues at work, or that unions provide perfect grievance systems when a violation occurs to a member.

20. Interview, South Bay Labor Council, May 16, 2006.

21. Interview, Building and Trades Council of Santa Clara and San Benito Counties, October 9, 2009.

22. Interview, Texas Workforce Commission, October 20, 2006.

23. The Department of Labor's Wage and Hour Division, the Occupational Safety and Health Administration, and the Equal Employment Opportunity Commission all have offices in Houston.

24. While official data from the 2007 annual report for the agency does report some job discrimination and wage/hour cases (36 and 35 respectively), these account for fewer than 2 percent of the overall 4,413 cases closed that year (LSLA 2007).

25. Interview, Lone Star Legal Aid, March 3, 2006.

26. Ibid.

27. Ibid.

28. Interview, Houston Interfaith Worker Justice, July 1, 2009.

29. The Industrial Areas Foundation was founded by Saul Alinsky in 1940 in industrial Chicago and has spawned a collaborative of over fifty-seven organizations throughout the United States and abroad. The central motto of IAF organizers is the "iron rule of organizing," "Never do for others what they can do for themselves," and the group emphasizes bottom-up leadership (Perry 1990).

30. According to the last provider, Neighborhood Centers Inc., "100% of CDBG funds were used for service delivery." Interview, Neighborhood Centers, March 9, 2006.

31. Interview, Mayor's Office of Immigrant and Refugee Affairs, March 6, 2006.

32. Interview, GANO-CARECEN, March 4, 2006.

33. Interview, Casa Juan Diego, March 9, 2006.

34. The official name for Justice and Equality in the Workplace has changed over the years. Fine (2006) refers to the Justice and Equality in the Workplace Program, and Karson (2004) refers to the Justice and Equality in the Workplace Partnership. Although earlier outreach material for the program from the Equal Employment Opportunity Commission refers to the Justice and Equality in the Workplace Program, the current website for the program simply uses "We Can Help Houston/Podemos Ayudar Houston: Justice and Equality in the Workplace." Throughout this book, I will refer to JEWP: Justice in Equality in the Workplace Program.

35. As of September 2009, the Lawyers Committee for Civil Rights had become inactive in the state of Texas (LCCR 2009).

36. Interview, CRECEN / America Para Todos, March 10, 2006

37. Though the agency eventually sent a liaison, his presence was minimal. This is largely due to the lack of presence of the TWC in Houston. Interview, Mayor's Office of Immigrant and Refugee Affairs, March 6, 2006.

38. Ibid.

39. Interview, Equal Employment Opportunity Commission, June 23, 2006.

40. One AFL-CIO organizer speculated that funders were probably more interested in backing interfaith efforts, rather than a union-driven project. Interview, Harris County AFL-CIO, July 2, 2009.

41. Interview, Worklife Institute / Worklife Ministry, March 7, 2006. See also Fussell and Valenzuela (2011).

42. In the last five years, several noteworthy resources have also emerged in New Orleans, including the New Orleans Workers' Center for Racial Justice, which has been instrumental in assisting low-wage native-born and immigrant workers seek compensation, including several high-profile cases on behalf of the growing ranks of guest workers (Evans 2009). See also Verma (2011).

43. Though it was clear that police department leadership was not implicated in incidents such as these, the inconsistency between the official supportive stance of the department and the behavior of rogue officers such as these was palpable and had a chilling effect in the community.

44. Interview, Worklife Institute / Worklife Ministry, March 7, 2006.

45. Houston Interfaith Worker Justice works closely with the Occupational Safety and Health Administration via the JEWP alliance, but the impression that claimants must be currently employed at the offending establishment and willing to give their full identifying information presents a significant deterrent for many workers.

46. Interview, Houston Interfaith Worker Justice, July 1, 2009.

47. In 2011, labor advocates won a major victory in Texas when Governor Rick Perry signed into law a wage theft bill that increased penalties for the crime of wage theft. Senate Bill 1024 was sponsored by Senator José Rodríguez, D-El Paso, and "closes a legal loophole that allowed employers to skirt enforcement if they'd paid just a portion of wages owed and makes it easier for police to arrest employers who fail to pay wages" (J. Smith 2011).

48. Interview, Houston Interfaith Worker Justice, 7/1/09

49. Ibid.

50. Ibid.

51. While successful union organizing drives such as SEIU's Justice for Janitors are not the sole focus of this book, JfJ provides several important lessons for crafting locally relevant campaigns. In both San Jose and Houston, JfJ's success had long-lasting impacts that reiterated the potential to organize immigrant workers, the importance of broad coalitions of support, and the persistent power of business interests. See Greenhouse (2008) for a riveting overview of the national campaign, as well a long line of scholarly case studies profiling the many local campaigns across the country.

52. Interview, South Bay Labor Council, May 19, 2006.

53. Drawn from the "Union Hotel Guide" compiled by the Hotel Workers Rising Campaign at http://www.hotelworkersrising.org/HotelGuide/.

54. Presentation by UNITE HERE Local 19 organizers, February 23, 2010. See also the "Boycott Woodfin Suites!" campaign in Emeryville (EBASE 2010).

55. Interview, Interfaith Council on Race, Religion, Economic and Social Justice, July 29, 2009.

56. Ibid.

57. Official estimates of the size of the march conflict. The San Jose Police Department and the *San Jose Mercury News* reported a turnout of 100,000. Yet the Spanish-language newspaper *El Observador* places the count at closer to 330,000 based on a photo taken from the eighteenth floor of the San Jose Municipal Building on Santa Clara Street by investigative journalist Sharat Lin (Vital 2010, 19).

58. Based on a phone call to the organization, May 4, 2010.

59. Interview, Harris County AFL-CIO affiliate (anonymity requested), 2006.

60. Interview, Sheet Metal Workers Local 54, March 8, 2006.

61. Interview, Carpenters Local 551, October 13, 2006.

62. Ibid.

63. Interview, Carpenters Local 405, May 24, 2006.

64. Interview, LIUNA Local 270, April 29, 2006, August 23, 2006, and September 9, 2006.

65. Interview, UNITE HERE Local 251, March 11, 2006.

66. Interview, Harris County AFL-CIO, March 3, 2006.

67. Some scholars have noted the distinctive nature of political activism in Houston. Cano (2009) argues that the city's proximity to the border and its sprawling geography (driven by its lack of a zoning policy) are important factors that account for the low levels of Mexican activism compared with other major gateway cities like Los Angeles and Chicago.

68. Interview, CRECEN / America Para Todos, March 10, 2006.

69. Nearly one thousand immigrant workers and their allies boarded buses from Seattle, Portland, San Francisco, Los Angeles, Las Vegas, Minneapolis, Chicago, Houston, Miami, and Boston from September 20 to October 4, 2003 (HERE 2003).

70. March organizers also included the newly formed Alianza Mexicana, which with the support of CRECEN has begun organizing with the Mexican community in Houston. Interview, Alianza Mexicana, July 1, 2009.

71. http://www.houstonunido.org/

72. Alongside its counterpart in Los Angeles, SCOPE (Strategic Concepts in Organizing and Policy Education) (SCOPE 2010), Working Partnerships USA is also a key partner in Building Partnerships USA (BPUSA 2010), also founded by Amy Dean.

73. Interview, People Acting in Community Together, summer 2004.

74. The program was later replicated by thirty other counties, and was used as a model for a statewide program (WPUSA 2010b).

75. A few years later, WPUSA also successfully raised funds in support of the creation of a health clinic to mitigate the loss of downtown's only hospital.

76. Interview, South Bay Labor Council, April 20, 2006.

77. Interview, Silicon Valley Toxics Coalition, May 31, 2006.

78. Interview, WorkSafe! October 9, 2009.

79. Interview, Silicon Valley Toxics Coalition, May 31, 2006.

80. Ibid.

81. Ibid.

82. Ibid.

83. Ibid.

84. Interview, WorkSafe! April 25, 2006.

85. For example, WorkSafe! has strongly endorsed the campaign in support of Martha and Lorena Reyes, two housekeepers who were fired from their jobs at the Hyatt Santa Clara after objecting to humiliating pictures of their faces on top of bikini-clad women displayed as part of "Housekeeper Appreciation Week" (UNITE-HERE! 2011).

86. The Houston Initiative on Worker Safety was pioneered by the WorkLife Institute, which was founded in 1988 as a "spiritual quality of work life center" that consults with business groups to encourage healthy and safe relations with their employees. The executive director of HIWS is a corporate chaplain and also the head of the National Institute of Business and Industrial Chaplains. Interview, Worklife Institute / Worklife Ministry, March 7, 2006.

87. Interview, Harris County AFL-CIO, March 3, 2006.

88. Interview, ACORN, July 6, 2009 (translated from Spanish).

89. ACORN, which endorsed Barack Obama for the presidency, was a frequent topic of controversy during the 2008 presidential election, in which opponents charged the group with promoting voter registration fraud. In 2009, the organization came under fire following an exposé released by a conservative activist that portrayed an ACORN employee advising a client on how to hide prostitution activity. The following year, the organization disbanded due to enormous

political scrutiny that led to loss of federal funds and support from many other significant donors. In November 2010, the organization filed for Chapter 7 bankruptcy. According to a final statement from the CEO, "The ongoing political onslaught caused irreparable harm. This effort was a clear attempt to cast a shadow over the historic 2008 Presidential election, and set up a far right counter offense. Through those attacks we re-tooled and re-organized. Then again came the right-wing media blitz. This time of edited videos that misrepresented our mission, and consequently misled the public. The pressure and cost of defending ourselves in multiple investigations as a result of the falsified videos has eroded our organization (Lewis 2010)." ACORN had been responsible for many campaigns to support working people, on issues ranging from housing, labor, poverty reduction, and immigrant rights.

90. Interview, AIR and TX-SIP, July 3, 2009.

91. Ibid.

92. Ibid.

93. Ibid.

94. In addition to the Houston Coalition for Immigration Reform, which has received substantial leadership from Pleasant Hill Ministries (a Baptist congregation in Houston's heavily African American and Hispanic 5th Ward), the Interfaith Coalition for Immigration Reform is active and spearheaded by The Metropolitan Organization (TMO), which works with congregations, schools, and other institutions through an Industrial Areas Foundation organizing model (interview, Pleasant Hill Ministries, September 27, 2011, and interview, The Metropolitan Organization, September 23, 2011).

95. Interview, Harris County AFL-CIO, March 3, 2006.

96. Interview, CRECEN, July 1, 2009.

97. On January 10, 2012, with support from the American Jewish Committee of Houston and the Kinder Institute for Urban Research at Rice University, leaders from the Greater Houston Partnership brought together a panel of speakers to discuss "Cost Savings of Implementing Immigration Reform" in the areas of business, law enforcement, health care, social services, and education. Representatives from the City of Houston, the Harris County AFL-CIO, and several immigrant rights organizations were in attendance (AJC 2012).

5. Advocating across Borders

1. See Benvenisti (1999), for example, which examines the role of supranational institutions such as the World Bank in shaping the actions of multinational corporations and their opponents; Winter (2006), which analyzes multilateral agreements that set global climate standards; and Varnis (2001), which highlights the growing need for international governance of transnational adoption.

2. A decade ago, Keck and Sikkink (1998) described the role that nongovernmental transnational advocacy groups can play in pressuring governments to respect the human rights of their citizens. These outside groups are able to pressure governments that are typically unresponsive to domestic demands through a "boomerang effect" by first pressuring their own government to wield influence over the violating government. See also Boli (2006).

3. While international relations scholars such as González Gutiérrez (1993) have explored the relevance of these institutions, civil society and labor scholars have paid less attention to their domestic influence.

4. A linchpin of this activity is the Instituto del Mexicano en el Exterior (Institute for Mexicans Abroad, IME), which was created to "'empower the Mexican diaspora abroad' through the organization of the Mexican emigrant community in the United States" (Laglagaron 2010, 10). This subministerial institution is affiliated with the Ministry of Foreign Affairs and has direct access to consular offices in the United States and Canada. The seventy-five IME staff working

abroad include both Foreign Service members and experienced local employees who have well-honed networks in the communities where consular offices operate. In 2009, IME's budget for programming was $2.8 million, supplemented by matching funds and in-kind donations from other government departments, businesses, individuals, nonprofits, and individuals in the community (13).

5. Interview, Consulado de México, San Francisco, March 26, 2006.

6. These include the Secretariat of Labor and Social Welfare of Mexico, the Mexican Social Security Institute, the Mexican Department of Health, and the Mexican Office of the Federal Attorney General for the Defense of Workers.

7. Solis herself is a daughter of Mexican and Nicaraguan immigrants and has interfaced for years with the local Mexican consulate through her work with organized labor and as a state senator and congressional representative of California's Thirty-second Congressional District (East Los Angeles and San Gabriel Valley) (Frank and Wong 2004).

8. The focus on construction stems not only from the large concentration of Latino immigrant workers in this industry but also from the historically strong focus that OSHA has placed on health and safety in this industry; it is also a response to the alarmingly high rate of fatalities among immigrant construction workers (Loh and Richardson 2004).

9. Interview, Equal Employment Opportunity Commission, San Francisco, August 4, 2006.

10. Interview, Consulado de México, Las Vegas, August 23, 2011.

11. Interview, Consulado de México, San Jose, May 9, 2006.

12. Translated from Spanish.

13. Interview, Consulado de México, San Jose, May 9, 2006.

14. Ibid.

15. Ibid.

16. Ibid.

17. Ibid, October 27, 2009.

18. The Texas Workforce Commission, which enforces wage/hour and discrimination protections, is not active locally and has chosen not to be a signatory to JEWP. The sole TWC office is located in Austin. Submitting claims to the state agency requires use of a mail-in process, and as a result most workers opt to utilize the federal bureaucracy.

19. Interview, Consulado de México, Houston, July 3, 2006.

20. Ibid.

21. Ibid., June 29, 2009.

22. Ibid.

23. Ibid.

24. Ibid.

25. These commonly occur when an employer does not carry insurance—which is not required by state law—and a worker has no other recourse than filing suit. Employers also often discourage workers from filing claims, in order to avoid increases in premiums, and insurers too are known to frequently challenge claims (Duncan 2003).

26. Interview, Consulado de México, San Jose, October 27, 2009.

27. Interview, Consulado de México, Denver, May 28, 2009.

28. Ibid.

29. Federal versus Colorado state minimum wage rates, respectively: $5.15 versus $5.15 (1998), $5.85 versus $6.85 (2007), $6.55 versus $7.02 (2008), and $7.25 versus $7.24 (2009) (CDLE 2010).

30. Interview, deputy district director, Equal Employment Opportunity Commission, Houston, June 28, 2006. The coalition has also received substantial press coverage (Sixel 2001, 2002).

31. Interview, Consulado de México, San Jose, October 27, 2009.

32. Interview, Consulado de México, San Francisco, March 26, 2009.

33. Interview, Ocucpational Safety and Health Administration, South Houston Office, January 12, 2012

34. Interview, Consulado de México, Sacramento, October 29, 2009.

35. Unlike the mobile consulate program, the "consulate on wheels" program relies on a separate staff and budget to reach outlying areas in the consulate's jurisdiction without redirecting existing consular resources.

36. Interview, Consulado de México, Denver, May 28, 2009.

37. Interview, Consulado de México, Houston, June 29, 2009.

38. Interview, TIGAAR representative, June 30, 2009.

39. Interview, Consulado de México, Houston, July 3, 2006.

40. Interview, Consulado de México, San Jose, May 9, 2006.

41. Ibid.

42. This is not to say that consular agencies do not also face funding cuts. For example, in late 2010, the Mexican secretary of foreign relations announced significant cuts to consular budgets, citing the expense of legal services in particular (Mendoza Aguilar 2010).

43. Interview, Equal Employment Opportunity Commission, Houston, June 23, 2006.

44. Interview, Consulado de México, Houston, July 3, 2006.

45. Interview, Consulado de México, San Jose, May 9, 2006.

46. Ibid.

Conclusion

1. However, local support should be understood as fluid and subject to shifts in administration and institutional arrangements. For example, although it had a long history of direct involvement with worker rights issues, the Houston Mayor's Office of Immigrant and Refugee Affairs, by summer 2011, was no longer taking part in managing the Justice and Equality in the Workplace hotline. That year the office was incorporated under the umbrella of the newly created Department of Neighborhoods, Office of International Communities, and went on to manage other programming priorities.

2. The Equal Employment Opportunity Commission has been the gold standard for tracing the success of charges over cities, states, and firms. Few other agencies make their administrative data as readily available, and understandable confidentiality concerns preclude any divulging of claimant characteristics. The Department of Labor's Wage and Hour Division's WHISARD database has been used by a limited number of researchers, such as Weil and Pyles (2005), but unlike the EEOC the DOL has no data-sharing arrangement with state and local agencies, making it difficult to compare claims-making in Houston (where the federal Department of Labor handles most wage and hour claims) to San Jose (where the California Division of Labor Standards Enforcement predominates). Though efforts at data sharing have begun under the Obama administration, scholarly research with these data is still fairly nascent. See also DOL (2010b).

3. As discussed in chapter 1, the disjointed nature of federal and state labor standards enforcement efforts makes comparisons across distinct regulatory contexts quite difficult. This is particularly true for the wage and hour violations. For example, while the Department of Labor's Wage and Hour Division plays a major regulatory role in Houston in the absence of widespread oversight by the Texas Workforce Commission, the California labor commissioner processes the overwhelming majority of wage and hour claims in San Jose. This bureaucratic disparity is revealed starkly through an assessment of recent wage and hour compliance data from the DOL Wage and Hour Division, which shows that between October 1, 2007, and June 30, 2011, 90 cases have been closed by the DOL-WHD in San Jose, compared with 891 in Houston (DOL 2011b). These counts are based on the author's calculation of Department of Labor WHISARD data released July 18, 2011, and accessed at http://ogesdw.dol.gov/raw_data_summary.php on July 26, 2011.

4. Similar to federal Department of Labor data, worker characteristics are not readily available from the Equal Employment Opportunity Commission, in order to protect claimant confidentiality.

5. Fifty-four total charges were filed in fiscal year 2011, compared with 244 in Houston. The foreign-born populations of San Jose and Houston are 352,966 (37.8 percent) and 610,563 (27.9 percent), respectively, and there are an estimated 228,738 and 400,522 immigrant workers in each city's labor force (U.S. Census Bureau 2011c, 2011d). Claims data are taken from a comparison of Metropolitan Statistical Areas no. 7400 (San Jose) and 3360 (Houston), using records for fiscal year 2011 through March 31, 2011. Based on the author's calculation of Equal Employment Opportunity Commission data provided through a Public Records Request on April 29, 2011. Population counts are based on 5-year estimates of 2005–9 American Community Survey data derived from Factfinder (U.S. Census Bureau 2011a).

6. During the same time period, 382 *total* charges were filed in San Jose, compared with 1,483 in Houston, and the overall labor force in each city was 488,792 and 1,130,656, respectively.

7. Further, just as there is significant debate among criminologists as to whether arrest rates represent crime levels or police enforcement, here we should similarly cautiously wonder whether the distinct political fields of immigrant worker rights in San Jose and Houston are yielding poorer workplace experiences or higher rates of legal mobilization, or both. I subscribe to the former view in Gleeson (2009), as do others such as McVeigh, Welch, and Bjarnason (2003). These analyses are able to arguably better control for spurious local variation through state-level analyses over time, and by controlling for key demographic, economic, and political factors in a multivariate context.

8. Reflecting a growing and more differentiated immigrant rights movement in Houston, as well as the increasingly powerful presence of the new worker center in the city, as of summer 2011, CRECEN was no longer directly involved in either the Justice and Equality in the Workplace Program or the Mayor's Advisory Committee on Immigrant and Refugee Affairs. Phone interview, CRECEN, July 1, 2011.

9. The classic conservative argument against an increased minimum wage contends that by increasing the costs of labor, employers will have to "cut corners" in other ways in order to respond to the rising costs of labor and in order to maintain their profit margin (Neumark and Wascher 2006).

10. After IRCA, states were responsible for providing the English/civics courses that applicants were required to complete in order to adjust their status (Cooper and O'Neil 2005), but nonprofit organizations played a significant role in the provision of these courses. Over the last decade, we have also seen a flurry of legal advocacy during the brief windows of 245(i) reauthorizations and extensions to Temporary Protected Status (Coutin 2000).

References

ABA, American Bar Association. 2006. "Legal Services Corporation Funding." American Bar Association fact sheet. Washington, DC. http://www.abanet.org/poladv/priorities/legal_services/LSCbackgrounder.pdf.

ACORN, Association of Community Organizations for Reform Now. 2009. National Living Wage Resource Center.

Adler Hellman, Judith. 2008. *The World of Mexican Migrants: The Rock and the Hard Place*. New York: New Press.

AFL-CIO, American Federation of Labor and Congress of Industrial Organizations. 2001. *A Nation of Immigrants* (Presented at the AFL-CIO 24th Biennial Convention: Conventions, Resolutions, and Executive Council Statements, Las Vegas, NV, December 2–6). Washington, DC.

——. 2006. "Procedure and Rules for Implementing the National Worker Center—AFL-CIO Partnership." Washington, DC. August. http://www.aflcio.org.

——. 2009a. "Labor in the Pulpits: A Shared Commitment to Justice." http://www.aflcio.org.

——. 2009b. "Safety and Health at Work." http://www.aflcio.org.

——. 2010. "AFL-CIO Solidarity Center Trip to Colombia—August 1–10, 2010." http://tx.aflcio.org/harriscounty/.

——. 2011. "Unions of the AFL-CIO." "About Us." http://www.aflcio.org.

Ahonen, Emily Q., and Fernando G. Benavides. 2006. "Risk of Fatal and Non-fatal Occupational Injury in Foreign Workers in Spain." *Journal of Epidemiology & Community Health* 60(5): 424–26.

AIR, Americans for Immigration Reform. 2009. "About Us." http://www.americans forimmigrationreform.com/about.

AJC, American Jewish Committee. 2012. "Immigration Summit: The Cost Savings of Implementing Immigration Reform." Rice University, Houston, TX.

Albiston, Catherine R. 2005. "Rights Consciousness, Claiming Behavior, and the Dynamics of Litigation." In *Handbook of Employment Discrimination Research: Rights and Realities*, ed. Laura B. Nielsen and Robert L. Nelson. Dordrecht: Springer.

Alderman, Jason, Gitanjali Gurudatt Borkar, Amanda Garrett, Lindsay Hogan, Janet Kim, Winston Le, Veronica Louie, et al. 2005. *The Most Conservative and Liberal Cities in the United States*. Berkeley, CA: Bay Area Center for Voting Research.

Aleinikoff, T. Alexander, David A. Martin, and Hiroshi Motomura. 2008. *Immigration and Citizenship Process and Policy*. Eagan, MN: Thomson West.

Alindor, Yolanda. 2007. Bay Area Day Labor Programs: Directory of Contacts and Services. Zellerbach Family Foundation. January.

Alvarado, Carol. 2007. "Council Member Alvarado Supports Mayor's Office of Immigrant & Refugee Affairs." Carol Alvarado Campaign press release. June 13. http://www.carolalvarado.com/0/303876/0/977D1095/.

Andersen, Ellen A. 2006. *Out of the Closets and into the Courts: Legal Opportunity Structure and Gay Rights Litigation*. Ann Arbor: University of Michigan Press.

Apple, Lauri. 2002. "The Theft of Wages Is Sin: Fighting for Migrant Workers." *Austin (TX) Chronicle*. December 27.

Armenta, Amada. 2012. "From Sheriff's Deputies to Immigration Officers: Screening Immigrant Status in a Tennessee Jail." *Law & Policy* 34(2): 191–210.

Arnow-Richman, Rachel S. 2010. "Just Notice: Re-Reforming Employment At-Will for the 21st Century." *UCLA Law Review* 58(1): 1–72.

Asher, Colin. 2007. "Victories in the New Labor Movement: Workers Groups Fight for the Rights of Young Transient Laborers in a Radically Changed Economy." *San Francisco Chronicle*. October 21.

Auerhahn, Louise, and Bob Brownstein. 2004a. *Building a Healthy Coyote Valley: A Proposal for Community Health Clinics*. San Jose: Working Partnerships USA.

———. 2004b. *The Economic Effects of Immigration in Santa Clara County and California*. San Jose: WPUSA, Working Partnerships USA. September.

Azaroff, Lenore S., Michael B. Lax, Charles Levenstein, and David H. Wegman. 2004. "Wounding the Messenger: The New Economy Makes Occupational Health Indicators Too Good to Be True." *International Journal of Health Services* 34(2): 271–303.

Bacon, David, and Bill Ong Hing. 2010. "The Rise and Fall of Employer Sanctions." *Fordham Urban Law Journal* 38(1): 77–105.

Baker-Cristales, Beth. 2009. "Mediated Resistance: The Construction of Neoliberal Citizenship in the Immigrant Rights Movement." *Latino Studies* 7(1): 60–82.

Baldas, Tresa. 2009. "EEOC Will Get $23 Million to Reduce 70,000-Case Backlog." *National Law Journal*. December 14.

Balderrama, Francisco. 1982. *In Defense of La Raza: The Los Angeles Mexican Consulate and the Mexican Community*. Tucson: University of Arizona Press.

Bandura, Albert. 1994. "Self-Efficacy." In *Encyclopedia of Human Behavior*, ed. V. S. Ramachaudran. New York: Academic Press.

Bardacke, Frank. 2012. Keynote lecture: remarks given at the Labor across the Food System conference. University of California, Santa Cruz, February 3.

Batalova, Jeanne. 2008. "Mexican Immigrants in the United States." U.S. in Focus. Washington, DC: Migration Policy Institute.

Bean, Frank D., Edward E. Telles, and B. Lindsay Lowell. 1987. "Undocumented Migration to the United States: Perceptions and Evidence." *Population and Development Review* 13(4): 671–90.

Benner, Chris. 2002. *Work in the New Economy: Flexible Labor Markets in Silicon Valley.* Malden, MA: Blackwell Publishing.

Benvenisti, Eyal. 1999. "Exit and Voice in the Age of Globalization." *Michigan Law Review* 98(1): 167–213.

Berberich, Steve. 2007. "Grocers Turn to Hand-Held Personal Scanners for Shoppers: Unions Decry New Technology." *Maryland Gazette*. Washington, DC. August 10.

Berk, Marc L., and Claudia L. Schur. 2001. "The Effect of Fear on Access to Care among Undocumented Latino Immigrants." *Journal of Immigrant Health* 3(3): 151–56.

Berman, Jennifer S. 2004. "The Needle and the Damage Done: How Hoffman Plastics Promotes Sweatshops and Illegal Immigration and What to Do about It." In bepress Legal Series.

Bernhardt, Annette. 2010. "Wage Policy from the Grassroots." *Huffington Post*. June 3.

Bernhardt, Annette, Heather Boushey, Laura Dresser, and Chris Tilly. 2008a. *The Gloves-off Economy: Workplace Standards at the Bottom of America's Labor Market.* Ithaca, NY: Cornell University Press.

——. 2008b. "An Introduction to the Gloves-off Economy." In Bernhardt et al., *Gloves-off Economy*, 31–64.

Bernhardt, Annette, and Siobhán McGrath. 2005. *Trends in Wage and Hour Enforcement by the U.S. Department of Labor, 1975–2004.* Economic Policy Brief. New York: Brennan Center for Justice. September.

Bernhardt, Annette, Ruth Milkman, Nik Theodore, Douglas Heckathorn, Mirabai Auer, James DeFilippis, Ana Luz González, et al. 2009. *Broken Laws, Unprotected Workers: Violations of Employment and Labor Laws in America's Cities.* Center for Urban Economic Development, National Employment Law Project, and the UCLA Institute for Research on Labor and Employment.

Betts, Albert, and Mike Geeslin. 2006. *Biennial Report of the Texas Department of Insurance to the 80th Legislature.* Austin, TX: Division of Workers' Compensation. December. http://www.tdi.state.tx.us/reports/dwc/documents/wc2006.pdf.

Biddle, Jeff. 2001. "Do High Claim-Denial Rates Discourage Claiming? Evidence from Workers Compensation Insurance." *Journal of Risk and Insurance* 68(4): 631–58.

Blankinship, Gary. 2009. Editorial: "Policies Play a Role in Houston Police Tragedy." *Houston Chronicle*. March 17.

BLS, Bureau of Labor Statistics. 2006. *Characteristics of Minimum Wage Workers: 2005.* Labor Force Statistics from the Current Population Survey. Washington, DC. May 19.

——. 2009a. "Industry Employment." *Occupational Outlook Quarterly (Online)* 53(4).

———. 2009b. *Occupational Outlook Handbook, 2010–11 Edition*. Washington, DC: United States Department of Labor. December 17.

———. 2010. Table 1. "Employment Status of the Foreign-Born and Native-Born Populations by Selected Characteristics, 2008–09 Annual Averages." Economic News Release. Washington DC: Department of Labor.

Bobo, Kim. 2008. *Wage Theft in America: Why Millions of Working Americans Are Not Getting Paid—and What We Can Do about It*. New York: New Press.

Boli, John. 2006. "International Nongovernmental Organizations." In *The Nonprofit Sector: A Research Handbook*, ed. W. W. Powell and R. Steinberg. New Haven, CT: Yale University Press.

Borjas, George. 2001. *Heaven's Door: Immigration Policy and the American Economy*. Princeton, NJ: Princeton University Press.

Bosniak, Linda. 2006. *The Citizen and the Alien: Dilemmas of Contemporary Membership*. Princeton, NJ: Princeton University Press.

Bourdieu, Pierre, and Loic Wacquant. 1992. *An Invitation to Reflexive Sociology*. Chicago: University of Chicago Press.

BPUSA, Building Partnerships USA. 2010. "Who We Are." http://building-partnerships. org/who_we_are_0.

Braley, Bruce. 2008. "Braley Continues Pressing for Answers on Status of Department of Labor Investigation into Agriprocessors, Inc." *United States Congressman Bruce Braley Serving Iowa's 1st Congressional District*. http://braley.house.gov/press-release/ braley-continues-pressing-answers-status-department-labor-investigation-agriproces.

Brecher, Jeremy. 1997. *Strike!* Cambridge, MA: South End Press.

Brehm, John, and Scott Gates. 1999. *Working, Shirking, and Sabotage: Bureaucratic Response to a Democratic Public*. Ann Arbor: University of Michigan Press.

Bridges, Amy. 1997. *Morning Glories: Municipal Reform in the Southwest*. Princeton, NJ: Princeton University Press.

Brownell, Peter. 2005. "The Declining Enforcement of Employer Sanctions." Washington, DC: Migration Policy Institute.

———. 2009. "Sanctions for Whom? The Immigration Reform and Control Act's 'Employer Sanctions' Provisions and the Wages of Mexican Immigrants." Ph.D. diss., University of California, Berkeley.

———. 2010. "Supreme Court Decisions regarding Workplace Remedies for Unauthorized Employees." Paper presented at the American Sociological Association Annual Meeting. Atlanta.

Brownstein, Bob. 2000. "Working Partnerships: A New Political Strategy for Creating Living-Wage Jobs." *WorkingUSA: The Journal of Labor and Society* 4(1): 35–48.

Buch, Jason. 2011. "States Diverging on Secure Communities: Controversy Swirls around Fingerprint Matching." *San Antonio (TX) Express News*. June 13.

Bumiller, Kristin. 1992. *The Civil Rights Society: The Social Construction of Victims*. Baltimore: John Hopkins University Press.

Byrd, Barbara, and Nari Rhee. 2004. "Building Power in the New Economy: The South Bay Labor Council." *WorkingUSA: The Journal of Labor and Society* 8(2): 131–53.

Byster, Leslie A., and Ted Smith. 2006. "From Grassroots to Global: The Silicon Valley Toxics Coalition's Milestones in Building a Movement for Corporate Accountability and Sustainability in the High-Tech Industry." In *Challenging the Chip: Labor Rights and Environmental Justice in the Global Electronics Industry*, ed. Ted Smith, David A. Sonnenfeld, and David N. Pellow. Philadelphia: Temple University Press.

CA-DFEH, California Department of Fair Employment and Housing. 2002. "Discrimination: Immigration Status." 2002 Legislative Summary. Sacramento. http://www.dfeh.ca.gov/res/docs/Publications/LegislativeSummaries/2002%20Legislative%20Summary.pdf.

CA-DIR, California Department of Industrial Relations. 2009. "Undocumented Worker Rights." http://www.dir.ca.gov/QAundoc.html.

Cal/OSHA, California Occupational Safety and Health Administration. 2005. *Respiratory Protection in the Workplace: A Practical Guide for Small-Business Employers*. Sacramento. http://www.dir.ca.gov/DOSH/dosh_publications/Respiratory.pdf.

Calavita, Kitty. 1992. *Inside the State: The Bracero Program, Immigration, and the INS*. New York: Routledge.

———. 2005. *Immigrants at the Margins: Law, Race, and Exclusion in Southern Europe*. Cambridge: Cambridge University Press.

Calderon-Barrera, Dennise A. 2003. "*Hoffman v. NLRB*: Leaving Undocumented Workers Unprotected under United States Labor Laws?" *Harvard Latino Law Review* 6:119–43.

Camarota, Steven A., and Roy Beck. 2002. *Elite vs. Public Opinion: An Examination of Divergent Views on Immigration*. Washington, DC: Center for Immigration Studies.

Cano, Gustavo. 2009. "¡Órale! Politics: Mobilization of Mexican Immigrants in Chicago and Houston." Ph.D. diss., Columbia University, New York.

Capps, Randy, Marc R. Rosenblum, Cristina Rodriguez, and Muzaffar Chishti. 2011. *Delegation and Divergence: A Study of 287(g) State and Local Immigration Enforcement*. National Center on Immigrant Integration Policy, U.S. Immigration Policy Program. Washington, DC: Migration Policy Institute. January.

Card, David. 2005. "Is the New Immigration Really So Bad?" *Economic Journal* 115(507): F300–323.

Carens, Joseph H. 1987. "Aliens and Citizens: The Case for Open Borders." *Review of Politics* 49(2): 251–73.

———. 2009. "The Case for Amnesty: Time Erodes the State's Right to Deport." *Boston Review*. May/June. http://bostonreview.net/BR34.3/carens.php.

Carroll, Susan. 2009a. "Geraldo Rivera Calls for End to Raids." *Houston Chronicle*. June 30.

———. 2009b. "HPD Will Train Jailers on Detaining Immigrants; but the Plan Troubles Immigrants' Advocates." *Houston Chronicle*. July 11.

———. 2009c. "HPD Rejects Immigration Screenings: HPD Won't Screen for Immigration, City Pulls Out of Controversial ICE Program." *Houston Chronicle*. October 17.

Carroll, Susan, and Renee C. Lee. 2009. "Immigrant Who Shot HPD Officer Was in U.S. Illegally; Wilfido Joel Alfaro, 29, Was Fatally Shot Last Week during Drug Raid." *Houston Chronicle*. March 10.

Caspers-Simmet, Jean. 2010. "Agri Star Promises Big Economic Effect in Postville." *Agri News*. April 29.

Castañeda, Xóchitl, and Patricia Zavella. 2003. "Changing Constructions of Sexuality and Risk: Migrant Mexican Women Farmworkers in California." *Journal of Latin American Anthropology* 8(2): 126–50.

Castellanos, Teresa. 2009. "Santa Clara County Model of Immigrant Integration: Overview of SCC County Programs." In *Latino Immigrant Civic Engagement Trends Conference*. Washington, DC: Mexico Institute, Woodrow Wilson International Center for Scholars.

CDLE, Colorado Department of Labor and Employment. 2010. "Minimum Wage History." *Wage and Hour Laws*. http://www.colorado.gov/cs/Satellite/CDLE-LaborLaws/CDLE/1251566749488.

Cedillo, Gil. 2003. SB 60. Sacramento: Senate Rules Committee. April 8. http://info.sen.ca.gov/pub/03–04/bill/sen/sb_0051–0100/sb_60_cfa_20030603_151552_sen_floor.html.

Chacón, Jennifer M. 2008. "Civil Rights, Immigrants' Rights, Human Rights: Lessons from the Life and Works of Dr. Martin Luther King, Jr." *New York University Review of Law and Social Change* 32(4): 465–84.

Chadwick, James D., and Bart G. Szafnicki. 1999. "Power of Partnership: INS and Local Law Enforcement Join Forces to Stop Criminal Illegal Aliens." *Police Chief* 66(8): 46–51.

Chammartin, Gloria Moreno-Fontes. 2004. "Women Migrant Workers' Protection in Arab League States." In *Gender and Migration in Arab States: The Case of Domestic Workers*, ed. Simel Esim and Monica Smith. Geneva: ILO, International Labor Organization.

Chaudry, Ajay, Randolph Capps, Juan Pedroza, Rosa Maria Castaneda, Robert Santos, and Molly M. Scott. 2010. "Facing Our Future: Children in the Aftermath of Immigration Enforcement." Washington, DC: Urban Institute.

Chavez, Leo R. 1998. *Shadowed Lives: Undocumented Immigrants in American Society*. Fort Worth, TX: Harcourt Brace College Publishers.

Chen, Ming Hsu. 2010. "From Civil Rights to Multiculturalism: Development of Language Rights in the US." Paper presented at the Law and Society Association Annual Meeting. Chicago, May 28.

Children's Health Initiative. 2010. "About CHI." http://www.chikids.org/aboutchi/whatschi.html.

Chishti, Muzaffar, and Claire Bergeron. 2009. "DHS Rescinds 'No-Match' Rule, Moves Forward with E-Verify as It Shifts Enforcement Focus to Employers." Policy Beat. Washington, DC: Migration Policy Institute.

Chiswick, Barry R. 2009. "Top Ten Myths and Fallacies Regarding Immigration." *IZA Policy Papers* 12.

Cho, Chi C., Jose Oliva, Erica Weitzer, Juan Nevarez, Joseph Zanoni, and Rosemary K. Sokas. 2007. "An Interfaith Workers' Center Approach to Workplace Rights: Implications for Workplace Safety and Health." *Journal of Occupational & Environmental Medicine* 49(3): 275–81.

Chun, Jennifer JiHye. 2001. "Flexible Despotism: The Intensification of Insecurity and Uncertainty in the Lives of Silicon Valley's High-Tech Assembly Workers." In *The Critical Study of Work: Labor, Technology, and Global Production*, ed. Rick Baldoz, Charles Koeber, and Philip Kraft. Philadelphia: Temple University Press.

CIPC, California Immigrant Policy Center. 2010. "About CIPC." http://www.caimmigrant.org/about.php.

City of Houston. 2005. Houston City Council Minutes, December 6. No. 2005–1160–1. http://www.houstontx.gov/citysec/agendas/2005/20051206.pdf.

———. 2006. Houston City Council Minutes, May 23. No. 2006–0386–1. http://www.houstontx.gov/citysec/agendas/2006/20060523.pdf.

———. 2007a. FY08 Budget Amendments. http://blogs.chron.com/cityhall/archives/budget_amend.pdf.

———. 2007b. Houston City Council Minutes, June 19. No. 2007–0591–1. http://www.houstontx.gov/citysec/agendas/2007/20070619.pdf.

———. 2012. Advisory Committee (MACIRA). Office of International Communities. http://www.houstontx.gov/intlcomms/index.html.

City of San Jose. 1997. Minutes of the City Council. January 21, 1997.

———. 2008. City Council Agenda: April 22, 2008, Amended Agenda. http://www.sanjoseca.gov/clerk/Agenda/042208/042208aa.pdf.

———. 2009a. "Statement from Mayor Chuck Reed regarding San José's Ranking as the Safest Big City in California, Fourth in the Nation." Press release. November 24, 2009. http://www.sanjoseca.gov/mayor/news/releases/09November/safecityRankings.pdf.

———. 2009b. "Strong Neighborhoods Initiative." http://www.strongneighborhoods.org/.

———. 2010. "San Jose Redevelopment Agency Forced to Pay $62 Million to Solve California's Budget Deficit and Pay State Obligations." Press release. San Jose Redevelopment Agency. http://www.sjredevelopment.org/PressRoom/SJRAForcedPayment051110.pdf.

———. 2012. "Successor Agency to the Redevelopment Agency of the City of San Jose." San Jose Redevelopment Agency. http://www.sjredevelopment.org/.

Clark, Jane Bennett. 2008. "No. 1: Houston, Texas." *Kiplinger's Personal Finance*. http://www.kiplinger.com/features/archives/2008/05/2008-best-city-houston.html.

Coleman, Mathew. 2009. "What Counts as the Politics and Practice of Security, and Where? Devolution and Immigrant Insecurity after 9/11." *Annals of the Association of American Geographers* 99(5): 904–13.

Colley, Jenna. 2006. "City Vote on Contract for Day Labor Site Operations Stalls Again." *Houston Business Journal*. May 24.

Construction Citizen. 2011. "Texas Agencies Consider Collaboration." January 11. http://constructioncitizen.com/blog/texas-agencies-consider-collaboration-emily-timm-twc/1101111.

Consulado General de México en Chicago. 2010. *¡Conozca sus Derechos en el Trabajo!* Ventanilla Laboral. Chicago. http://portal.sre.gob.mx/chicago/pdf/060109ManualLaboral2.pdf.

Consulado General de México en San José. 2009. "Finaliza con éxito la 'Semana de Derechos Laborales.'" Press release. San Jose. http://www.consulmexsj.com/.

Cooper, Betsy, and Kevin O'Neil. 2005. "Lessons from the Immigration Reform and Control Act of 1986." Migration Policy Institute. Policy brief. August 2005(3).

Corchado, Alfredo. 2009. "Mexican Consulate Investigation Focused on Former Employee." *Dallas Morning News*. August 17.

Cornelius, Wayne A. 1998. "The Structural Embeddedness of Demand for Mexican Immigrant Labor: New Evidence from California." In *Crossing: Mexican Immigration in Interdisciplinary Perspectives*, ed. Marcelo M. Suarez-Orozco, 113–56. Cambridge, MA: David Rockefeller Center for Latin American Studies, Harvard College.

Cornfield, Dan. 2006. "Immigration, Economic Restructuring, and Labor Ruptures: From the Amalgamated to Change to Win." *WorkingUSA: The Journal of Labor and Society* 9(2): 215–23.

Cottman, Michael H. 2006. "NAACP, Obama Call for Earned Citizenship for Undocumented." *New America Media*. April 5.

Coutin, Susan B. 2000. *Legalizing Moves: Salvadoran Immigrants' Struggle for US Residency*. Ann Arbor: University of Michigan Press.

Crowe, Robert. 2006. "Loopholes Still Open for Immigrant Repeat Offenders; Slayings Show New HPD Rules, Even Deportation Offer No Guarantee." *Houston Chronicle*. October 13.

CTW, Change to Win. 2009. "Change to Win and AFL-CIO Unveil Unified Immigration Reform Framework." Press release. April 14.

Cunningham-Parmeter, Keith. 2008. "Fear of Discovery: Immigrant Workers and the Fifth Amendment." *Cornell International Law Journal* 41–81: 27.

Daniels, Roger. 2008. "The Immigration Act of 1965: Intended and Unintended Consequences." *Historians on America*. U.S. Department of State. http://www.america.gov/st/educ-english/2008/April/20080423214226eaifas0.9637982.html.

Dávila, Arlene M. 2001. *Latinos, Inc: The Marketing and Making of a People*. Berkeley and Los Angeles: University of California Press.

Dean, Amy B. 2011. "Breaking Down the Silos: Iowa Citizens for Community Improvement." *Truthout*. July 14.

Dean, Amy B., and Wade Rathke. 2008. "Beyond the Mutual Backscratch: A New Model for Labor-Community Coalitions." *New Labor Forum* 17(3): 47–56.

Dean, Amy B., and David B. Reynolds. 2010. *A New New Deal: How Regional Activism Will Reshape the American Labor Movement*. Ithaca, NY: Cornell University Press.

DeBolt, Daniel. 2010. "A New Era Dawns for Day Worker Center." *Mountain View (CA) Voice*. May 27.

Decker, Scott H., Paul G. Lewis, Doris M. Provine, and Monica Varsanyi. 2009. "On the Frontier of Local Law Enforcement: Local Police and Federal Immigration Law." In *Immigration, Crime, and Justice*, ed. Mathieu Deflem, 261–276. Bingley, UK: Emerald Group Publishing.

De Genova, Nicholas. 2002. "Migrant 'Illegality' and Deportability in Everyday Life." *Annual Review of Anthropology* 31: 419–47.

de Graauw, Els. 2008. "Nonprofit Organizations and the Urbanized Politics of Immigrant Representation in San Francisco." In *Racial and Ethnic Politics in California*, ed. Sandra Bass, Bruce E. Cain, and Jaime A. Regalado, 175–95. Berkeley, CA: Institute of Governmental Studies Press.

———. 2009. "The Identity Crisis of Undocumented Immigrants and Intergovernmental Tensions over Municipal ID Cards in San Francisco." Paper presented at the Law and Society Association Annual Meeting. Denver.

de Graauw, Els, and Caroline Andrew. 2011. "Immigrant Political Incorporation in American and Canadian Cities." In *Immigrant Geographies of North American Cities*, ed. Carlos Teixeira, Wei Li, and Audrey Kobayashi, 179–206. Don Mills, ON: Oxford University Press.

Delaney, Kathryn. 2002. "As Part of a Nationwide Effort, OSHA Is Exploring New Ways to Reach Hispanics in the Lone Star State." Hispanic Outreach: Delivering the Safety and Health Message. OSHA, Occupational Safety and Health Administration. http://www.osha.gov/Publications/JSHQ/summer2002/hisp.htm.

Délano, Alexandra. 2009. "From Limited to Active Engagement: Mexico's Emigration Policies from a Foreign Policy Perspective (2000–2006)." *International Migration Review* 43(4): 764–814.

DeLeon, Richard. 1992. *Left Coast City: Progressive Politics in San Francisco (1975–1991)*. Lawrence: University Press of Kansas.

DHS, Department of Homeland Security. 2010. *2009 Yearbook of Immigration Statistics*. Washington, DC. http://www.dhs.gov/xlibrary/assets/statistics/yearbook/2009/ois_yb_2009.pdf.

Dickey, Jim. 1994. "Law Center Assists Immigrants Fights for the Rights of Low-Income Workers." *San Jose (CA) Mercury News*. October 17.

DOL (Department of Labor). 2002a. *Annual Report, Fiscal Year 2002*. Washington, DC.

——. 2002b. Ministerial Consultations Joint Declaration between the Department of Labor of the United States of America and the Secretariat of Labor and Social Welfare of the United Mexican States Concerning U.S. NAO Public Communications 9901 and 2000–01 Mexican NAO Public Communication 9804. Bureau of International Labor Affairs. Washington, DC.

——. 2002c. "U.S.-Mexico Joint Statement on Ministerial Consultations under the North American Agreement on Labor Cooperation." News release. June 12. Washington, DC.

——. 2003. "Federal Agencies and Partners Launch Asian American Worker Protection Program in Houston." News release. July 23. Washington, DC.

——. 2004a. "U.S. Labor Department Distributes $725,000 in Back Wages to Los Angeles Garment Workers." News release. August 6. Washington, DC.

——. 2004b. "U.S. Labor Secretary Elaine L. Chao and Mexican Foreign Secretary Luis Ernesto Derbez Sign Joint Declaration to Improve Working Conditions for Mexican Workers." News release. July 21. Washington, DC.

——. 2005. "U.S. Department of Labor Collects $40,000 in Back Wages for 59 California Chicken Processing Employees." News release. April 6. http://www.dol.gov/opa/media/press/opa/archive/OPA20050708.htm.

——. 2006. "Northridge Apparel Firm Ordered to Pay Nearly $120,000 in Back Wages, Damages." April 13. Washington, DC.

——. 2008. "Fact Sheet #48: Application of U.S. Labor Laws to Immigrant Workers: Effect of Hoffman Plastics Decision on Laws Enforced by the Wage and Hour Division." http://www.dol.gov/whd/regs/compliance/whdfs48.pdf.

——. 2009a. "Minimum Wage Laws in the States." Data drawn from historical table. http://www.dol.gov/whd/minwage/america.htm.

——. 2009b. "Wage and Hour Division District Office Locations." http://www.dol.gov/whd/america2.htm.

——. 2010a. "Statement of US Secretary of Labor Hilda L. Solis on pressing need for comprehensive immigration reform." News release. Washington, DC: Department of Labor. July 1.

——. 2010b. "Wage and Hour Investigative Support and Reporting Database." Office of the Chief Information Officer. Washington, DC.

——. 2010c. "We Can Help." http://www.dol.gov/wecanhelp/.

——. 2011a. "Minimum Wage Laws in the States—January 1, 2011." Data drawn from historical table. http://www.dol.gov/whd/minwage/america.htm.

——. 2011b. Wage and Hour Compliance Action Data. Data Enforcement. Washington, DC.

DOS, Department of State. 2009. "The Immigration and Nationality Act of 1952 (The McCarran-Walter Act)." In Timeline of U.S. Diplomatic History. http://www.state.gov/r/pa/ho/time/cwr/87719.htm.

Down with Wage Theft Campaign. 2012. Campaign letter. http://downwithwagetheft.org/about/campaign-letter/.

Drash, Wayne. 2008. "Mayor: Feds Turned My Town 'Topsy Turvy.'" CNN. October 14.

Dugan, Ianthe Jeanne. 2009. "Working Two Jobs and Still Underemployed." *Wall Street Journal*. November 30.

Duncan, Grant. 2003. "Workers' Compensation and the Governance of Pain." *Economy and Society* 32(3): 449–77.

Durand, Jorge, and Douglas S. Massey. 2006. *Crossing the Border: Research from the Mexican Migration Project*. New York: Russell Sage Foundation.

Durand, Jorge, Douglas S. Massey, and Emilio A. Parrado. 1999. "The New Era of Mexican Migration to the United States." *Journal of American History* 86(2): 518–36.

DWU, Domestic Workers United, and Datacenter. 2006. *Home Is Where the Work Is: Inside New York's Domestic Work Industry*. New York: Domestic Workers United & Datacenter.

Dyer, R. A. 1996. "$100,000 Contributed to Fight Wage Boost; Restaurant Group Leads in Donations." *Houston Chronicle*. December 24.

Dyer, R. A., Dan Feldstein, and Salatheia Bryant. 1997. "Voters Reject $6.50 Wage, Proposition A on Taxes." *Houston Chronicle*. January 19.

EBASE, East Bay Alliance for a Sustainable Economy. 2010. "Immigrant Housekeepers' David vs. Goliath Fight at Woodfin Hotel."

Ebinger, Fritz. 2008. "Exposed to the Elements: Workers' Compensation and Unauthorized Farm Workers in the Midwest." *Drake Journal of Agricultural Law* 13: 263–84.

Edelman, Lauren B. 1992. "Legal Ambiguity and Symbolic Structures: Organizational Mediation of Civil Rights Law." *American Journal of Sociology* 97(6): 1531–76.

EEOC, Equal Employment Opportunity Commission. 2001. *Facts about Discrimination Based on Sexual Orientation, Status as a Parent, Marital Status and Political Affiliation*. Washington, DC.

——. 2002a. EEOC Compliance Manual. Section 13: "National Origin Discrimination." Washington, DC.

——. 2002b. "EEOC Reaffirms Commitment to Protecting Undocumented Workers from Discrimination." Press release. Washington, DC. June 28.

——. 2003. "EEOC Expands Mediation with New FEPA Pilot Program." Press release. Washington, DC. April 24.

——. 2008. "About National Origin Discrimination." http://www.eeoc.gov/laws/types/nationalorigin.cfm.

——. 2009a. "Sexual Harassment Charges, EEOC and FEPAs Combined: FY 1997–FY 2008." Enforcement & Litigation Statistics. Washington, DC.

——. 2009b. "Willamette Tree Wholesale Sued by EEOC for Severe Sexual Harassment Retaliation." Press release. Washington, DC. June 18.

——. 2010. "EEOC Reaches Voluntary Settlement for Sexual Harassment with Koreatown Restaurant." Press release. Washington, DC. July 1.

Embajada de México en Estados Unidos. 2010. "El Embajador Arturo Sarukhan y la Secretaria del Trabajo de Estados Unidos, Hilda L. Solis Suscriben una Declaración Conjunta en Materia de Derechos Laborales." Washington, DC. May 5.

Epp, Charles R. 1998. *The Rights Revolution: Lawyers, Activists, and Supreme Courts in Comparative Perspective*. Chicago: University of Chicago Press.

——. 2010. *Making Rights Real: Activists, Bureaucrats, and the Creation of the Legalistic State*. Chicago: University of Chicago Press.

Esquivel, Paloma. 2011. "Seven Democrats Ask Brown to Suspend California's Participation in Secure Communities." *Los Angeles Times*. June 11.

Estreicher, Samuel. 2006. "Disunity within the House of Labor: Change to Win or to Stay the Course?" *Journal of Labor Research* 27(4): 505–11.

Evans, Desiree. 2009. "New Orleans Day Laborers Want Wage Theft Criminalized." *Facing South: A New Voice for a Changing South*. Durham, NC: Institute for Southern Studies.

Evans, Peter B., Dietrich Rueschemeyer, and Theda Skocpol. 1985. *Bringing the State Back In*. Cambridge: Cambridge University Press.

Ewick, Patricia, and Susan S. Silbey. 1998. *The Common Place of Law: Stories from Everyday Life*. Chicago: University of Chicago Press.

Fan, Chuncui Velma, and Jeanne Batalova. 2007. "Foreign-Born Wage and Salary Workers in the US Labor Force and Unions." US in Focus. Washington, DC: Migration Policy Institute.

Fantasia, Rick, and Kim Voss. 2004. *Hard Work: Remaking the American Labor Movement*. Berkeley and Los Angeles: University of California Press.

Feagin, Joe R. 1988. *Free Enterprise City: Houston in Political-Economic Perspective*. Piscataway, NJ: Rutgers University Press.

Félix, Adrián. 2011. "Posthumous Transnationalism: Postmortem Repatriation from the U.S. to México." *Latin American Research Review* 46(3): 157–79.

Felstiner, William L. F., Richard L. Abel, and Austin Sarat. 1980. "The Emergence and Transformation of Disputes: Naming, Blaming, Claiming." *Law and Society Review* 15(3–4): 631–54.

Fernández, Valeria. 2010. "Domestic Violence Victims Silenced by SB 1070." New America Media. July 15.

Fine, Janice. 2006. *Worker Centers: Organizing Communities at the Edge of the Dream*. Ithaca, NY: Cornell University Press.

Fishback, Price V. M., and Shawn E. Kantor. 2006. *A Prelude to the Welfare State: The Origins of Workers' Compensation*. Chicago: University of Chicago Press.

Fisher, Robert. 1990. "The Urban Sunbelt in Comparative Perspective: Houston in Context." In *Essays on Sunbelt Cities and Recent Urban America*. College Station: Texas A&M University Press.

Fisk, Catherine, Laura Cooper, and Michael J. Wishnie. 2005. "The Story of *Hoffman Plastic Compounds, Inc. v. NLRB*: Labor Rights without Remedies for Undocumented Immigrants." Duke Law School Faculty Scholarship Series, Paper 20.

Fitzgerald, David. 2008. *A Nation of Emigrants: How Mexico Manages Its Migration*. Berkeley and Los Angeles: University of California Press.

Fleury-Steiner, Benjamin, and Laura B. Nielsen. 2006. *The New Civil Rights Research: A Constitutive Approach*. Burlington, VT: Ashgate Publishing.

Fligstein, Neil, and Doug McAdam. 2003. "A Political and Cultural Approach to the Study of Strategic Action." Paper presented at the Annual Meetings of the American Sociological Association. Atlanta, August.

———. 2011. "Toward a General Theory of Strategic Action Fields." *Sociological Theory* 29(1): 1–26.

Folmar, Kate. 2002. "Labor's Fiercest Fighter: South Bay Council Head Has Become Political Force." *San Jose (CA) Mercury News*. November 18.

Fox, Jonathan, and Xóchitl Bada. 2008. "Migrant Organization and Hometown Impacts in Rural Mexico." *Journal of Agrarian Change* 8(2): 435–61.

Frank, Larry, and Kent Wong. 2004. "Dynamic Political Mobilization: The Los Angeles County Federation of Labor." *WorkingUSA: The Journal of Labor and Society* 8(2): 155–81.

Freeman, Gary P. 1998. "The Decline of Sovereignty? Politics and Immigration Restriction in Liberal States." In *Challenge to the Nation-State: Immigration in Western Europe and the United States*, ed. Christian Joppke, 86–108. Oxford: Oxford University Press.

Frosch, Dan. 2010. "Immigrants Claim Wal-Mart Fired Them to Provide Jobs for Local Residents." *New York Times*. February 8.

Fuller, Hugh Alexander. 2006. "Immigration, Compensation and Preemption: The Proper Measure of Lost Future Earning Capacity Damages after *Hoffman Plastic Compounds, Inc. v. NLRB*." *Baylor Law Review* 58: 985–1009.

Fussell, Elizabeth, and Abel Valenzuela. 2011. "Construction Work in Post-Katrina New Orleans: Race and Immigration Status." Paper presented at the Law and Society Association Annual Meeting. San Francisco, June 3.

Gambetta, Ricardo, and Zivile Gedrimaite. 2011. *Municipal Innovations in Immigrant Integration: 20 Cities, 20 Good Practices*. American Cities Series. National League of Cities Municipal Action for Immigrant Integration.

GAO, Government Accountability Office. 2006. "Illegal Immigration: Border-Crossing Deaths Have Doubled since 1995, Border Patrol's Efforts to Prevent Deaths Have Not Been Fully Evaluated." GAO-06–770. Washington, DC. August. http://www.gao.gov/new.items/d06770.pdf.

———. 2009a. "Wage and Hour Division Needs Improved Investigative Processes and Ability to Suspend Statute of Limitations to Better Protect Workers against Wage Theft." Department of Labor. GAO-09–629. Washington, DC. June 23.

———. 2009b. "Wage and Hour Division's Complaint Intake and Investigative Processes Leave Low Wage Workers Vulnerable to Wage Theft." Department of Labor. GAO-09–458T. Washington, DC. March 25.

———. 2009c. "Enhancing OSHA's Records Audit Process Could Improve the Accuracy of Worker Injury and Illness Data." Workplace Safety and Health. GAO-10–10. Washington, DC. October 15.

Gibson, R. Sebastian. 2009. "DFEH Complaints, EEOC Complaints, DLSE and DIR Complaints for Discrimination, Harassment and Retaliation—How a California Labor Attorney Can Decide Which to File." Law Firm of R. Sebastian Gibson. April 13. http://www.hg.org/article.asp?id=6212.

Glaberson, William. 1987. "Is OSHA Falling Down on the Job?" *New York Times*. August 2.

Gleeson, Shannon. 2007. "State Variation in Labor Violations in the U.S." UC Berkeley Department of Demography Brown Bag Series. October 3.

———. 2009. "From Rights to Claims: The Role of Civil Society in Making Rights Real for Vulnerable Workers." *Law & Society Review* 43(3): 669–700.

———. 2010. "Labor Rights for All? The Role of Undocumented Immigrant Status for Worker Claims-Making." *Law and Social Inquiry* 35(3): 561–602.

———. 2011a. "Assessing Processes of Legal Mobilization amongst Low-Wage Immigrant Workers: Findings from the San Francisco Bay Area." Paper presented at the Law and Society Association Annual Meeting, Citizenship and Immigration Collaborative Research Network Session. San Francisco.

———. 2011b. "To Protect One, We Must Protect All: Bureaucratic Scripts for Protecting Undocumented Workers." Persistent Puzzles in Immigration Law Symposium. University of California, Irvine School of Law. February 17–18.

Golash-Boza, Tanya. 2009. "The Immigration Industrial Complex: Why We Enforce Immigration Policies Destined to Fail." *Sociological Compass* 3(2): 295–309.

Gomez, Alan. 2012. "Immigration Enforcement Program to Be Shut Down." *USA Today*. February 17.

Gómez, Natalia. 2005. "Reimprimirá SRE 'Guía del migrante.'" *El Universal*. México, DF. January 22.

Gonzales, Roberto. 2008. "Born in the Shadows: The Uncertain Futures of the Children of Unauthorized Mexican Migrants." Ph.D. diss., University of California, Irvine.

Gonzalez, Arturo. 2007. "Day Labor in the Golden State." *California Economic Policy* 3(3). San Francisco: Public Policy Institute of California. July.

González, Daniel. 2006. "Phoenix Treats Cheating Laborers as a Criminal Act." *Arizona Republic*. Phoenix. February 11.

Gonzalez, Gilbert G. 1999. *Mexican Consuls and Labor Organizing: Imperial Politics in the American Southwest*. Austin: University of Texas Press.

González Gutiérrez, Carlos. 1993. "The Mexican Diaspora in California: Limits and Possibilities for the Mexican Government." In *The California-Mexico Connection*, ed. Abraham F. Lowenthal and Katrina Burgess. Stanford, CA: Stanford University Press.

Gordon, Jennifer. 2007. *Suburban Sweatshops: The Fight for Immigrant Rights*. Cambridge, MA: Belknap Press of Harvard University Press.

Gould, Deborah B. 2009. *Moving Politics: Emotion and ACT UP's Fight against AIDS*. Chicago: University of Chicago Press.

Govtrack. 2011. "H.R. 3303: Wage Theft Prevention Act." Legislation. http://www.govtrack.us/congress/bill.xpd?bill=h111–3303.

Greater Houston Partnership. 2009. "Houston Foreign Consulate Representation." Partnership Research. Houston. September 15. http://www.houston.org/pdf/research/18AW001.pdf.

——. 2010. "Doing Business Here." Houston. http://www.houston.org/.

Greenhouse, Steven. 1999. "The Most Innovative Figure in Silicon Valley? Maybe This Labor Organizer." *New York Times*. November 14.

——. 2003. "Suit Claims Discrimination against Hispanics on Job." *New York Times*. February 9.

——. 2005. "Beyond the Bargains, Grievances." *New York Times*. June 6.

——. 2008. *The Big Squeeze: Tough Times for the American Worker*. New York: Random House.

Greer, Ian. 2007. "Special Interests and Public Goods: Organized Labor's Coalition Politics in Hamburg and Seattle." In *Labor in the New Urban Battlegrounds: Local Solidarity in a Global Economy*, ed. Lowell Turner and Daniel P. Cornfield, 193–210. Ithaca, NY: Cornell University Press.

Hagan, Jacqueline Mariaw. 1994. *Deciding to Be Legal: A Maya Community in Houston*. Philadelphia: Temple University Press.

Hamlin, Rebecca. 2008. "Immigrants at Work: Labor Unions and Non-Citizen Members." In *Civic Hopes and Political Realities: Immigrants, Community Organizations, and Political Engagement*, ed. S. Karthick Ramakrishnan and Irene Bloemraad, 300–322. New York: Russell Sage Foundation Press.

Harris, Ben. 2008a. "Agriprocessors Raid Fallout Continues: Jewish Liberals Plan Rally in Postville." *JewishJournal.com*. July 22.

——. 2008b. "Child Labor Allegations in Postville Agriprocessors." *Jewish Review*.

Harris County Clerk's Office Elections Division. 2008. "Cumulative Report (Official), Harris County, Texas, General and Special Elections, November 4, 2009." http://www.harrisvotes.org/HISTORY/110408/Cumulative/cumulative.htm.

Hasan, Najeeb. 2004a. "Hide and Seek: Playing Find-the-Documents with the Valley's Cagey Labor Council." *Metro*. San Jose, CA. April 14.

——. 2004b. "The Six Million Dollar Woman." *Metro*. Washington, DC. March 24.

Haugen, Steven E. 2009. "Measures of Labor Underutilization from the Current Population Survey." BLS Working Papers. Working Paper 424. Washington, DC: U.S. Department of Labor, Bureau of Labor Statistics, Office of Employment and Unemployment Statistics. March. http://www.bls.gov/ore/pdf/ec090020.pdf.

Hawes, Amanda, and David N. Pellow. 2006. "The Struggle for Occupational Health in Silicon Valley: A Conversation with Amanda Hawes." In Smith, Sonnenfeld, and Pellow, *Challenging the Chip*.

Henderson, O. Kay. 2010. "Postville Mayor Says Community Still Recovering from Immigration Raid." *Radio Iowa*. April 14. http://www.radioiowa.com/2010/04/14/postville-mayor-says-community-still-recovering-from-immigration-raid/.

HERE, Hotel Employees and Restaurant Employees International Union. 2003. "Immigrant Workers Freedom Ride: September 20–October 4, 2003." http://www.immigrantworkersfreedomride.com.

Hill, Laura, and Hans P. Johnson. 2011. *Unauthorized Immigrants in California: Estimates for Counties*. San Francisco: Public Policy Institute of California. July.

Hirsch, Barry T., and David A. Macpherson. 2009. "Union Membership and Coverage Database from the CPS." Georgia State University and Trinity University. http://www.unionstats.com/.

Hirsh, C. Elizabeth. 2008. "Settling for Less? Organizational Determinants of Discrimination-Charge Outcomes." *Law & Society Review* 42(2): 239–74.

Hirsh, C. Elizabeth, and Sabino Kornrich. 2008. "The Context of Discrimination: Workplace Conditions, Institutional Environments, and Sex and Race Discrimination Charges." *American Journal of Sociology* 113(5): 1394–1432.

HIWJ, Houston Interfaith Worker Justice Center. 2008. "HIWJ Mission Statement." Houston. http://www.hiwj.org/.

———. 2010. *Working without Pay, Fighting for Justice: A Report on Wage Theft in Houston and How We Can Stop It*. Houston. http://www.hiwj.org/images/stories/wage_theft_report__11.16.10.pdf.

Ho, Christopher, and Jennifer C. Chang. 2005. "Drawing the Line after *Hoffman Plastic Compounds, Inc. v. NLRB*: Strategies for Protecting Undocumented Workers in the Title VII Context and Beyond." *Hofstra Labor Law Journal* 22(1): 473–531.

Hollyfield, Amy. 2011. "SJPD's New Chief Reviews Racial Profiling Tactics." KGO-TV. http://abclocal.go.com/kgo/story?section=news/local/south_bay&id=7972725.

Holmes, Seth M. 2006. "An Ethnographic Study of the Social Context of Migrant Health in the United States." *PLoS Med* 3(10): e448.

Houston Guide. 2010. "About Houston." http://www.houstonguide.com/houston.html.

Houston Press. 2001. "Best Activist: Benito Juárez." http://www.houstonpress.com/bestof/2001/award/best-activist-30662/.

HPD, Houston Police Department. 1992. General Order No. 500–5. June 25.

———. 2008. Circular: Theft of Service Involving Failure to Document Day Laborers. No. 08–0214–028.

HRW, Human Rights Watch. 2005a. *Submission by Human Rights Watch to the Office of the United Nations High Commissioner for Human Rights Committee on Migrant Workers*. New York. December 15.

———. 2005b. Submission to the United Nations Office of the High Commissioner for Human Rights (OHCHR) regarding the Protection of the Rights of the Child in the Context of Migration. New York.

———. 2010. VII: Health and Safety—Sexual Harassment and Violence. Fields of Peril. May 5. http://www.hrw.org/en/node/90125/section/10.

Hsu, Spencer S. 2008. "Immigration Raid Jars a Small Town: Critics Say Employers Should Be Targeted." *Washington Post*. May 18.

Huq, Chaumtoli, Amelia Toledo, Naomi Zauderer, and Monika Batra. 2006. *Rights Begin at Home: Defending Domestic Workers' Rights in California*. Asian American Legal Defense and Education Fund (AALDEF) and the National Employment Law Project (NELP). October.

ICE, Immigration and Customs Enforcement. 2006. Section 287(g) Immigration and Nationality Act. Fact sheet. Washington, DC: U.S. Department of Homeland Security. August 16.

——. 2008a. Delegation of Immigration Authority Section 287(g) Immigration and Nationality Act. Programs. Washington, DC: Department of Homeland Security. August 18.

——. 2008b. "Harris County Sheriff's Office First of Several Sites in the Nation to Receive Full Interoperability Technology to Help Identify Criminal Aliens— Departments of Homeland Security and Justice Providing More Identity Information to Local Officers about Non U.S. Citizen Criminal Arrests." News releases. Washington, DC: Department of Homeland Security. October 29.

——. 2008c. "Harris County Sheriff Deputies Complete ICE 287(g) Immigration Enforcement Training." News releases. Washington, DC: Department of Homeland Security. August 15.

——. 2011a. Fact Sheet: Updated Facts on ICE's 287(g) Program. Enforcement and Removal: 287(g). Washington, DC: Department of Homeland Security.

——. 2011b. Revised Memorandum of Understanding between the Departments of Homeland Security and Labor Concerning Enforcement Activities at Worksites. Washington, DC. Signed by John Morton (director, U.S. Immigration and Customs Enforcement, Department of Homeland Security) and M. Patricia Smith (solicitor of labor, Department of Labor). March 31.

IME, Instituto de los Mexicanos en El Exterior. 2005. "Matrícula Consular." http://www.ime.gob.mx/.

——. 2012a. "Deportes." http://www.ime.gob.mx/.

——. 2012b. "Directorio de Organizaciones y Clubes de Oriundos." http://www.ime.gob.mx/.

——. 2012c. "Educación Financiera." http://www.ime.gob.mx/.

——. 2012d. "Remesas." http://www.ime.gob.mx/.

——. 2012e. "Semana Binacional de Salud." http://www.ime.gob.mx/.

——. 2012f. "Servicios Consulares." http://www.ime.gob.mx/.

——. 2012g. "Ventanilla de Salud." http://www.ime.gob.mx/.

ImmigrantInfo.org. 2004. "Economic Empowerment: Wages and Working Conditions." *Bridging Borders in Silicon Valley, Summit on Immigrant Needs and Contributions*. http://www.immigrantinfo.org/borders/index.html.

INCITE! Women of Color against Violence. 2007. *The Revolution Will Not Be Funded*. Brooklyn, NY: South End Press.

IOM, International Organization for Migration. 2008a. "Global Estimates and Trends." http://www.iom.int/jahia/Jahia/lang/en/pid/241.

——. 2008b. "Migration in the Twenty-First Century." http://www.iom.int/jahia/Jahia/lang/en/pid/241.

IWFRC, Immigrant Workers Freedom Ride Coalition. 2003. "Endorsements." Washington, DC: Immigrant Workers Freedom Ride Coalition.

IWJ, Interfaith Worker Justice. 2009. "State and Local Campaigns." http://www.wagetheft.org/campaignmap/campaignmap.html#California.

Jackson, Melinda. 2009a. *Omnibus Survey Report*. San Jose, CA: San Jose State University, Survey Policy Research Institute. Spring.

——. 2009b. *Silicon Valley Pulse Survey Report*. San Jose, CA: San Jose State University, Survey Policy Research Institute. Fall.

Jacobson, David. 1997. *Rights across Borders: Immigration and the Decline of Citizenship*. Baltimore: Johns Hopkins University Press.

Jacobson, Robin, and Kim Geron. 2008. "Unions and the Politics of Immigration." *Socialism and Democracy* 22(3): 105–22.

Jayaraman, Saru. 2005. "'ROCing' the Industry: Organizing Restaurant Workers in New York." In *The New Urban Immigrant Workforce: Innovative Models for Labor Organizing*, ed. Saru Jayaraman and Immanuel Ness, 143–52. Armonk, NY: M. E. Sharpe.

Johnson, Kevin R. 2004. "Driver's Licenses and Undocumented Immigrants: The Future of Civil Rights Law." *Nevada Law Journal* 5: 213.

Johnston, Paul. 1994. *Success while Others Fail: Social Movement Unionism and the Public Workplace*. Ithaca, NY: Cornell University Press.

Jones-Correa, Michael. 2007. "Fuzzy Distinctions and Blurred Boundaries: Transnational, Immigrant and Ethnic Politics." In *Latino Politics: Identity, Mobilization and Representation*, ed. Rodolfo Espino, David Leal, and Kenneth Meier, 44–60. Charlottesville: University of Virginia Press.

——. 2008. "The Bureaucratic Incorporation of Immigrants in Suburbia: The Role of Bureaucratic Norms in Education." In *New Faces in New Places: The Changing Geography of American Immigration*, ed. Doug Massey, 308–10. New York: Russell Sage Foundation.

Jordan, Miriam. 2005. "Employers Requiring Workers to Speak English Face Suits." *Wall Street Journal*. November 9.

Joyce, Amy. 2004. "EEOC Sues Virginia Hotel over English Fluency Policy." *Washington Post*. October 6.

Kane, Will. 2010. "Tesla Reopens Fremont's Former Nummi Plant." *San Francisco Chronicle*. October 28.

Kaplan, Esther. 2007. "Liar, Liar: The New Propaganda War against Unions." *New Labor Forum* 16(1): 105–13.

Karson, Tom. 2004. "Confronting Houston's Demographic Shift: The Harris County AFL-CIO." *WorkingUSA: The Journal of Labor and Society* 8(2): 207–27.

Keck, Margaret E., and Kathryn Sikkink. 1998. *Activists beyond Borders: Advocacy Networks in International Politics*. Ithaca, NY: Cornell University Press.

Kennett, Jim. 2005. "Houston, Illegal Immigrant Haven, Pushed to Get Tough." Bloomberg. New York. December 7.

KGACLC, Katharine and George Alexander Community Law Center. 2010. "About Us." http://law.scu.edu/kgaclc/about-us.cfm.

Khashu, Anita. 2009. *The Role of Local Police: Striking a Balance between Immigration Enforcement and Civil Liberties*. Washington, DC: Police Foundation. April.

Kheel Center. 2011. "Story of the Fire." Remembering the Triangle Factory Fire. http://www.ilr.cornell.edu/trianglefire/story/introduction.html.

Krikorian, Mark. 2011. "Worksite Enforcement: Audits Are Not Enough." Testimony before the Committee on the Judiciary Subcommittee on Immigration Policy and Enforcement. Washington, DC: Center for Immigration Studies.

LaFranchi, Howard. 2010. "Obama and Calderón Agree: Arizona Immigration Law Is Wrong." *Christian Science Monitor*. May 19.

Laglagaron, Laureen. 2010. *Protection through Integration: The Mexican Government's Efforts to Aid Migrants in the United States*. Washington, DC: Migration Policy Institute; National Center on Immigrant Integration Policy.

Lagos, Marisa. 2010. "Governor Vetoes Farmworkers Overtime Bill." *San Francisco Chronicle*. July 29.

Landon, Simone. 2008. "Immigration Raid Breaks Up Organizing Drive at Iowa Meatpacking Plant: Employers Are Using Immigration Enforcement by ICE to Hurt Workers, Both Natives and Migrants." *Labor Notes*. http://www.alternet.org/story/97842/?page=2.

Langford, Terri. 2011. "Suspect's Immigration Status Surfaces in HPD Officer's Death: Federal Immigration Officials Won't Confirm, but There's a 'Detainer' on His Arrest Records." *Houston Chronicle*. May 30.

La Nueva Raza. 2010. "Houston: May 1 March for Immigrant Rights." April 15. http://nuevaraza.wordpress.com/2010/04/15/houston-may-1-march-for-immigrant-rights/.

Larsen, Erik. 2009. *Reaching "Hard to Reach" Populations: Seven Trees "Cafecitos," a Tale of Two Schools*. San Jose, CA: Strong Neighborhood Initiative.

Lashuay, Nan, Barbara J. Burgel, Robert Harrison, Leslie Israel, Jacqueline Chan, Catherine Cusic, Jane Chao Pun, Ken Fong, and Young Shin. 2002. *We Spend Our Days Working in Pain: A Report on Workplace Industries in the Garment Industry*. Oakland, CA: AIWA, Asian Immigrant Women Advocates.

Lazarovici, Laureen. 2010. "Houston: We Have a Union Hotel." America@work. http://www.aflcio.org/aboutus/thisistheaflcio/publications/magazine/0205_houston.cfm.

LCCR, The Lawyers' Committee for Civil Rights under Law. 2009. "About Us." http://www.lawyerscommittee.org/about?id=0016.

Lee, Stephen. 2009. "Private Immigration Screening in the Workplace." *Stanford Law Review* 61: 1103.

Legislative Counsel of California. 2011. *Bill Analysis: AB 889 (Ammiano)*. http://www.leginfo.ca.gov/pub/11-12/bill/asm/ab_0851-0900/ab_889_cfa_20110825_131735_sen_comm.html.

Let Justice Roll Living Wage Campaign. 2009. "States and Cities with Minimum Wages above $6.55 Federal Rate: Effective and Scheduled Rates as of July 1, 2009." "Resources."

Lewis, Bertha. 2010. "The End of an Era: ACORN Files Chapter 7 Bankruptcy." Feature story. Association of Community Organizations for Reform Now (ACORN). November 2, 2010. http://www.acorn.org/node/712.

Lewis, Paul G., and S. Karthick Ramakrishnan. 2007. "Police Practices in Immigrant-Destination Cities: Political Control or Bureaucratic Professionalism?" *Urban Affairs Review* 42(6): 874.

Leys, Tony. 2010. "Postville Packing Plant to Hire 150 Workers." *Des Moines Register*. January 30.

Lichtenstein, Nelson. 2002. *State of the Union: A Century of American Labor*. Princeton, NJ: Princeton University Press.

Lin, Sharat. 2009. "San José Police Department Targets Latinos, Photo Survey Shows." *Indy Bay—South Bay*. San Jose, CA. May 20.

Lipsky, Michael. 1980. *Street Level Bureaucrats*. New York: Russell Sage Foundation.

Loh, Katherine, and Scott Richardson. 2004. "Foreign-Born Workers: Trends in Fatal Occupational Injuries, 1996–2001." *Monthly Labor Review*. June: 42–53.

LSLA, Lone Star Legal Aid. 2007. *Justice in Action—Lone Star Legal Aid Year in Review, 2007*. Houston.

Luce, Stephanie. 2004. *Fighting for a Living Wage*. Ithaca, NY: Cornell University Press.

Mack, Kristen. 2005. "Union Makes a Statement in One City Council Race." Your Government. *Houston Chronicle*. December 16.

MacLaury, Judson. 2009. *The Occupational Safety and Health Administration: A History of Its First Thirteen Years, 1971–1984*. Washington, DC: Office of the Assistant Secretary for Administration and Management, U.S. Department of Labor.

Maestrelli, Teresa. 2010. "Miami-Dade County Passes New Wage Theft Ordinance." March 4. http://www.wagehourblog.com/2010/03/articles/wage-and-hour-policies/miamidade-county-passes-new-wage-theft-ordinance/.

Majority Staff. 2008. *Discounting Death: OSHA's Failure to Punish Safety Violations That Kill Workers*. United States Senate Health, Education, Labor and Pensions Committee (Edward M. Kennedy, chairman). Washington, DC. April 29.

Mangaliman, Jessie. 2001. "Hate Free Group Has a Sense of Urgency." *San Jose (CA) Mercury News*. December 24.

——. 2003. "San Jose 'Freedom Riders' Begin Tour for Immigrant Worker Rights." *San Jose (CA) Mercury News*. September 24.

——. 2007. "Unions Call Attention to Worker Abuses at Mercados." *San Jose (CA) Mercury News*. April 20.

Marrow, Helen B. 2010. "Deserving to a Point: Undocumented Immigrants in San Francisco's Universal Access Healthcare Model." First Annual Research Training Workshop of the UC Center of Expertise on Migration and Health (COEMH), University of California, San Diego, May 13–14.

Marshall, T. H. 1950. *Citizenship and Social Class and Other Essays*. Cambridge: Cambridge University Press.

Martin, John Levi. 2003. "What Is Field Theory?" *American Journal of Sociology* 109(1): 1–49.

Martin, Philip. 2005. "Mexico-US Migration." In *NAFTA Revisited: Achievements and Challenges*, ed. Gary Clyde Hufbauer and Jeffrey J. Schott, 441–66. Washington, DC: Institute for International Economics.

——. 2009. "Recession and Migration: A New Era for Labor Migration?" *International Migration Review* 43(3): 671–91.

Martin, Philip L., Michael Fix, and J. Edward Taylor. 2006. *The New Rural Poverty: Agriculture and Immigration in California*. Washington, DC: Urban Institute Press.

Mascaro, Lisa, and Michael Mishak. 2009. "Feds' Appraisal of Nevada OSHA Practices Damning: Probe of Agency's Response to Worker Deaths Turns Up Serious Problems." *Las Vegas Sun*. October 21.

Mashaw, Jerry L. 1985. *Bureaucratic Justice: Managing Social Security Disability Claims*. New Haven, CT: Yale University Press.

Massey, Douglas S. 1996. "The Age of Extremes: Concentrated Affluence and Poverty in the Twenty-First Century." *Demography* 33(4): 395–412.

Massey, Douglas S., Jorge Durand, and Nolan J. Malone. 2003. *Beyond Smoke and Mirrors*. New York: Russell Sage Foundation.

Massey, Douglas S., and Kristin E. Espinosa. 1997. "What's Driving Mexico-U.S. Migration? A Theoretical, Empirical and Policy Analysis." *American Journal of Sociology* 102(4): 939–99.

Matthews, Glenna. 2003. *Silicon Valley, Women, and the California Dream: Gender, Class, and Opportunity in the Twentieth Century*. Palo Alto, CA: Stanford University Press.

Maynard-Moody, Steven, and Michael C. Musheno. 2003. *Cops, Teachers, Counselors: Stories from the Front Lines of Public Service*. Ann Arbor: University of Michigan Press.

Mayor Watch. 2006. "Is Chuck Reed a Closeted Republican?" http://mayorwatch. blogspot.com/2006/08/is-chuck-reed-closeted-republican.html.

McCann, Michael W. 1994. *Rights at Work: Pay Equity Reform and the Politics of Legal Mobilization*. Chicago: University of Chicago Press.

McCarthy, Allison L. 2009. "The May 12, 2008 Postville, Iowa Immigration Raid: A Human Rights Perspective." *Transnational Law and Contemporary Problems* 19: 293–315.

McElhone, Sharon. 2006. "Chuck Reed and His Plans to 'Reboot' the Way San Jose Does Business." *La Oferta*. San Jose, CA. February 3.

McGreevy, Patrick, and Anthony York. 2011. "Brown Vetoes Farmworker Bill: Despite Pressure, He Rejects Measure Making It Easier for Laborers to Organize." *Los Angeles Times*. June 29.

McVeigh, Rory, Michael R. Welch, and Thoroddur Bjarnason. 2003. "Hate Crime Reporting as a Successful Social Movement Outcome." *American Sociological Review* 68(6): 843–67.

Mehta, Chirag, Nik Theodore, and Marielena Hincapié. 2003. *Social Security Administration's No-Match Letter Program: Implications for Immigration Enforcement and Workers' Rights*. Center for Urban Economic Development. Project no. 490. Chicago: University of Illinois at Chicago. November.

Meissner, Doris. 2009. Testimony of Doris Meissner, Director, U.S. Immigration Policy Program, Migration Policy Institute, Hearing on "Comprehensive Immigration Reform in 2009, Can We Do It and How?" Before the Committee on the Judiciary, Subcommittee on Immigration, Border Security and Citizenship, U.S. Senate. Washington, DC: Migration Policy Institute. April 30.

Mendoza Aguilar, Gardenia. 2010. "Se Reducen los Recursos a Los Migrantes." *La Opinión*. Los Angeles. October 14.

Merry, Sally Engle. 1988. "Legal Pluralism." *Law & Society Review* 22(5): 869–96.

———. 1990. *Getting Justice and Getting Even: Legal Consciousness among Working-Class Americans*. Chicago: University of Chicago Press.

Meyerson, Harold. 2004. "A Tale of Two Cities: In the Past Couple of Decades, Los Angeles and Houston Have Both Seen Huge Growth in Their Latino Populations—and in Latino Poverty. But That's Where the Similarities End." *American Prospect*. May 17.

Michaels, David. 2007. "Is OSHA Working for Working People?" Statement of David Michaels, PhD, MPH, Research Professor and Acting Chairman, Department of

Environmental and Occupational Health, George Washington University, School of Public Health and Health Services, and Director, Project on Scientific Knowledge and Public Policy, before the Subcommittee on Employment and Workplace Safety, U.S. Senate Committee on Health, Education, Labor and Pensions. April 26.

Milkman, Ruth. 2000. *Organizing Immigrants: The Challenge for Unions in Contemporary California*. Ithaca, NY: Cornell University Press.

——. 2006a. *L.A. Story: Immigrant Workers and the Future of the U.S. Labor Movement*. New York: Russell Sage Foundation.

——. 2006b. "Labor and the New Immigrant Rights Movement: Lessons from California." Social Science Research Council. http://www.ssrc.org/.

Milkman, Ruth, Joshua Bloom, and Victor Narro. 2010. *Working for Justice: The LA Model of Organizing and Advocacy*. Ithaca, NY: Cornell University Press.

Miller Center of Public Affairs. 2010. "Public Opinion Surveys on Immigration Policy." http://millercenter.org/public/debates/immigration/surveys.

Miller, Doug. 2006. "City Passes Controversial Day Labor Site Contract." KHOU Houston. May 31. http://www.khou.com/topstories/stories/khou060531_gj_daylaborcontract.3f1f8564.html.

Minkoff, Debra. 1995. *Organizing for Equality: The Evolution of Women's and Racial-Ethnic Organizations in America, 1955–1985*. New Brunswick, NJ: Rutgers University Press.

Miraftab, Faranak, and Shana Wills. 2005. "Insurgency and Spaces of Active Citizenship." *Journal of Planning Education and Research* 25(2): 200.

Mishel, Lawrence, and Matthew Walters. 2003. "How Unions Help All Workers." Briefing paper 143. Washington, DC: Economic Policy Institute. August.

Mitra, Diditi. 2005. "Driving Taxis in New York City: Who Wants to Do It?" In *The New Urban Immigrant Workforce: Innovative Models for Labor Organizing*, ed. Saru Jayaraman and Immanuel Ness, 33–56. Armonk, NY: M. E. Sharpe.

Morris, Monique. 2010. "Do Undocumented Immigrants Take African-American Jobs?" http://naacpblogs.naacp.org/blog/?p=551.

MTA-ABAG, Metropolitan Transportation Commission and Association of Bay Area Governments. 2011. Table 1: County-to-County Commuting in the San Francisco Bay Area, 1960–2000. Oakland. http://www.mtc.ca.gov/maps_and_data/datamart/census/county2county/table1coco.htm.

Mundy, Karen, and Lynn Murphy. 2001. "Transnational Advocacy, Global Civil Society? Emerging Evidence from the Field of Education." *Comparative Education Review* 45(1): 85–126.

Muñiz, Karina. 2010. "The Janitorial Industry and the Maintenance Cooperation Trust Fund." In *Working for Justice: The LA Model of Organizing and Advocacy*, ed. Ruth Milkman, Joshua Bloom, and Victor Narro, 211–231. Ithaca, NY: Cornell University Press.

Murolo, Priscilla, A. B. Chitty, and Joe Sacco. 2001. *From the Folks Who Brought You the Weekend: A Short, Illustrated History of Labor in the United States*. New York: New Press.

Nash, James L. 2003. "OSHA Expands Outreach to Hispanic Workers." *Occupational Hazards* 65(5): 12.

National Law Journal. 2011. "Plaintiffs' Immigration Status 'Irrelevant' to Their Wage Claims, Mass. Judge Rules." April 1.

Nazario, Sonia, and Doug Smith. 2008. "Inspectors Find Dirt on Books at Southern California Carwashes." *Los Angeles Times*. March 22.

NCOSH, National Council for Occupational Safety and Health. 2009. "What Is the National Council for Occupational Safety and Health ('The National COSH')." "About Us." http://www.coshnetwork.org/.

NCSL, National Conference of State Legislatures. 2011. "2011 State Immigration-Related Bills." Immigration Policy Project. Washington, DC. http://www.ncsl.org/default.aspx?tabid=19897.

NELP, National Employment Law Project. 2009a. "Independent Contractor Misclassification and Subcontracting." http://www.nelp.org/site/issues/category/independent_contractor_misclassification_and_subcontracting.

——. 2009b. "Unemployment Rate Jumps Past 10% Plateau." Press release. Washington, DC. http://www.nelp.org/page/-/UI/PR.Oct09.Jobs.pdf?nocdn=1.

Ness, Immanuel. 2005. *Immigrants, Unions, and the New US Labor Market*. Philadelphia: Temple University Press.

Neumark, David, and William Wascher. 2006. "Minimum Wages and Employment: A Review of Evidence from the New Minimum Wage Research." National Bureau of Economic Research Working Paper no. W12663.

——. 2008. "Minimum Wages and Low-Wage Workers: How Well Does Reality Match the Rhetoric?" *Minnesota Law Review* 92: 1296–1316.

Nevins, Joseph. 2002. *Operation Gatekeeper: The Rise of the "Illegal Alien" and the Making of the US-Mexico Boundary*. New York: Routledge.

Ngai, Mae M. 2004. *Impossible Subjects: Illegal Aliens and the Making of Modern America*. Princeton. NJ: Princeton University Press.

Nielsen, Laura B., and Robert L. Nelson. 2005. *Handbook of Employment Discrimination Research: Rights and Realities*. New York: Springer.

Nielsen, Laura B., Robert L. Nelson, and Ryon Lancaster. 2008. "Uncertain Justice: Litigating Claims of Employment Discrimination in the Contemporary United States." 3rd Annual Conference on Empirical Legal Studies Papers. American Bar Foundation research paper. September 13. http://ssrn.com/paper=1093313.

NILC, National Immigration Law Center. 2002a. "Courts Continue Rejecting Defendants' Post-Hoffman Inquiries into Plaintiffs' Immigration Status." *Immigrants' Rights Update* 16(6). October 21.

——. 2002b. "*Rodriguez v. The Texan, Inc.*: Defendant's Failure to Raise Plaintiffs' Failure to 'Mitigate Damages' Precludes Introducing Immigration Status Evidence at Trial." *Immigrants' Rights Update* 16(6). October 21.

——. 2003. "*Sanchez et al. v. Eagle Alloy, Inc.*: Michigan Court of Appeals Limits Workers' Compensation Recovery in Cases Involving Undocumented Workers." *Immigrants' Rights Update* 17(1). February 21.

——. 2005. "New Hampshire Supreme Court: Undocumented Workers May Recover Lost Earnings at U.S. Wage Levels in Limited Circumstances." *Immigrants' Rights Update* 19(5). October 5.

——. 2008a. "Facts about the Social Security 'No-Match' Letter." Los Angeles. March 26.

——. 2008b. "Laws, Resolutions and Policies Instituted across the U.S. Limiting Enforcement of Immigration Laws by State and Local Authorities." Los Angeles.

——. 2009a. "Basic Pilot / E-Verify: Why Mandatory Employer Participation Will Hurt Workers, Businesses, and the Struggling U.S. Economy." Los Angeles. February.

——. 2009b. "Facts about the Social Security 'No-Match' Letter" (updated October 2009). Los Angeles. November.

——. 2010. "SB 1070, Arizona: U.S. Department of Justice Files Lawsuit against Arizona's Racial Profiling Law, NILC and Other Groups Also Challenging Law Laud Obama Administration's Action." Washington, DC. July 6.

NLRB, National Labor Relations Board. 2002. Procedures and Remedies for Discriminatees Who May Be Undocumented Aliens after *Hoffman Plastic Compounds, Inc.* Memorandum GC 02–06. Washington, DC. July 19.

——. 2011. "Board Holds That Supreme Court Decision Forecloses Backpay Remedy for Undocumented Immigrant Workers." News releases. Washington, DC. August 9.

No More Deaths. 2011. "Deaths on AZ Border Oct. 2010–Apr. 2011." http://www.nomoredeaths.org/Information/deaths.html.

Normand, Vrinda. 2007. "Selling Sanctuary." *MetroActive*. San Jose, CA. June 27.

Noy, Darren. 2009. "When Framing Fails: Ideas, Influence, and Resources in San Francisco's Homeless Policy Field." *Social Problems* 56(2): 223–42.

NRA, National Restaurant Association. 2008. "Restaurant Industry—Facts at a Glance." http://www.restaurant.org.

NRTWO, National Right to Work Organization. 2007. "Right to Work States." http://www.nrtw.org/rtws.htm.

OECD, Organisation for Economic Co-operation and Development. 2008. "Growing Unequal? Income Distribution and Poverty in OECD Countries." Summary in English. OECD Multilingual Summaries. http://www.oecd.org/dataoecd/45/42/41527936.pdf.

OEHHA, Office of Environmental Health Hazard Assessment. 2007. "Proposition 65." http://www.oehha.org/prop65.html.

Office of the Mayor. 2009. Letter from Bill White (mayor of the City of Houston, Texas) to John P. Torres (acting assistant secretary, U.S. Department of Homeland Security). March 16.

Office of the Mayor Chuck Reed. 2009. "Mayor Reed's Green Vision for San José." San Jose, CA. http://www.sanjoseca.gov/mayor/goals/environment/GreenVision/GreenVision.asp.

Office of U.S. Senator Russ Feingold. 2006. "Senators Call on Chertoff to Explain ICE's Refusal to Disavow Enforcement Practice That Undermines Workplaces Protections." Washington, DC. http://feingold.senate.gov/releases/06/03/20060307.html.

Oliart, Patricia. 2008. "Indigenous Women's Organizations and the Political Discourses of Indigenous Rights and Gender Equity in Peru." *Latin American and Caribbean Ethnic Studies* 3(3): 291–308.

Olson, Bradley, and R. G. Ratcliffe. 2009. "White Kicks Off His Campaign for Governor: But Perry Has Little to Say about the Houston Mayor's Bid." *Houston Chronicle*. December 4.

OMB, Office of Management and Budget. 2010. "U.S. Department of Labor." Washington, DC. http://www.whitehouse.gov/omb/fy2010_department_labor/.

Orozco, Manuel, and Manuel Rouse. 2007. "Migrant Hometown Associations and Opportunities for Development: A Global Perspective." Inter-American Dialogue. Washington, DC: Migration Policy Institute. February. http://www.migrationinformation.org/feature/display.cfm?ID=579.

Orum, Anthony M., and Joe R. Feagin. 1991. "A Tale of Two Cases." In *A Case for the Case Study*, ed. Joe R. Feagin, Anthony M. Orum, and Gideo Sjoberg. Chapel Hill: University of North Carolina Press.

OSHA, Occupational Safety and Health Administration. 2003a. "Agreement Establishing an Alliance between the Occupational Safety and Health Administration, U.S. Department of Labor Denver and Englewood Area Offices, the U.S. Department of Labor Wage and Hour Division Denver District Office, the Equal Employment Opportunity Commission Denver District Office, and the Consulado General De Mexico En Denver, Colorado." Washington, DC.

———. 2003b. "Justice, Safety & Equality in the Workplace: Dallas, Texas." Washington, DC. http://www.osha.gov/dcsp/success_stories/compliance_assistance/jsew_accord_20030610.html.

———. 2003c. "State Incentives: Promoting Voluntary Compliance." http://www.osha.gov/dcsp/osp/oshspa/2003_report/state_promoting.html.

———. 2003d. "State Initiatives: Reducing Workplace Risks." http://www.osha.gov/dcsp/osp/oshspa/2003_report/state_promoting.html.

———. 2004a. ACCSH (Advisory Committee on Construction Safety and Health) Transcripts: October 20. Washington, DC.

———. 2004b. Annual Report on the Alliance Program, October 1, 2003, to September 30, 2004. Washington, DC.

———. 2005a. Agreement between the U.S. Department of Labor's Occupational Safety and Health Administration, Region II, and the Consulate General of Mexico in New York, New York. Washington, DC. October 12.

———. 2005b. Agreement Establishing an Alliance between the Occupational Safety and Health Administration, U.S. Department of Labor Austin Area Office and Consulate General of Mexico in San Antonio and Associated General Contractors of America. Washington, DC. January 28.

———. 2005c. Agreement Establishing an Alliance between the Occupational Safety and Health Administration, U.S. Department of Labor Austin Area Office, and Consulate General of Mexico in Austin, and Construction Safety & Health, Inc. Washington, DC. January 21.

———. 2005d. Annual Alliance Report, the Consulate of El Salvador, Long Island, New York. Washington, DC. July 1.

———. 2005e. Arrangement Establishing an Alliance between the U.S. Department of Labor's Occupational Safety and Health Administration Region II and the Consulate General of Guatemala in New York, New York. Washington, DC. October 13.

———. 2005f. "OSHA Joins with Guatemalan Consulate to Enhance Safety and Health for Hispanic Workers in New York and New Jersey." Region 2 news release. Washington, DC. November 9.

———. 2006. Arrangement Establishing an Alliance between U.S. Department of Labor Occupational Safety and Health Administration Houston Area Offices and Consulate General of Mexico in Houston. March 24.

———. 2007a. Arrangement Establishing an Alliance between the U.S. Department of Labor's the Occupational Safety and Health Administration, U.S. Department of Labor Des Moines Area Office, the United States Department of Labor's Wage and Hour Division, U.S. Department of Labor Des Moines District Office, the Iowa Division of Labor, and the Consulate of Mexico in Omaha, Nebraska. Washington, DC.

———. 2007b. The Consulate of Mexico in Seattle, Annual Alliance Report. Washington, DC. April 3.

———. 2007c. "Region IV and Mexican Consulate Alliance Establish Helpline to Assist Hispanic Workers in the Southeast." Washington, DC. December.

———. 2008a. Annual Alliance Report, Kansas City Area Office, Wage and Hour Division, Kansas City District Office, and the Consulate of Mexico in Kansas City, Missouri. Washington, DC. October 15.

———. 2008b. Arrangement Establishing an Alliance between the United States Department of Labor's Occupational Safety and Health Administration, Omaha Area Office, the United States Department of Labor's Wage and Hour Division Omaha Area Office, the Nebraska Workers' Compensation Court, Nebraska Workforce Development, and the Consulate of Mexico in Omaha, Nebraska. Washington, DC. October 23.

———. 2009a. Mexican Consulate / Wage and Hour / Iowa Division of Labor, Annual Alliance Report. January 22.

———. 2009b. "Region V's Chicago North Area Office Reaches Out to Thousands of Hispanics at the Binational Health Week." Washington, DC. March.

———. 2010. National Action Summit for Latino Worker Health & Safety.

———. 2011. State Occupational Safety and Health Plans. Washington, DC.

PACT, People Acting in Community Together. 2010. "Survey Shows Widespread Racial Profiling in San Jose." Media Alerts, San Jose. September 14.

Pánuco, Cindy. 2008. "Assessing the Rights of Undocumented Workers: Rejecting Federal Preemption of State Labor Protections." *Los Angeles Public Interest Law Journal* 1: 285–311.

Paoletti, Sarah, Rebecca Smith, Claudia Flores, Lenora Lapidus, Chandra Bhatnagar, Steve Watt, Ann Beeson, Jennifer C. Chang, and Lucas Guttentag. 2006. Petition Alleging Violations of the Human Rights of Undocumented Workers by the United States of America. Report to the Inter-American Commission on Human Rights, Organization of American States. American Civil Liberties Union. November 1.

Papademetriou, Demetrios G., and Aaron Terrazas. 2009. "Immigrants in the United States and the Current Economic Crisis." Washington, DC: Migration Policy Institute. April.

Parker, Wendy. 2005. "Lessons in Losing: Race and National Origin Employment Discrimination Litigation in Federal District Court." Wake Forest University Legal Studies Paper. February 1.

Parks, James. 2007. "Immigrant Union Membership Grew 30 Percent in Last Decade." *AFL-CIO Now Blog*. August 30.

———. 2010. "Trumka's Speech on Immigration Available Now in Video Excerpts." Washington, DC. June 24.

Passel, Jeffrey S. 2006. "Size and Characteristics of the Unauthorized Migrant Population in the U.S." Washington, DC: Pew Hispanic Center. March 7.

Passel, Jeffrey, and D'Vera Cohn. 2009. "A Portrait of the Unauthorized Migrants in the United States." Washington, DC: Pew Hispanic Center. April 14.

———. 2010. "U.S. Unauthorized Immigration Flows Are Down Sharply since Mid-Decade." Washington, DC: Pew Hispanic Center. September 1.

———. 2011. "Unauthorized Immigrant Population: National and State Trends, 2010." "Data and Resources." Washington, DC: Pew Hispanic Center. February 1.

Pellow, David N., and Glenna Matthews. 2006. "Immigrant Workers in Two Eras: Struggles and Successes in Silicon Valley." In Smith, Sonnenfeld, and Pellow, *Challenging the Chip*.

Pellow, David N., and Lisa S. H. Park. 2003. *The Silicon Valley of Dreams: Environmental Injustice, Immigrant Workers, and the High-Tech Global Economy*. New York: NYU Press.

Peri, Giovanni. 2007. "How Immigrants Affect California Employment and Wages." *California Counts: Population Trends and Profiles* 8(3). San Francisco: Public Policy Institute of California. February.

Perry, Cynthia. 1990. "IAF, 50 Years Organizing for Change." Chicago: Industrial Areas Foundation.

PHC, Pew Hispanic Center. 2006. "The State of American Public Opinion on Immigration in Spring 2006: A Review of Major Surveys." Fact sheet. Washington, DC. May 17.

———. 2007. "2007 National Survey of Latinos: As Illegal Immigration Issue Heats Up, Hispanics Feel a Chill." December.

———. 2009. "Hispanics of Guatemalan Origin in the United States, 2007." Fact sheet. October 15.

Pinkerton, James. 2007a. "Day Labor Center Saved from Closure; Although the City Didn't Renew Its Contract, Private Funds Will Keep It Open Another Year." *Houston Chronicle*. July 3.

———. 2007b. "Day Workers Plagued by Wage Theft: Local Advocates Hope to Recoup Pay in Problem Plaguing Nation." *Houston Chronicle*. July 30.

———. 2009a. "Parts of ICE Plan Worry Hurtt." *Houston Chronicle*. May 20.

———. 2009b. "Police, Mayor Square Off over Policy—Union Wants Ban against Asking about Immigration Status Overturned." *Houston Chronicle*. July 3.

Pinkerton, James, and Susan Carroll. 2007. "City Ends Funding for Day-Labor Hall: Site in East End Was at the Center of 2006 Debate about Immigration Policy." *Houston Chronicle*. June 21.

Piore, Michael J. 1979. *Birds of Passage: Migrant Labor and Industrial Societies*. Cambridge: Cambridge University Press.

Pipes, Paula, and Nestor Rodriguez. 2007. *A Research Review of Characteristics and Contributions of Foreign-Born Labor*. Texans for Sensible Immigration Policy. January 2007. http://www.txsip.com/resources/research-review.

Pitti, Stephen J. 2002. *The Devil in Silicon Valley: Northern California, Race, and Mexican Americans*. Princeton, NJ: Princeton University Press.

Preston, Julie. 2010. "Illegal Workers Swept from Jobs in 'Silent Raids.'" *New York Times*. July 9.

Preston, Rudy. 2004. "'Justice for Janitors' Not 'Compensation for Custodians': The Political Context and Organizing in San Jose and Sacramento." In *Rebuilding Labor: Organizing and Organizers in the New Union Movement*, ed. R. Milkman and K. Voss. Ithaca, NY: Cornell University Press.

Ramos, José. 2008. "Postville Raids Hit Iowa Hard." *Hola America: The Midwestern English Spanish Newspaper*. May 21.

Ray, Raka. 1999. *Fields of Protest: Women's Movements in India*. Minneapolis: University of Minnesota Press.

Re-Elect San José Mayor Chuck Reed. 2010. "Endorsements." http://www.mayorreed2010.com/Endorsements.aspx.

Reese, April. 2009. "U.S.-Mexico Fence Building Continues despite Obama's Promise to Review Effects." *New York Times*. April 16.

Reich, Robert. 2011. "Why Inequality Is the Real Cause of Our Ongoing Terrible Economy." *New York Times*. September 4.

Reyes, Belinda I., Hans P. Johnson, and Richard Van Swearingen. 2002. *Holding the Line? The Effect of the Recent Border Build-up on Unauthorized Immigration*. San Francisco: Public Policy Institute of California.

Reynolds, David, and Jen Kern. 2004. "Labor and the Living-Wage Movement." *WorkingUSA: The Journal of Labor and Society* 5(3): 17–45.

Rhee, Nari. 2004. "Living Wage Jobs and Quality of Life: The Community Benefits Initiative in San Jose." *Perspectives on Work: The Magazine of the Labor and Employment Relations Association*. Fall.

——. 2007. "Searching for Working Class Politics: Labor, Community and Urban Power in Silicon Valley." Ph.D. diss., University of California, Berkeley.

Rhee, Nari, and Julie Anna Sadler. 2007. "Building an Inclusive City: Labor-Community Coalitions and the Struggle for Urban Power in San Jose." In *Labor in the New Urban Battlegrounds: Local Solidarity in a Global Economy*, ed. Lowell Turner and Daniel P. Cornfield, 178–92. Ithaca, NY: Cornell University Press.

Rhor, Monica, and Peter Prengaman. 2008. "Immigration Debate Takes Back Seat as Southeast Texas Looks to Latinos in Rebuilding from Ike." Associated Press. Pasadena, TX. September 22.

Riccardi, Nicholas. 2006. "New Denver Law Aims to Ensure Pay for Immigrant Day Laborers." *Los Angeles Times*. January 3.

Ridgley, Jennifer. 2008. "Cities of Refuge: Immigration Enforcement, Police, and the Insurgent Genealogies of Citizenship in US Sanctuary Cities." *Urban Geography* 29(1): 53–77.

Rising Together. 2009. "About." http://risingtogether.wordpress.com/about/.

Robinson, Lisa, and Andrew Grant-Thomas. 2004. *Race, Place, and Home: A Civil Rights and Metropolitan Opportunity Agenda*. Cambridge, MA: Civil Rights Project at Harvard University.

ROC-NY, Restaurant Opportunities Center of New York. 2005. *Behind the Kitchen Door: Pervasive Inequality in New York City's Thriving Restaurant Industry*. New York: Restaurant Opportunities Center of New York and the New York City Restaurant Industry Coalition. January 25. http://www.urbanjustice.org/pdf/publications/ BKDFinalReport.pdf.

——. 2009. *The Great Service Divide: Occupational Segregation and Inequality in the New York City Restaurant Industry*. New York: Restaurant Opportunities Center of New York and the New York City Restaurant Industry Coalition.

Rodriguez, Cristina, Muzaffar Chishti, and Kimberly Nortman. 2007. *Testing the Limits: A Framework for Assessing the Legality of State and Local Immigration Measures*. National Center on Immigrant Integration Policy. Washington, DC: Migration Policy Institute.

Rodriguez, Joe. 2010. "San Jose to Boycott Arizona, Sort Of." *San Jose (CA) Mercury News*. June 8.

Rodriguez, Lori. 2006. "Will Missteps End Rise of a Political Natural? Alvarado's Hopes for Higher Office May Have Vanished, Some Observers Say." *Houston Chronicle*. March 27.

Rodriguez, Robert. 2010. "Heat Is On to Enforce Farm Heat Safety Rules: Advocacy Group Visits Valley Farms to Ensure Compliance." *Fresno (CA) Bee*. July 3.

Rosenberg, Gerald N. 1991. *The Hollow Hope: Can Courts Bring About Social Change?* Chicago: University of Chicago Press.

Ruckelshaus, Catherine K. 2007. Providing Fairness to Workers Who Have Been Misclassified as Independent Contractors. Testimony of Catherine K. Ruckelshaus, National Employment Law Project Hearing before the U.S. House of Representatives Committee on Education and Labor Subcommittee on Workforce Protections. National Employment Law Project. March 27. http://www.nelp.org/page/-/Justice/ IndependentContractorTestimony2007.pdf.

Rusk, Karina. 2006. "San Jose Mayoral Candidate Profile: Cindy Chavez." ABC-KGO. May 23. http://abclocal.go.com/kgo/story?section=news/assignment_7&id= 4198815.

Rytina, Nancy. 2002. "IRCA Legalization Effects: Lawful Permanent Residence and Naturalization through 2001." Paper presented at "The Effects of Immigrant Legalization Programs on the United States: Scientific Evidence on Immigrant Adaptation and Impacts on U.S. Economy and Society." The Cloister, Mary Woodward Lasker Center, NIH Main Campus, Bethesda, MD. October 25.

Rytina, Nancy, and John Simanksi. 2009. Apprehensions by the U.S. Border Patrol: 2005–2008. Fact sheet. Washington, DC: Department of Homeland Security.

Salamon, Lester M. 1987. "Partners in Public Service: The Scope and Theory of Government-Nonprofit Relations." In *The Nonprofit Sector: A Research Handbook*, ed. W. W. Powell, 99–117. New Haven, CT: Yale University Press.

——. 2002. "The New Governance and the Tools of Public Action: An Introduction." In *The Tools of Government: A Guide to the New Governance*, ed. Lester M. Salamon. New York: Oxford University Press.

Salcido, Olivia, and Madelaine Beth Adelman. 2004. "He Has Me Tied with the Blessed and Damned Papers: Undocumented-Immigrant Battered Women in Phoenix, Arizona." *Human Organization* 63(2): 162–72.

Sallaz, Jeffrey J., and Jane Zavisca. 2007. "Bourdieu in American Sociology, 1980–2004." *Annual Review of Sociology* 33: 21–41.

San Jose City Council. 2007. Resolution No. 73677: A Resolution of the Council of the City of San Jose Supporting Public Safety and Immigrant Rights. San Jose, CA. March 6. http://www.sanjoseca.gov/clerk/ORDS_RESOS/RESO_73677.pdf.

Santa Clara County (CA) Registrar of Voters. 2009. November 4, 2008, Presidential Election Official Final Results. http://www.sccgov.org/elections/results/nov2008/.

Sarkar, Saurav. 2011. "Houston's Revolution Will Not Be Televised." *Next American City*. Washington, DC. http://americancity.org/magazine/article/houstons-revolution-will-not-be-televised-sarkar/.

Saxenian, AnnaLee. 2007. *The New Argonauts: Regional Advantage in a Global Economy*. Cambridge, MA: Harvard University Press.

SBLC, South Bay AFL-CIO Labor Council. 2007. "Principles on Comprehensive Immigration Reform." Labor Net. May 21.

——. 2008. "San Jose Council Approves Higher Standards at Airport." October 29.

——. 2009. "11th Year of Labor in the Pulpits Faith Reaches Most Worshipers Ever." September 15.

——. 2010a. "Political Advocacy and Endorsement: Our Political Priorities." http://www.atwork.org/.

——. 2010b. "What Is the Labor Council?" http://www.atwork.org/.

——. 2012. "A Packed Council Chambers Reacts to Discussion on a Pension Reform Ballot Measure." http://www.atwork.org/.

SCC, Santa Clara County 2005. Legislative Committee, Thursday, September 15, 2005, Minutes. San Jose, CA: Santa Clara County Board of Supervisors. http://www.sccgov.org.

——. 2006. Board of Supervisors, Tuesday, April 11, Minutes. San Jose, CA: Santa Clara County Board of Supervisors. http://www.sccgov.org.

SCC-OHR, Santa Clara County Office of Human Relations. 2009. "Citizenship Still a High Priority for Immigrants; More Than One Thousand People Attend 20th Citizenship & Immigrant Pride Day." eNewsletter. March/April.

——. 2010. "Citizenship Day 2008." http://www.sccvote.org.

SCCOSH, Santa Clara Center for Occupational Safety and Health, and South Bay AFL-CIO Labor Council SBLC. 2000. "OSHA's Turnaround." Op-Ed. *Washington Post*. January 18.

SCOPE, Strategic Concepts in Organizing and Policy Education 2010. "About Us." http://www.scopela.org/section.php?id=3.

Seipel, Tracy. 2009. "San Jose Mayor Angers Labor Groups with Ethics Proposals." *San Jose (CA) Mercury News*. December 13.

SEIU, Service Employees International Union. 2009. "What Is Justice for Janitors?" Property Services FAQ. http://www.seiu.org/a/propertyservices/property-services-faq.php.

——. 2010. "Justice for Janitors ¡Si Se Puede!" http://seiu-usww.org/campaigns/justiceforjanitors/default.aspx.

Sellers, Jeffrey M. 2007. "Unions and the Strategic Context of Local Governance: A Comparative Overview." In *Labor in the New Urban Battlegrounds: Local Solidarity in a Global Economy*, ed. Lowell Turner and Daniel P. Cornfield, 35–52. Ithaca, NY: Cornell University Press.

Semana Binacional de Salud. 2005. "Binational Health Week 2006 Will Close after Holding Over 1,000 Activities for the Underserved Latino Population." Press advisory. Washington, DC: Consulado General de México and the California-Mexico Health Initiative.

Sensenbrenner, F. James. 2005. House Bill 4437: The Border Protection, Antiterrorism, and Illegal Immigration Control Act of 2005. Washington, DC. http://thomas.loc.gov/cgi-bin/bdquery/z?d109:h.r.04437.

Singer, Audrey. 2003. "The Rise of New Immigrant Gateways." Immigration, Demographics, Ethnicity, Race. Washington, DC: Center on Urban and Metropolitan Policy, the Brookings Institution.

Singer, Audrey, Susan W. Hardwick, and Caroline Brettell. 2008. *Twenty-first Century Gateways: Immigrant Incorporation in Suburban America*. Washington, DC: Brookings Institution Press.

Singh, Ajit, and Ann Zammit. 2004. "Labour Standards and the 'Race to the Bottom': Rethinking Globalization and Workers' Rights from Developmental and Solidaristic Perspectives." *Oxford Review of Economic Policy* 20(1): 85.

SIREN, Services, Immigrant Rights and Education Network. 2012a. "Policy Advocacy." http://www.siren-bayarea.org/advocacy.html.

——. 2012b. "The South Bay Raid Response Network." http://www.siren-bayarea.org/southbay.html.

Sixel, L. M. 1998. "Union Buscapade Hands Out 'Awards.'" *Houston Chronicle*. June 26.

——. 1999. "AFL-CIO Says Hispanics Paid Less." *Houston Chronicle*. June 25.

——. 2001. "Immigrants Getting Rights Information." *Houston Chronicle*. July 20.

——. 2002. "Hispanic Workers to Be Told of Rights; OSHA Involved in Getting Info Out." *Houston Chronicle*. April 4.

SJPD, San Jose Police Department. 2008. Duty Manual 2008: San Jose Police Department Policies, Rules, Procedures. http://www.sjpolice.org/download/Duty_Manual_2008_Electronic_Distribution.pdf.

Smiley, Lauren. 2010. "Undocumented Immigrants Barred from Visiting Loved Ones in Prison." *SF Weekly*. San Francisco. February 17.

Smith, Barton. 1996. *The Impact of the Proposed Local Minimum Wage upon the Houston Economy* (prepared for Save Houston Jobs). Summer.

Smith, Jordon. 2011. "A Pay Day from Perry: Perry Signs Law Targeting Wage Theft." *Austin (TX) Chronicle*.

Smith, Rebecca, Amy Sugimori, and Luna Yasui. 2004. "Low Pay, High Risk: State Models for Advancing Immigrant Workers' Rights." *New York University Review of Law & Social Change* 28: 597.

Smith, Ted, David A. Sonnenfeld, and David N. Pellow. 2006. *Challenging the Chip: Labor Rights and Environmental Justice in the Global Electronics Industry*. Philadelphia: Temple University Press.

Solis, Hilda. 2010. "Secretary Solis' Labor Day Address." U.S. Department of Labor. August 30. http://www.youtube.com/watch?v=UsXxMbFbZWQ.

Sonn, Paul K. 2006. "Citywide Minimum Wage Laws: A New Policy Tool for Local Governments." Economic Policy Brief. No. 1. New York: Brennan Center for Justice. May.

Sperling, Valerie, Myra Marx Ferree, and Barbara Risman. 2001. "Constructing Global Feminism: Transnational Advocacy Networks and Russian Women's Activism." *Signs* 26(4): 1155–86.

SRE, Secretaría de Relaciones Exteriores. 2004. "Acuerdo Marco." http://www.conapo. gob.mx/micros/infavance/2004/17.pdf.

———. 2012. "Consulares Honorarios." http://www.sre.gob.mx/.

Staff. 2008a. "Houston Mayor Announces U.S. Senate Bid." *Houston Business Journal.* December 17. http://houston.bizjournals.com/houston/stories/2008/12/15/daily25. html.

———. 2008b. "Striking Silicon Valley Janitors to Take Message to SEIU Convention." *Silicon Valley / San Jose Business Journal.* May 27.

———. 2009. "Asesoran a migrantes mexicanos sobre derechos laborales." *El Universal.* August 31. http://www.eluniversal.com.mx/notas/623328.html.

Stalker, Peter. 2000. *Workers without Frontiers: The Impact of Globalization on International Migration.* Boulder, CO: Lynne Rienner Publishers.

Steward Research Group. 2004. "Racial Profiling: Texas Traffic Stops and Searches." Texas Criminal Justice Reform Coalition, the ACLU of Texas, NAACP of Texas, and Texas LULAC. February.

Stiles, Matt. 2010. "Annise Parker: Houston Isn't a Sanctuary City." *Texas Tribune.* March 29.

Stranahan, Susan Q. 2002. "The Clean Room's Dirty Secret." *Mother Jones.* March/April.

SVAIR, Silicon Valley Alliance for Immigration Reform. 2012. "Info." https://www.facebook. com/pages/Silicon-Valley-Alliance-for-Immigration-Reform-SVAIR/149164630851.

SVTC, Silicon Valley Toxics Coalition. 2009. *AXT: Pollute, Exploit, and Move On: The Common Story of the High-Tech Industry.* San Jose, CA. http://svtc.svtc.org.

Talbott, John R. 2008. *Obamanomics: How Bottom-Up Economic Prosperity Will Replace Trickle-Down Economics.* New York: Seven Stories Press.

Terrazas, Aaron. 2010. *Salvadoran Immigrants in the United States.* Washington, DC: Migration Policy Institute. http://www.migrationinformation.org/USFocus/display. cfm?ID=765.

Terrazas, Aaron, and Jeanne Batalova. 2009. "Frequently Requested Statistics on Immigrants and Immigration in the United States." US in Focus. Washington, DC: Migration Policy Institute. October. http://www.migrationinformation.org/USFocus/ display.cfm?ID=747#9b.

Theriault, Denis C. 2008. "More Than 1,100 Arrested throughout California in Immigration Raids." *San Jose (CA) Mercury News.* September 29.

Thompson, James. 2009. "Justice Bus Rolls to Stop Wage Theft." *People's World.* November.

Tilly, Charles. 1990. *Where Do Rights Come From?* New York: Center for Studies of Social Change, Columbia University.

Torget, Andrew J. 2011. "Texas Slavery Project." http://www.texasslaveryproject.org/.

Torpey, John. 2000. *The Invention of the Passport: Surveillance, Citizenship and the State.* Cambridge: Cambridge University Press.

Tramonte, Lynn. 2011. "Debunking the Myth of 'Sanctuary Cities': Community Policing Policies Protect American Communities." Washington, DC: Immigration Policy

Center, American Immigration Council. April. http://www.immigrationpolicy.org/special-reports/debunking-myth-sanctuary-cities.

Treviño, Guillermo. 2008. "The Untold Story of Postville, Iowa." *Hola America: The Midwestern English Spanish Newspaper*.

Tsai, Jenny H. C., Mary K. Salazar, and Faan Cohn-S. 2007. "Occupational Hazards and Risks Faced by Chinese Immigrant Restaurant Workers." *Family & Community Health* 30: S71–79.

Turner, Lowell, and Daniel B. Cornfield. 2007. *Labor in the New Urban Battlegrounds: Local Solidarity in a Global Economy*. Ithaca, NY: Cornell University Press.

TX-SIP, Texans for Sensible Immigration Policy. 2009. "A Reasonable Plan for Immigration Reform." http://www.txsip.com/.

——. 2011. "This Is a Plea to the GOP   Together We Can Save America in 2012!" September. http://txsip.com/plea-gop-together-we-can-save-america-2012.

U.S. Census Bureau. 1961. "Consumer Income: Average Income of Families up Slightly in 1960." Current Population Reports. No. 36. Washington, DC. http://www2.census.gov/prod2/popscan/p60–036.pdf.

——. 2009a. 2005–2007 American Community Survey 3-Year Estimates, Custom Table. *American Factfinder*. http://factfinder2.census.gov.

——. 2009b. Table 588. Employed Workers with Alternative and Traditional Work Arrangements. *Statistical Abstract of the United States*. http://www.census.gov/compendia/statab/.

——. 2010. Table 47. Estimated Unauthorized Immigrants by Selected States and Countries of Birth. www.census.gov/compendia/statab/2010/tables/10s0047.xls.

——. 2011a. 2005–2009 American Community Survey 5-Year Estimates, Custom Table. *American Factfinder*. http://factfinder.census.gov.

——. 2011b. "Income Inequality" Historical Income Tables. http://www.census.gov/hhes/www/income/data/historical/inequality/index.html.

——. 2011c. S0501. Selected Characteristics of the Native and Foreign-Born Populations: Houston City, Texas. *American Factfinder*. http://factfinder.census.gov.

——. 2011d. S0501. Selected Characteristics of the Native and Foreign-Born Populations: San Jose City, California. *American Factfinder*. http://factfinder.census.gov.

——. 2011e. S1903: Median Income in the Past 12 Months (in 2010 Inflation-Adjusted Dollars) 2008–2010 American Community Survey 3-Year Estimates. *American Factfinder*. http://factfinder2.census.gov.

UNITE-HERE! 2009. "Hotel Workers Rising! About the Campaign." http://www.hotelworkersrising.org/Campaign/.

——. 2011. "Hyatt Strips Housekeepers of Their Dignity." November 18. http://www.unitehere.org/detail.php?ID=3484.

Urban Research Center of Houston. 2009. "The Houston Area Survey, Central Findings from Year 28." Houston: Rice University.

Valenzuela, Abel, Jr. 2003. "Day Labor Work." *Annual Review of Sociology* 29(1): 307–33.

Valenzuela, Abel, Jr., Nik Theodore, Edwin Melendez, and Ana Luz Gonzalez. 2006. *On the Corner: Day Labor in the United States*. Los Angeles: UCLA Center for the Study of Urban Poverty. January.

van der Leun, Joanne. 2003. *Looking for Loopholes: Processes of Incorporation of Illegal Immigrants in the Netherlands*. Amsterdam: Amsterdam University Press.

Van Hook, Jennifer, and Frank D. Bean. 2009. "Explaining the Distinctiveness of Mexican-Immigrant Welfare Behaviors: The Importance of Employment-Related Cultural Repertoires."*American Sociological Review* 74(3): 423–44.

Varnis, Steven L. 2001. "Regulating the Global Adoption of Children." *Social Science & Public Policy* 38(2): 39–46.

Varsanyi, Monica. 2007. "Documenting Undocumented Migrants: The Matrículas Consulares as Neoliberal Local Membership." *Geopolitics* 12(2): 299–319.

Varsanyi, Monica W. 2008. "Immigration Policing through the Backdoor: City Ordinances, the 'Right to the City' and the Exclusion of Undocumented Day Laborers." *Urban Geography* 29(1): 29.

Varsanyi, Monica W., Paul G. Lewis, Doris Marie Provine, and Scott Decker. 2012. "A Multilayered Jurisdictional Patchwork: Immigration Federalism in the United States." *Law & Policy* 34(2): 138–58.

Ventanilla de Salud. 2010. "Sobre VDS." http://ventanillas.org/index.php/es/?lang=es.

Verga, Rita J. 2005. "An Advocates Toolkit: Using Criminal 'Theft of Service' Laws to Enforce Workers' Right to Be Paid." *New York City Law Review* 8: 283.

Verma, SaunJuhi. 2011. "A Legal Bind: Employer Networks within the Guest Worker Program." Paper presented at the Law and Society Association Annual Meeting. San Francisco, June 3.

Vital, Rosario. 2010. *Coming Out and Making History: Latino Immigrant Civic Participation in San Jose*. Translated by Leslie Lopez. Reports on Latino Immigrant Civic Engagement. No. 7. Washington, DC: Woodrow Wilson International Center for Scholars.

Voss, Kim, and Irene Bloemraad, eds. 2011. *Rallying for Immigrant Rights*. Berkeley and Los Angeles: University of California Press.

Wachholz, Sandra, and Baukje Miedema. 2000. "Risk, Fear, Harm: Immigrant Women's Perceptions of the 'Policing Solution' to Woman Abuse." *Crime, Law and Social Change* 34(3): 301–17.

Waldinger, Roger, Eric Popkin, and Hector Aquiles Magana. 2008. "Conflict and Contestation in the Cross-Border Community: Hometown Associations Reassessed." *Ethnic and Racial Studies* 31(5): 843–70.

Walsh, Diana. 2006. "Reed Claims Mayoral Victory San Jose: Reed Rolls into Mayor's Job." *San Francisco Chronicle*. November 8.

Watanabe, Teresa. 2010. "For Immigrant Employers in L.A., EEOC Begins Training Seminars on U.S. Anti-Discrimination Laws." *Los Angeles Times*. July 11.

WCRI, Workers Compensation Research Institute. 2010. Workers' Compensation Laws. WC-10–52. October.http://www.wcrinet.org/studies/public/abstracts/wclaws_3rd-ab.html.

Webby, Sean. 2011a. "San Jose Police Change Definition of 'Racial Profiling.'" *San Jose (CA) Mercury News*. February 22.

——. 2011b. "San Jose: Two Federal Immigration Agents to Help in City's Anti-Gang Crackdown." *San Jose (CA) Mercury News*. June 24.

Weil, David. 2003. "OSHA: Beyond the Politics." *Frontline*. Washington, DC: PBS. http://www.pbs.org/wgbh/pages/frontline/shows/workplace/osha/weil.html.

Weil, David, and Amanda Pyles. 2005. "Why Complain? Complaints, Compliance, and the Problem of Enforcement in the U.S. Workplace." *Comparative Labor Law and Policy Journal* 27: 59.

Weinberg, Roger and Rosenfeld (law firm). 2009. "Department of Homeland Security Rescinds No-Match Rule." Oakland, CA. July 8. http://www.unioncounsel.net/status_of_no_match_litigation.html.

Weintraub, Sidney. 1992. "US-Mexico Free Trade: Implications for the United States." *Journal of Interamerican Studies and World Affairs* 34(2): 29–52.

Weise, Julie M. 2008. "Mexican Nationalisms, Southern Racisms: Mexicans and Mexican Americans in the U.S. South, 1908–1939." *American Quarterly* 60(3).

Weissbrodt, David. 2007. "Remedies for Undocumented Noncitizens in the Workplace: Using International Law to Narrow the Holding of *Hoffman Plastic Compounds, Inc. v. NLRB*." *Minnesota Law Review* 92: 1424–45.

Willen, Sarah S. 2007. "Toward a Critical Phenomenology of Illegality: State Power, Criminalization, and Abjectivity among Undocumented Migrant Workers in Tel Aviv, Israel." *International Migration* 45(3): 8–38.

Williams, Roy L. 2009. "EEOC Official Seeks to Help Migrant Hispanic Female Laborers." *Birmingham (AL) News*. August 27.

Winter, Gerd, ed. 2006. *Multilevel Governance of Global Environmental Change: An Interdisciplinary Approach*. Cambridge: Cambridge University Press.

Wishnie, Michael J. 2007. "Prohibiting the Employment of Unauthorized Immigrants: The Experiment Fails." *University of Chicago Legal Forum* 2007: 193–217.

Wolgin, Phil. 2011. "Seen and (Mostly) Unseen: The True Costs of E-Verify." Immigration. Washington, DC: Center for American Progress. http://www.americanprogress.org/issues/2011/06/e_verify.html.

Woolfok, John. 2010. "San Jose Mayor, Council Members Tee Off on Arizona Immigration Law." *San Jose (CA) Mercury News*. May 7.

Workplace Fairness. 2009. "Overtime—State Laws." Your Rights. http://www.workplacefairness.org/overtime_statelaws?agree=yes.

Worksafe! A California Coalition for Worker Occupational Safety Health Promotion. 2012. "About Us." Oakland, CA. http://www.worksafe.org/about/index.html.

WPUSA, Working Partnerships USA. 2008a. "Accomplishments." San Jose, CA. http://www.wpusa.org/.

——. 2008b. "The Interfaith Council on Religion, Race, Economic and Social Justice." San Jose, CA.

——. 2009. "The Contingent Workers Project." San Jose, CA.

——. 2010a. "About Us." San Jose, CA.

——. 2010b. "Health Care . . . Affordable, Quality Access for All." San Jose, CA.

Yale-Loehr, Stephen. 2006. "Immigration Issues in Personal Injury Cases." Ithaca, NY: Miller Mayer. http://www.millermayer.com/.

YWU, Young Workers United. 2009. "Main Cases That the WJC & CJT Has Addressed over the Last Few Years." "Cases." San Francisco. http://www.youngworkersunited.org.

Zabin, Carol, and Isaac Martin. 1999. *Living Wage Campaigns in the Economic Policy Arena: Four Case Studies from California*. Berkeley: University of California–Berkeley, Labor Center. Zlolniski, Christian. 2006. *Janitors, Street Vendors, and Activists: The Lives of Mexican Immigrants in Silicon Valley*. Berkeley and Los Angeles: University of California Press.

Zolberg, Aristide R. 1999. "Matters of State: Theorizing Immigration Policy." In *The Handbook of International Migration: The American Experience*, ed. Charles Hirschman, Philip Kasinitz, and Josh DeWind, 71–92. New York: Russell Sage Foundation.

Zwick, Mark, and Louise Zwick. 2005. *The Catholic Worker Movement: Intellectual and Spiritual Origins*. Mahwah, NJ: Paulist Press.

———. 2011. *Mercy without Borders: The Catholic Worker and Immigration*. Mahwah, NJ: Paulist Press.

Index